THE COMPLETE IDIOT'S GUIDE® TO

Self-Publishing

by Jennifer Basye Sander

ALPHA

A member of Penguin Group (USA) Inc.

D1312427

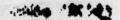

For all the creative people in the world—get out and share your talents!

ALPHA BOOKS

Published by the Penguin Group

Penguin Group (USA) Inc., 375 Hudson Street, New York, New York 10014, U.S.A.

Penguin Group (Canada), 10 Alcorn Avenue, Toronto, Ontario, Canada M4V 3B2 (a division of Pearson Penguin Canada Inc.)

Penguin Books Ltd., 80 Strand, London WC2R 0RL, England

Penguin Ireland, 25 St Stephen's Green, Dublin 2, Ireland (a division of Penguin Books Ltd.)

Penguin Group (Australia), 250 Camberwell Road, Camberwell, Victoria 3124, Australia (a division of Pearson Australia Group Pty Ltd.)

Penguin Books India Pvt Ltd., 11 Community Centre, Panchsheel Park, New Delhi—110 017, India

Penguin Group (NZ), cnr Airborne and Rosedale Roads, Albany, Auckland 1310, New Zealand (a division of Pearson New Zealand Ltd.)

Penguin Books (South Africa) (Pty) Ltd., 24 Sturdee Avenue, Rosebank, Johannesburg 2196, South Africa

Penguin Books Ltd., Registered Offices: 80 Strand, London WC2R 0RL, England

Copyright © 2005 by Jennifer Basye Sander

International Standard Book Number: 1-59257-358-4
Library of Congress Catalog Card Number: 2005928076

07　06　05　8　7　6　5　4　3　2　1

Interpretation of the printing code: The rightmost number of the first series of numbers is the year of the book's printing; the rightmost number of the second series of numbers is the number of the book's printing. For example, a printing code of 05-1 shows that the first printing occurred in 2005.

Printed in the United States of America

Note: This publication contains the opinions and ideas of its author. It is intended to provide helpful and informative material on the subject matter covered. It is sold with the understanding that the author and publisher are not engaged in rendering professional services in the book. If the reader requires personal assistance or advice, a competent professional should be consulted.

The author and publisher specifically disclaim any responsibility for any liability, loss, or risk, personal or otherwise, which is incurred as a consequence, directly or indirectly, of the use and application of any of the contents of this book.

Most Alpha books are available at special quantity discounts for bulk purchases for sales promotions, premiums, fundraising, or educational use. Special books, or book excerpts, can also be created to fit specific needs.

For details, write: Special Markets, Alpha Books, 375 Hudson Street, New York, NY 10014.

Publisher: *Marie Butler-Knight*
Editorial Director: *Mike Sanders*
Senior Managing Editor: *Jennifer Bowles*
Senior Acquisitions Editor: *Renee Wilmeth*
Development Editor: *Nancy D. Lewis*
Production Editor: *Janette Lynn*

Copy Editor: *Krista Hansing*
Cartoonist: *Chris Eliopoulos*
Cover/Book Designer: *Trina Wurst*
Indexer: *Tonya Heard*
Layout: *Angela Calvert*
Proofreading: *Mary Hunt*

Contents at a Glance

Contents

10   Legal Matters   115

Part 3:   Getting Down to Business—How a Book Is Made   129

11   The Parts of a Book   131

Foreword

Words. What are words? It's been said that words are the architect of the mind. Words determine the way the world works. Words assembled properly can change the way people think. Imagine how powerful words become when put together to create a book. Books have the power to change the world.

I'm thankful for my astonishing publishing success—over 100 million *Chicken Soup for the Soul* books sold (and we're not done yet!). What does it take to make a book a success? Creating a successful book calls for uncommon skills. I'm here to tell you that you can develop the skills you will need to make your book a success, too. With the help of *The Compete Idiot's Guide to Self-Publishing* you are off to a fabulous start.

My first book was self-published. So was my second. And my third. When you publish your own books, tapes, CDs, and DVDs you keep 100% of the profits! Is that great or what? Be sure and pick a niche no one else is messing with. I'm a big believer in growing rich in a niche.

Here is my wish for you—I want your self-publishing journey to take you to a place of workstasy. Bob Allen and I coined that term in our book *Cracking the Millionaire Code*. Workstasy is that wonderful moment when your work becomes ecstasy. Seeing your own words and thoughts made real on the page, holding a finished book that you have published on your own … workstasy indeed.

Are you a little nervous at this stage of your publishing journey? Of course you are, I was too. My old mentor Dr. R. Buckminster Fuller used to say that a book is like a baby, and only you can give birth to it and love it like one of your own kids. Get ready for a new member of your family soon.

And get started now! I want you to take a cue from the late comedian, songwriter, writer, composer Steve Allen, whom I had the great privilege to know. He sometimes worked on a mind-boggling 28 projects at once! Once you have completed your first self-publishing project you will soon be on to the next. Build an empire.

On your self-publishing journey, listen to what your skillful guide, Jennifer Basye Sander, has to share with you. Bountifully helpful, Jennifer is one of the smartest and funniest people in the publishing business. She is the insider's insider on two levels—as a former top acquisitions editor of a big publishing house, and as the author, co-author, and packager of over a hundred titles. Jennifer routinely creates bestselling book ideas for herself, her friends, and her clients and knows the publishing world well. I'm certain that with the solid information she has compiled in this book, you'll be well on the way to success.

See you at the bookstore!

Mark Victor Hansen is the mega bestselling co-author of the *Chicken Soup* series, the founder of MEGA Book Marketing University and Building Your MEGA Speaking Empire. Both are annual conferences where Mark coaches and teaches new and aspiring authors, speakers and experts on building lucrative publishing and speaking careers. www.megabookmarketing.com

Introduction

Well, it happened again today. In the paper, yet another story which featured a self-published book! Today the news was about the late romance writer Barbara Cartland, how her heirs are now bypassing publishers to bring her last works directly to her fans and readers. Yesterday the story was about Amy Fisher, the Long Island Lolita who has written and published her autobiography herself through iUniverse, a print-on-demand company. The focus of these news stories was not the fact that they had been self-published—that was completely beside the point. It was referred to simply as a business decision the writers had made on the road to bringing their product to market.

I've been in the book business for 20 long years now, doing everything from book packaging to book publicity, acquisitions to editing, creating book marketing materials and catalog copy, and writing my own *New York Times* bestsellers. But what was my very first book project? *The Sacramento Women's Yellow Pages*, a business directory I spotted a need for, created, and then brought to market. My first taste of publishing was as a self-publisher. And what was my favorite, out of the 30-plus books I've written for major publishers such as Penguin, William Morrow, and Andrews McMeel? *The Air Courier's Handbook*, a small self-published booklet that gave me a reason (and a write-off) for exotic travel.

Does that surprise you? That my favorite project didn't involve a high-powered literary agent (I have one), a six-figure advance (I've received them), a major New York publisher (I know them all), and a fancy book tour (been there, done that), but rather my own computer and countless trips to Kinko's, the post office, and the bank? Trust me, once you get a taste of publishing your own work, it won't surprise you at all.

As a publishing consultant and the co-author of *The Complete Idiot's Guide to Getting Published*, I speak to writers' groups and conferences on a monthly basis. More often than not, at some point during a talk, I am asked, "should I self-publish my work?" My answer varies, according to who has asked. As you will learn in the following pages, the decision to self-publish is different for everyone. What needs to be constant, though, is that you need to be businesslike. You need to be realistic about your expectations. And you need to be ready to work.

You must be ready to do the work because you picked up this book! Congratulations on taking your first steps toward becoming a published author. As you read through these chapters, please remember that although I am blunt about the process and what it takes to make it work, I'm not here to hurt your feelings or belittle your ideas. I want you to be happy and fulfilled by the process of self-publishing, not unhappy, bitter, and broke. Sadly, I've seen more than a few self-publishers who are, and I'm here to help you avoid that ending. So let's get started now. The sooner you take the plunge, the sooner you'll be holding your first book in your hands!

How to Use This Book

To simplify the otherwise complicated self-publishing process, I've broken this book into several large parts:

Part 1, "Before You Begin," introduces you to the world of publishing and explains who does what and why. This overview of the process will help ease you into the real work of publishing your book.

Part 2, "Getting Started," presents you with some of the decisions you'll have to make on the way to a finished book and walks you through making them. Hardcover or softcover? Book doctor or developmental editor? Short-run printer or print-on-demand? It's all here, explained in an easy-to-understand way.

Part 3, "Getting Down to Business—How a Book Is Made," walks you through the production process. From explaining the different parts of a book itself to designing an effective cover and rounding up your paperwork and registration, you will be an informed publisher in no time.

Part 4, "My Book Is Done, Now What? Publicizing and Selling a Self-Published Book," gives you all the information you need to publicize and sell your self-published book. Talk of distributors and booksellers might be daunting to you now, but soon the mystery will fall away. You will also learn marketing techniques to move books, publicity techniques to catch the attention of a producer, and sales techniques to move even more books. This self-publishing thing might be so enjoyable that you'll want to go on and publish more books—this section will help you make an informed decision there, too.

Extras

Look for the little asides and comments I've added throughout the chapters to fill this book with the inside knowledge you need to succeed as a self-publisher.

Pro Style

These are quick pieces of professional advice from me or my many contacts in the publishing world.

By the Way

Occasionally I share an observation or story from the publishing trenches to help shed light on the topic at hand.

Wise Words

These are the glossary definitions of publishing terms you will need to know.

Cautionary Tales

These are warnings about the typical pitfalls that can be avoided.

Acknowledgments

I am indebted to so many in the self-publishing world who have generously helped me with this project: Mahesh Grossman of Authors Team, Brian Taylor of Pneuma Books, Eric Kampmann of Midpoint Distributors, Diane Gedymin of iUniverse, and others too numerous to mention.

Lynne Rominger has shared her book publicity knowledge with me both in person and on the printed page, and I am thankful. Mark Victor Hansen continues to share his knowledge, wisdom, and enthusiasm for the business of publishing with me on a regular basis. The editors at Alpha Books are always a joy, and I'm thankful to have had yet another chance to work with Renee and her team. And to my husband, Peter, and our sons, Julian and Jonathan, you guys are the best.

Jennifer Basye Sander
Granite Bay, California

Special Thanks to the Technical Reviewer

The Complete Idiot's Guide to Self-Publishing was reviewed by an expert who double-checked the accuracy of what you'll learn here, to help us ensure that this book gives you everything you need to know about getting ready for publishing your own book. Special thanks are extended to Robin Hood.

Robin C. Hood has worked in the publishing industry for 30 years. Her company, Professional Publishing Services, specializes in all aspects of book production for publishers and self-publishers.

Trademarks

All terms mentioned in this book that are known to be or are suspected of being trademarks or service marks have been appropriately capitalized. Alpha Books and Penguin Group (USA) Inc. cannot attest to the accuracy of this information. Use of a term in this book should not be regarded as affecting the validity of any trademark or service mark.

Part 1

Before You Begin

Self-publishing means a lot of things to a lot of people—what exactly does it mean to you? By examining your reasons for self-publishing and your expectations of what it will achieve, you can set the best course to proceed. Learn how the self-publishing world has changed and how the latest advances can help you reach your goals.

When you clarify your reason to self-publish your work, it might turn out that you can skip the book itself! Read up on the many ways to broadcast your message in nonbook form that might be an even faster way into print than a book.

Chapter 1

Self-Publishing: The Big Picture

In This Chapter

- ◆ Self-publishing defined
- ◆ What commercial publishers do (and don't do)
- ◆ Different types of self-publishing
- ◆ Attitudes toward self-publishing have changed
- ◆ The major players involved in the self-publishing business
- ◆ The best reasons to self-publish

Welcome to the world of self-publishing! In the following chapters, you will find all of the information you need to take the words in your head to the printed page, and into the hands of a reader.

But before you rush your manuscript off to the printer, let's start at the beginning and take a closer look at the big picture of self-publishing. There is much to be learned, so let the learning begin!

What Exactly Is Self-Publishing?

You picked up this book because you'd like to become a self-published author. Self-published? What exactly does that mean? If you look up the word *publish* in the dictionary, the standard definition runs something like this: to issue copies of a book to the public. So, if you are a self-publisher, you are the person issuing copies of your book to the public. Another way to look at it is this: the world of publishing is a world of money and business, and the role of publisher goes to the person with the checkbook. If you are a self-publisher, you are the person paying for the copies of your book that you are issuing to the public.

To many, the notion of being a publisher sounds quite glamorous. The publisher, he's that guy in the tweed jacket and the old leather chair in the corner office, staring silently off into space as he ponders the next brilliant literary move his publishing company will make …. Glamour, schlamour. A publisher runs a publishing business. Instead of being the person grappling with literary issues, the publisher is the person grappling with the unglamorous issues of paper prices, printing contracts, and the bottom line of profit and loss. All issues that you will personally deal with once you decide to become your own publisher.

Acting in the role of your own publisher, you will be making decision after decision regarding your book, from editing through design and production, from printing to marketing and publicity. As you work through the chapters in *The Complete Idiot's Guide to Self-Publishing* on the various topics the process involves, you might well ask yourself, "Should I make this particular decision with my wallet or my heart? One or the other, or, perhaps, at times, both?"

> **By the Way**
>
> Publishers really are business people, not editorial types. The employee of a publishing company who rises through the ranks to become the publisher usually comes up from the business side, through sales or marketing, rather than editorial. Keep this reality in mind as you contemplate your future as the publisher of your own work—it will come in handy.

Have I already got you worried about the size of the task just one or two paragraphs into this book? Don't worry, self-publishing is something you can do quite well on your own. The rewards are manifold, and we will be looking at those closely. Before we do, though, why not dispense with any nagging notion you might have that being your own publisher is somehow inferior to being published by someone else. The second choice, a fallback position, not the grand triumph you had hoped your writing would achieve. As a former editor with a major New York publishing house and the author of more than 30 books myself, let me pull back the curtain of mystery and let you all peek inside ….

Commercial Publishers: What They Do, What They Don't Do!

Some writers daydream endlessly about how wonderful life could be if only a major publisher would pick up their work. All the writer would have to do would be write, and the publisher would handle the process from the moment the manuscript was finished. In fact, *commercial publishers* do exactly that—take delivery of the finished manuscript from an author that they have under contract and handle the process (and the bills) from then on.

Being published by a large commercial publisher or small independent publisher can be a terrific experience for a writer. It can also be a wrenching experience for some, involving a frustrating loss of control over the book project you have nurtured for so long. Unless you are a major name like James Patterson or Nora Roberts, here is what authors who have signed a standard contract with a commercial publisher *don't* get to do:

Wise Words

A **commercial publisher** is a book publishing company, large or small, that assumes the full costs of producing, distributing, marketing, and selling the books it publishes. Commercial publishers pay authors for the right to publish their work.

- Choose the final title of their book
- Choose a cover design
- Decide what material ultimately gets in the book
- Decide when the book comes out in the marketplace
- Decide how to best position the book in the marketplace
- Determine when the life of the book has ended

Each one of these will be explained in the sections that follow.

Say Good-Bye to Your Favorite Title

Can you imagine that? You've worked for years on a book that you have given the perfect title, only to lose control and see the book published and on the shelves with a title you hate. Ask any author who has been published by a major house, and they can quickly reel off a list of the times they've wished their book had gone in a different direction. I've sold books to major publishers with titles I loved, only to see them changed at the last minute. A collection of quotes and poems about jealousy and revenge I sold to a large publisher under the name *Green-Eyed Prose*, what I thought was a cool and classy title, was published under the name *Love Stinks*. Oooo, do you think I tell many of my friends (let alone my husband) that I'm the author of a book with that name? Not often! *Self-publish, and you will have total control over the title of your book.*

Yikes! Where Did That Cover Come From?

Some books have wonderful covers; some do not. Imagine how you could feel if your book is finally published with a cover that makes you cringe in embarrassment. Why don't authors have control over their covers? Because commercial publishers feel that this is a critical part of how well a book sells and that they have the knowledge to determine it. *Self-publish, and you are in charge of your cover!*

Am I Missing a Chapter?

Sign a standard book contract, lose control over the content of your book. It is as basic as that. Once you begin the editing process, you might well find that the publishing house editor has a vastly different idea about how long your book needs to be and whether all of your hard work actually needs to see the light of day. Paper costs sometimes determine the final length of a book. If a manuscript is running a few pages too long, then some of your hard work may be axed in lieu of spending money for more pages. Chances are you won't get to weigh in on what gets cut, either. *Self-publish, and your book can be as long as you want it to be.*

Skipping Christmas

Publishing schedules at commercial publishers rule the day, and your idea of when your book has to be out doesn't count for much in the decision-making process. Hope it would be on the shelves for the holidays? Maybe, if it fits in their overall pan. Need your book published in time for a big business presentation? Sorry, not a big enough factor to move it forward. *Self-publish, and it will be done when you want it, and when you need it.*

Position Number One

You wrote a book for working moms, but your publisher positioned it in the marketing materials and *press releases* as appealing to stay-at-home moms? It could happen. Authors have little input (and are seldom asked for their opinion) into the entire marketing, sales, and publicity process. That's not what happens when you are running your own show! *Self-publish, and you determine how your book is positioned in the marketplace.*

Wise Words

A **press release** is a one-page announcement distributed to the press. It contains the five W's—who, what, where, when, and why.

The Remains of the Day

Your book was published to great reviews but didn't sell as well as the publisher had planned. So although you would like to see it available for the next few years, your publisher wants to quickly write this off as a failure and dump the overstock books on sale tables around the country. Your book could end up pulled off the market, and the rights might not automatically revert to you. No product, no ability to resell it. Needless to say, this is not a situation a self-publisher would ever fall into! *Self-publish, and you have total control over how long they keep your work in print and available.*

So while being published by a commercial publisher doesn't cost the author any money (in fact, they pay you advances and royalties, of which an average 15 percent goes to an agent if you use one), there is certainly a cost to the amount of control you have lost over your beloved book project. Something to consider and weigh very carefully if you have strong feelings about the way you want your book to read, to look, and to be marketed.

A self-publisher, then, is someone who is assuming the costs of issuing copies of a book to the public, while maintaining control of that work, determining how and when it is brought to market, and deciding how long it stays there. And that sounds pretty good, doesn't it?

Variations on a Theme of Self-Publishing

There are as many ways to self-publish as there are topics on which to write. If you are an entrepreneurial sort of person, you might well decide to plunge in and manage every aspect of the process from start to finish. If you are a little more hesitant about your managerial or business skills, you might opt to go with one of the new businesses that cater to self-publishers. You might even decide, after examining all of the options, to bypass the print process altogether and self-publish online!

So that this book has enough solid information for everyone, I'm assuming that many of you will want to handle it all by yourself. After reading all the way through and learning about the many aspects, you might well decide that there are things you will want some extra help with. A few of you might even throw up your hands and want someone to manage the entire process for you! Let's take a look at the different variations of self-publishing.

Do-It-All-Yourself

In this can-do world of ours, there are many writers who enjoy managing the entire process of publishing their book from start to finish. Searching out the best printer, locating the most appropriate cover designer, finding a distributor, and then calling bookstores around the country to alert them to a brand new book—no detail is too large or small for the do-it-yourselfers. You might well be cut out to do it all this way, on your own. You might find, however, that there are tasks you either don't enjoy (negotiating with printers) or are reluctant to do (promote yourself to the media). In these chapters, I am assuming that you will want to handle all of the details on your own, and plan to give you the information you need in order to do that effectively. If after reading through the book you decide to do some, but not all, of the process yourself, no matter. You will be an extremely informed and educated buyer.

Hiring Help

For those writers who do sense the need to involve a few experts in their project from the very beginning, there are plenty of ways to go. From book doctors and editors who will help you get your manuscript into readable shape, to print brokers and cover designers to help with some of the production aspects, to the new emergence of companies like iUniverse and AuthorHouse who work with self-publishers to produce *print-on-demand* books, if you need help, you will be able to find it. Companies like iUniverse and AuthorHouse are one-stop-shopping experiences for the fledgling self-publisher and can assign one person to guide you

> **Wise Words**
>
> **Print-on-demand,** or POD, is a new process by which books are printed as needed on a copy-by-copy basis rather than in large quantities.

through the entire process. None of this comes free, of course, there are fees involved from the start.

Vanity Press

It seems quaint in this day and age, but vanity presses still do exist. I still see the words "manuscripts wanted" or "publish your book now" in literary magazines. Although the term *vanity press* does bring a certain sort of image to mind, vanity presses are more accurately described as "subsidy publishers." That is, the author, you, are subsidizing the publication of your book, either in part or in total.

Here is how it is described on the website of Vantage Press, a major subsidy publisher: "You, the author, pay for the publication of your book. The amount varies with each manuscript, depending upon length and other factors which contribute to production costs. In return for the fee you pay, we publish your book and you receive 40 percent of the retail price of every book sold at standard discounts." The information on the site also cautions, "Sales vary widely, from a few to a few thousand copies or more. There is no guarantee of financial success. You may not even earn back your publishing fee."

How does this differ from working with a company that will help you produce print-on-demand copies? The biggest difference is one of control. You are in the driver's seat with a company like iUniverse, choosing from the menu of services and determining how many books you'd like and how fancy you'd like them to be. With most subsidy publishers, they still operate on the printed book standard, and you will finish up the process with cases of bound books stacked in your garage.

Pro Style

Diane Gedymin has worked in the book-publishing industry for many years. As a senior editor with a New York house, an independent literary agent, and the publisher of a well-known imprint, she has said no to authors more than once. "I've rejected a lot of books," Diane says about her earlier career, "not necessarily because they weren't good, but most often because of the realities of today's publishing marketplace." What does she do now? She is the editorial director of iUniverse, part of a team that helps authors self-publish.

Nonbook Self-Publishing

Nonbook? What exactly is a nonbook? What I mean is information that is delivered to customers in a form other than a professionally printed book. Perhaps the book you've written doesn't really need to be a book. It might work better as an e-book or as a binder marketed to professionals in your field. An audiotape? A CD of your speeches? We live in a world in which information is king, and there are many ways of selling information. In Chapter 5, I'll help you decide whether taking a different publishing route might work better for you.

No Longer in the Shadows

In my introduction, I said that hardly a day goes by without yet another mention of a self-published book in the media. I wasn't exaggerating. I do see stories on a very regular basis in which it is clear to me as a book industry pro that the book being mentioned was self-published. The remarkable thing is that, in most cases, the fact that it was self-published is not a major point in the story. What was once a stigma, a mark that someone had had to *pay* to see a work in print, is now an accepted business practice.

"Privately printed" or "privately published" were two rather classy ways of referring to self-published memoirs or books of poetry published by gentlemen of leisure. While the term *vanity publisher* still does have a certain sting to it, the term *self-published* sounds vigorous and daring, entrepreneurial and bold. Modern, almost, compared to the stodgy notion that your book is published by someone else.

Book reviewers might still be hesitant to work with self-published books (we'll deal with that topic at length in the chapters on print publicity), but other members of the media seem not at all bothered by the notion that self-published means second class.

All over the country there are writers and businesspeople who never try to submit their work elsewhere, but plan from the get-go to publish it themselves. Josh Ortega, the author of the self-published novel *Frequencies*, was inspired by the example of hip-hop recording artists who recorded, produced, and then distributed their own CDs out of their cars. Handling all of the details himself seemed more like the mark of a true artist, rather than risk allowing others to make decisions about his literary work.

Self-publishers like Josh Ortega have much in common with Mark Twain, Gertrude Stein, and Edith Wharton. All published their own work at one point in their careers. More recently, best-selling young writer Dave Eggers decided to follow up his book *A Heartbreaking Work of Staggering Genius* by publishing his second book on his own. Stephen King dipped his toe into the e-book world a few years back by offering one of his new works directly to readers online. "Bypassing the system" seems like a daring thing to do nowadays and isn't taken as a sign that you have failed elsewhere. Who wouldn't want to be part of a club with such distinguished members?

Why the Change in Attitude?

How did the idea of self-publishing go from a sign of failure to a sign of success? The emergence of the web and online journalism is a large factor. Years ago, in order to be considered an expert in anything, you needed to go to an impressive college, spend years working for established organizations, and then slowly build up your name among your peers before being accepted on the national level. That doesn't really seem to be the case anymore. Put up a website, send out an e-zine, begin a blog, and the world will at least notice, if not take you seriously. Self-publishers have certainly benefited from the change in what constitutes the "media" and who constitutes a "writer" or "journalist." Outsider status is now highly sought after rather than sneered at.

Attitudes always shift when big players and big money get involved. The publishing business in general has shifted over the last few decades from one controlled by a few wealthy and well-read men to one in which major conglomerates are in charge of the purse strings. Some of those same conglomerates have invested in the burgeoning world of self-publishing.

New Players on the Self-Publishing Team

Some of the biggest names in the book business are now owners or investors in businesses that cater to self-publishers. Random House Ventures, the investment arm of the Random House publishing firm, is a major owner of Xlibris, one of the early print-on-demand companies. Ingram Book Group, the giant book wholesaler and distributor, is an owner of Lightning Source, another POD company. Bookselling behemoth Barnes & Noble has made significant investments over the years in various ventures, some of which still exist (the POD company iUniverse) and some of which do not (MightyWords, an e-book company).

Technology Difference

Not only has the emergence of print-on-demand technology made a big difference in how much it costs to self-publish, but the other major technological difference that affects self-publishers is the emergence of new distribution and sales methods. Not only did the old-style self-publisher have to order a print run of several thousand books (which filled many a writer's garage), but they also faced an endless round of sales calls to bookstores and other outlets to stock the book, followed by endless phone calls to check up on stock or request payment.

Cautionary Tales _____

Although major publishing companies are investing in self-publishing-related ventures, they are quick to point out that using these services is no shortcut in through their corporate back door. On the Xlibris website FAQs section, the question "Does this mean my book is being published by Random House?" is answered with a terse "No." Some of the early dotcom bubble investments that publishing companies made were spoken of as potential "farm teams" for the publishing houses, a new pool of potential projects that editors could cull through and look for projects they'd want for the big house, so to speak. This optimistic talk soon faded, no doubt discouraged by the editors themselves!

Nowadays a self-publisher can sell directly to a customer online through a website or e-mail newsletter. Combined with the existence of online bookstores like Amazon.com and others that can be accessed anywhere, anytime, by a customer seeking your book, the business life of the self-publisher has been completely changed for the better.

Diane Gedymin, editorial director of iUniverse, echoes my own theory in explaining why she thinks self-publishing is more accepted today:

> A few years ago, if you told someone you bought a used leather jacket (so what if it was Armani?) they'd turn up their noses as though they smelled something musty from a thrift store. Then came eBay. Now if you tell someone you bought an Armani on eBay, they think it's cool. It's a combination of the technology and e-world bargaining that drove acceptance of this age-old practice. Print-on-demand is similar. Used to be that vanity publishers charged a fortune and the quality of the titles was very bad—the proverbial biography of someone's pet poodle. Now [with] the acceptance and success of "indy" music and film, books naturally fit into a growing wave of taking control of all aspects of one's creative work, from the control of the content to its sales, promotion, and marketing.

The Entrepreneurial Edge

Entrepreneurism is celebrated now more than ever, and self-publishers are the ultimate entrepreneurs. Not only are you risking yourself emotionally by putting your thoughts and theories down on paper, but then you step up and take a business risk by publishing it yourself and assuming responsibility for the entire process. Instead of being perceived as failed writers who couldn't get a publisher interested in their work, self-publishers are often seen as creative businesspeople who believe in their own work enough to risk money on it.

By the Way

My favorite self-publishing project was a travel booklet called *The Air Courier's Handbook*. It is amazing to think back now on the low-tech way I produced it only 10 years ago. Every year I changed the cover—once it was an old map of Asia in the background, then a leopard skin print, and the final edition was tiger striped. I had covers printed in quantities of 100 on card stock (heavy paper). When I got orders in the mail for the book, I'd walk down the street to the copy shop and do much of the production myself—copy the pages I'd laid out on stiff design board and collate the pages in the proper order. Saddle-stitched (small booklets that are stapled) books need to be done by a large stapler, so I'd hand over as many covers as needed and pay the copy shop 10¢ each to do that for me. It was such a satisfying way to spend an evening, assembling books that I'd ship out the next day. I was never behind in my print bills, as I'd already been paid for the booklets I was shipping out!

Because so many aspects of the self-publishing world have had businesses built up around them, like in other businesses some folks are ready to deal. If you decide to go the route of working with one of the major POD firms, don't decide too hastily. Get quotes from several, add your name to a mailing list or two, and sit back and wait for the special offers to roll in. Sign up by this date and save! Or buy a special package, regularly priced at X, available this week for Y! You might be able to shave 10 or 20 percent off your total costs if you hold out for a special price. And when talking to companies directly, always ask, "Are there any specials coming up that I should know about?"

The Best Reasons to Self-Publish

Have I got you pumped up yet about how rewarding it can be to control your own creative product? Have I reassured you that this is a new era of self-publishing, one without the lingering stigma of amateurism that existed before? If the idea of self-publishing still seems daunting, if you are worried that perhaps you will be taking on more than you can handle, let me share a quick top five reasons to self-publish:

5. You'll keep control of your creative product.

4. You'll keep on schedule.

3. You'll keep more on your bottom line.

2. You'll get your novel published quickly.

1. You'll see your name in print.

Each one of these reasons will be explained in the sections that follow.

Keep Control, Keep on Schedule

I touched on this topic earlier when I was describing what happens to books that are under contract with a commercial publisher. The author has zero control over how quickly the project is published or when it appears in the marketplace. I've known novelists whose books were turned in to the editor one year but were not published for another two years. Imagine waiting for two or more years to see the fruits of your labors finally arrive. As a self-publisher, the pace, timing, and scheduling of your book are left entirely up to you. Need your book for a major business presentation where you will have the chance to sell to 1,000 attendees in the back of the room? Great, you can plan for that and make sure you have enough self-published product to handle it.

The Bottom Line

Let me give you the facts about commercial publishing. As a much-published writer and a former acquisitions editor, I am all too familiar with the standard *royalty* contracts. Of course, you can make a handsome living from a commercially published book, if the sales are big enough. Be warned, though, that this rarely happens. For books that sell only modestly, it is a tough way to make a living.

> **Wise Words**
>
> **Royalty** is the percentage of the proceeds the commercial publisher pays the author for each copy sold.

A self-published book that sells only modestly can still make a handsome profit for the author, though. As the publisher of your own material, you have the opportunity to make the lion's share of the profit. Let's take a quick look at how I did as the publisher of my own travel booklet:

- My cost was $1 per book. An envelope and shipping was another $1. The retail price was $10, so I made $8 profit per book. Over the years and six editions, I sold 5,000 copies. $5,000 \times \$8 = \$40,000$.

- A standard publishing contract pays the author a royalty of 8 percent of the retail price. So I would have made 80¢ for each book sold. $5,000 \times 80¢ = \$4,000$.

Gee, $40,000, or $4,000—which one was the better deal? I think you can figure that one out pretty quickly!

Cash flow is another great aspect of self-publishing that can really work in your favor. The potential for money in your mailbox every day, what a feeling! That's a feeling that I experienced on a delightfully regular basis with the six editions I published of *The Air Courier's Handbook.* Royalty checks from the books I've sold to commercial publishers arrive only a scant two times a year (if that), but my book income from this little booklet went on steadily throughout the year, due to press releases I'd send to travel editors. It was a simple formula: articles about the book would appear in newspapers and magazines, and a few days later, checks would appear in my mail. If you publish and market your books aggressively, you might well get used to the thrilling sight of a mailbox stuffed full of checks.

Novels, Memoirs, and Children's Books

A recent study by the Jenkins Group discovered that 81 percent of Americans feel they have a book in them. What on Earth are we all working on? Probably not cookbooks and travel books, but rather novels, our own memoirs, and children's books. What categories are the hardest for first-time writers to sell to publishers? Drum roll, please—novels, memoirs, and children's books. If you truly want to see your creative work in print, publishing your own novel, memoir, or children's book might be the way to go.

Memoirs are perfect for the print-on-demand process. You have the satisfaction of seeing your own story in print and can purchase just enough copies to share with your family and friends. No need to buy large quantities that might just gather dust. If your goal is to see your memoir published by a large publisher, you will have a finished book that just might catch an editor's eye.

Your Name in Print!

What better feeling could there be to hold a book in your hands that is truly yours? A book that you wrote, a book whose production and design you were involved with, a book that you now intend to promote for years to come? A book of your very own?

Now that you have a grasp of the big picture of self-publishing, it is time to move on and focus less on the actual idea of self-publishing and more on you personally as a self-publisher.

The Least You Need to Know

- Self-publishing no longer carries a stigma in the marketplace.
- New methods and new players make it easier and faster than ever before.

♦ Self-publishers can keep control over their book's destiny.

♦ Self-publishers can make money but can also lose money.

♦ Self-publishing is the fastest way to get a book with your name on it.

2

Self-Publishing and You

In This Chapter

- ◆ What self-publishing means financially
- ◆ Ideas to defray expenses
- ◆ How self-publishing can boost your career
- ◆ What kind of personality makes a good publisher?
- ◆ The self-publisher aptitude test

By now I hope I've given you an overall sense of what self-publishing is about, but what does all of this mean to *you*? What will self-publishing your work mean to you financially, in terms of both potential cost and potential rewards? What will it mean to you professionally, to your career? And what does it mean to you on a personal and emotional basis as you tackle this enormously creative yet complicated task?

Each and every one of us comes to self-publishing for a different reason, with different ideas about what we hope to achieve with the experience. Let's start looking at what self-publishing can mean to you on a financial level. It's not free, you know ….

Publishing Books for Fun and Profit

You can make money with books, I will affirm that potential now. You can also lose money easily, I will affirm that just as strongly! Self-publishing your work can also affect you on a financial level due to the costs associated with seeing your project through from beginning to end, and the potential for lost income as you divert your attention to this project. You'll need to carefully balance the time you take away from your own career while writing and publishing your book. Try not to count too much on an increased income after your book is published. If it happens, wonderful! But if it doesn't, you don't want to kick yourself over work you turned away in the meantime. Publishing a book is a gamble, not a guarantee.

On a more positive note, there is also potential for increased income due to increased professional visibility. For example, JoDee Senekar is the author and publisher of *Making Time for Each Other: A Couple's Guide to Living and Loving*. She and her husband, Phil, teach six-week courses to couples about how to create a closer relationship. Her newly self-published book is a critical part of that plan. Not only does she now have a book that can be found in bookstores that will serve as a "brochure" of sorts and lead-generator to direct future paying customers to their course, but the book itself is also a terrific tool that is included in the course price and can be used as the textbook to teach the course. And who would you rather take a course from—someone who claims to be an expert, or someone who not only is an expert but can hand you a professionally produced book to back it up?

But What Is This Going to Cost Me?

Ah, wondering just how much of a financial impact self-publishing can have on your pocketbook? It is easy to get caught up in the vision of self-publishing your work and not let your imagination settle too much on the hard reality. Publishing costs money. Sometimes it costs a lot of money—huge amounts, in fact.

Depending on your own financial resources and your overall reasons for publishing, money matters are something that I urge you to carefully consider. Please do not jeopardize yourself or your family to self-publish your work.

JoDee Senekar's book, *Making Time for Each Other*, is beautiful. The paper cover includes shiny red, embossed letters in the subtitle and a romantic photo to set the mood. It's 148 pages long and 6 inches by 9 inches, with no interior photos and black ink. It is clear that she worked with professional designers both on the cover, as well as the interior.

So JoDee … how much? "From start to finish, I'd say it cost me about $14,000. I had 3,000 copies printed up, but the total cost includes everyone who helped in the design and also some professional seminars I attended to learn more about the process." That $14,000 is not a sum to sneeze at. Your project might cost far less, or you might well be heading toward an even larger sum.

Does it always have to cost that much to self-publish? Certainly not. Remember my little travel pamphlet that cost me a dollar each to produce at Kinko's? I'm just giving you a cursory overview of the money angle right now. In future chapters, we will delve headfirst into the dollars and cents of publishing. But when we talk about "self-publishing and you," I need to point out that you will soon be making big decisions regarding "self-publishing, your money, and you."

You will learn in the printing chapters that much affects the cost of each actual book you have printed. The type of paper, the type of binding, what color ink and how many inks—all of these affect the price per book. The single biggest factor, though, is the size of the print run. An important piece of information you should keep in mind now is that the price you pay per book depends on how many books you are printing up each time. The more you print, the less you will pay per individual book. When you daydream about the day you see your book in print, make sure you are realistically visualizing how many copies you will have ordered!

 Pro Style _____

To publish books, you need a printer. And not just any printer, mind you, but a printer who specializes in printing books. Using your local printer is a nice community gesture, but chances are, he doesn't have the right equipment or knowledge to print and bind books. You might end up with a substandard product that will disappoint you and not fit into the marketplace.

Is there any way to somehow lessen the big sticker shock of self-publishing? Is there a way to somehow defray the costs and make it more affordable? Here are three ideas I'd like to share with you.

Sell Advertising—I Did!

My first foray into publishing was a business directory. Before designing mine, I looked at the best available example—the telephone yellow pages. And what did I find? Pages and pages of advertising. So in my business directory, *The Sacramento Women's Yellow Pages*, I sold ads. It brought in a tidy sum of money that helped pay for the typesetting, designing, and printing of the book. By the time I had actual books to sell, the money I made from book sales was pure profit because all of my bills had been taken care of by ad revenues. Wouldn't that be great? Is there a way that you could sell advertising in your book, too?

The kinds of books that lend themselves to advertising are regional books (dining guides, travel guides, local business histories, anything with a local bent that will sell to folks who live in one region). In the 1980s, commercial publisher Chris Whittle shocked the industry with his plan to sell ads in his books. He published "big thought" books by important writers that were subsidized by one major corporate sponsor. Me, I wasn't shocked. I thought it was smart publishing. Anytime you can get someone else to help defray your costs, I say, go for it.

Advertising is always based on circulation, of course. No one will buy an ad in a book that will have only limited circulation, so you will have to commit to really getting copies out there. A best-case scenario for selling advertising would be if you are publishing a book that will be given free to high-end customers of a bank, for instance, or a stockbroker. Wouldn't a fancy steakhouse or a custom tailor like to have an ad in a book that will be going to that kind of clientele?

Cash Up Front

Another way to come up with the money to self-publish is to sell books before you print them. With *The Sacramento Women's Yellow Pages*, not only was I selling advertising, but I took advance orders in the month before the book was actually released. That's right, a few hundred people were willing to fill out order forms and attach checks for a book that they wouldn't receive right away. This won't work with every kind of book; there would need to be a compelling reason for your customers to order early and pay in advance. If you are working on a family history, for instance, it is a reasonable request to ask relatives to pay early so that you won't have to foot a big print bill alone.

Cautionary Tales _____

Over the years, I've met hundreds of self-publishers, some successful, some bitter and unhappy. Who makes it? The ones who are serious about what they are undertaking. The ones who study the book business, make connections any way they can, and approach their self-publishing project like a business. And who ends up bitter? The folks who thought that the world would beat a path to their door, that success would come looking for them once their book was published. It doesn't work that way. You create your own success with a self-published book; no one does it for you.

Should I Just Go Electronic?

I'm making this whole self-publishing thing sound both risky and expensive, aren't I? I'm really not trying to frighten you. I'm just trying to make sure you know what you are embarking on. If all you want is to share your opinions with the world, there might be other less expensive ways to go about it.

In Chapter 4, I'll introduce you to the world of e-books and let you consider more fully if that is a viable plan for you. It is less expensive than producing and printing an actual book, so if money is a consideration, an e-book might be the answer.

Or maybe you should look into blogging. Writing a daily journal that is available to be read online will get your ideas out into the world quickly and with a lot less money. More on that in Chapter 21.

A Book and Your Career

What might it mean to you professionally once you have a book out? Here are just a few of the places a book can take you: on a cruise, on television and radio, on the witness stand, or even on the stage.

Imagine being invited to sail the world to exotic ports and cruise for free, just for giving a short talk or two in return? It happens all the time to published authors on topics as varied as tax planning, crafts, cooking, and even one of my favorite topics—indulgence! Hotels are also starting to book guest lecturers in exchange for free stays. I've been asked to lecture on cruise ships and give classes at a Ritz-Carlton in exchange for a room. A free stay at the Ritz? A small indulgence, indeed.

Would it help your career to be seen on television regularly, or to be heard nationwide on the radio talking about your work? Imagine how much more you can raise your fees once you become a nationally recognized figure. Or how quickly you might gain a promotion once your employer sees what a dynamo you are.

Perhaps you can see yourself on the witness stand, testifying as an expert witness in a high-stakes trial? It can happen. I've been asked to testify in intellectual property cases, and expert parachuting author Dan Poynter has testified many times in cases involving parachutes.

If you can't see yourself in the witness stand, perhaps you like to picture yourself on the stage? Many self-publishers have built successful speaking careers after publishing their books. Developing into a high-powered speaker in your professional specialty will put your career into high gear.

Can You Really Handle It?

Okay, let's move away from the money and career issues for a while and take a closer look at your personality. It takes a certain sort of person to embrace the self-publishing experience and thrive in the midst of it. Not everyone is really cut out for the process. Despite the fact that I have self-published my own work twice and been successful both times, the honest truth is that I really don't have all of the traits it takes to be a self-publisher. I have a short attention span. I'm impatient. I'm lazy.

Here are a few tough questions to consider. Not only are these drawn from my own publishing experiences, but I also talked to other self-publishers to make sure I wasn't overlooking some important trait. Sit down with a cup of coffee or a glass of wine and consider the following:

- **Can I afford to do this?** Self-publishing costs money. Will I be jeopardizing some other part of my life if I spend money publishing books that might not sell? Another way to look at this question is, can I afford to *lose* money to do this?

- **Do I enjoy handling multiple tasks?** Publishing is a complicated process. There will be times when you need to be doing several things at once—checking into distributors and negotiating printing prices, and trying to put the final touches on the manuscript … it can be crazy.

- **Can I be patient with the process?** Publishing can also be very, very slow …. Trying to get all of the other players to do their parts in a timely fashion can happen at a maddeningly slow pace. Are you okay with that? Some self-publishers end up angry and frustrated by how long it takes others to respond. Your book, your work, is of prime importance to you, but it's only one of many books to a bookstore, a distributor, a printer, a publicist. You will have to accept that what is important to you is less important to others.

- **Can I take criticism?** This is a big deal. You are putting your work out into the world. What if some parts of the world don't like it? Will you be able to handle it if your work is criticized by a reviewer or lambasted by a neighbor? I just noticed that on Amazon.com that there is a new comment about one of my books. "This book is silly," it says. Ouch, that stings. How will you feel if someone thinks what you have done is silly? Writers and publishers need thick skins in order to survive.

- **Can I take the sound of silence?** Just like you might run into criticism once you've published your work, you might also run into … nothing. Nothing at all. What if you publish your book and nothing happens? No one reviews it, no one comments on it, no one wants to interview you. I've had that happen once or twice myself, and it isn't pretty. Will you be okay if, to paraphrase Emily Dickenson, "I wrote a letter to the world, who never answered me." Think about this possibility long and hard.

- **Can I talk about myself?** Self-publishers need to be major *self-promoters*. Do you have what it takes to talk about yourself? Sounds easy, I know, but it really isn't. We are raised from birth to not brag about ourselves and our exploits, yet you will have to as a self-published author. This is not a pursuit for shy persons. You might have written and published an amazing book, but if you aren't cut out to promote it, the world will never know about your work.

> **Wise Words**
>
> A **self-promoter** is a person who is able to enthusiastically promote themselves and their work unapologetically and without hesitation.

- **Do I really have the time?** Self-publishing a book takes a great deal of time. Not just the actual writing of the book, but also producing, distributing, promoting—it all takes hours and hours. If your life is already filled to the brim with other responsibilities, do you really have the time to do this effectively?

- **Can I stop?** Can you stop writing and start publishing? Can you set deadlines for yourself and your project, and stick to them? Not everyone can! Some writers have been tinkering for years with their work, and it is *almost* right, they are *almost* ready to start publishing, but yet …. Will you be able to let your work go and put an end to endless changes? Once you start the publishing process, changes cost money. You'll learn the pricey facts once we start talking about production and printing.

- **Can I ask for help?** Will you be able to ask for help if you feel overwhelmed? There are plenty of professionals available in the publishing world to help you if you need it. Be clear-eyed about deciding where your talents lie and turning over tasks that you aren't good at. You might write a wonderful book, but you might not be a skilled copyeditor.

♦ **Am I passionate about my work?** To be happily self-published requires that you are passionate about what you are trying to achieve. Do you have the passion and the drive to keep going in the face of delays and obstacles? There might well be days when you feel like chucking the whole project! Do you have the passion to see this through to the end? You will need it.

Do you have to have all of these traits in order to succeed as a self-publisher? No. I've already confessed that I don't have them all. But you need to have enough of them to be able to see your book project through to a finished product.

Your Book and You

"I just couldn't believe it," JoDee Senekar said, "when I finally held a copy of my book in my hands. Just unbelievable, the feeling of accomplishment. My son is so proud, he took a copy to school to show off and is now talking about writing and publishing a book himself. I told him he could do it if that is what he put his mind to."

Imagine how it will feel for *you*—the thrill of accomplishment, the sense of achievement, and a job well done. Not to mention the relief you will feel that the actual publishing part of the process is finally over. And now the fun will begin—promoting your work! Promoting yourself! Selling your book and actually making some money!

"I'm ready to do it again," JoDee told me. "I have all these other ideas for new books." Self-publishing can be addictive, be warned. Once you absorb the feelings of pride and accomplishment, you just might be reaching for your laptop to get started on yet another book ....

The Least You Need to Know

♦ Publishing books can be a risky financial proposition.

♦ Publishing books can be a rewarding financial proposition.

♦ You might be able to lower your costs through advance sales or selling advertising.

♦ A book can have a dramatic positive effect on your professional career.

♦ Not everyone is cut out to be a self-publisher; you need to be focused, thick-skinned, patient, and a risk taker.

♦ Holding a finished book in your hands is well worth the effort.

Chapter 3

Evaluate Your Idea

In This Chapter

- ◆ Why you should evaluate your idea now
- ◆ Book genres defined
- ◆ Assess your idea for commercial potential
- ◆ Tweak your idea to maximize potential
- ◆ How do you define success?

Now that you have a clearer idea of what is involved with the process of self-publishing, I'd like to focus on the actual book project you have in mind. I recommend we hit the Pause button for a chapter here and take a step back. You bought this book because you have an idea for a book or have already written a book, and are making plans to self-publish. Let's take the time now to evaluate your idea in a clear-eyed fashion. After reading this chapter, you might decide to do your book differently, or you might decide not to change a thing.

You plan to self-publish and call all your own shots, so why do you need to evaluate your idea? Because it might be that what you plan to publish doesn't match up with your reasons for publishing. As a major fan of self-publishing, I don't want you to think I'm trying to discourage you from proceeding. I just want all prospective self-publishers to think long and hard about their reasons for publishing, their expectations, their budget, and their vision of what lies ahead. As many authors can tell you, writing and publishing books is an extremely satisfying thing to do. It is also a good way to get your heart broken, your dreams dashed, and your pocketbook depleted. The more you evaluate your project from a business perspective, the better you will be prepared for your journey.

What Kind of Book Are You Writing?

It is vitally important that from the get-go, you have an understanding of exactly what kind of book you are writing and publishing. We live in a world that likes to categorize, from defining our foods as low carb or high protein, to categorizing our cars as SUVs or hybrids, to divvying up our country and its voters into red and blue states. What exactly *is* that food, that car, that voter, we want to know. The same is true for the books we read. "What is *this?*" customers will ask when happening upon your finished book. "Is this a cookbook," they will wonder, flipping through the pages. "Is it meant to inspire me?" Readers will connect with your work based on their quick understanding of what they have stumbled across.

Wise Words

Nonfiction books are works that are fact based, containing true information or observation. **Genre** is a particular kind or style of literature.

Books are first divided by whether they contain true information—whether they are fiction or *nonfiction*. Within those two broad categories, they are further divided into smaller categories:

- **Novel.** A novel is fiction, not fact. Some self-published projects have fictionalized a factual life (the author's own, perhaps), but the resulting product is still called fiction. Here are the major fiction *genres*. Remember, your potential readers will gravitate toward the type of novel they like most, so try to stick with one genre. Blending romance with suspense, for instance, or horror with Western, might be fun for the writer but will have a hard time finding an audience.

- **Mainstream fiction.** Mainstream fiction is a catchall phrase for fiction that doesn't fall neatly into another fiction category. Philip Roth's new novel, *The Plot Against America*, is a mainstream novel. Anne Tyler writes mainstream fiction; so does Anita Shreve. Usually published first in hardcover, mainstream fiction is fiction suited for a large general audience.

Pro Style

Bridget Kinsella, West Coast correspondent for trade magazine *Publishers Weekly*, always advises writers and self-publishers to spend time doing a comparison of the competition. "You need to know what else is already published in that category and what the strengths and weaknesses are of the books already out there." Don't assume that yours is the first book ever published on a particular topic, but make sure you know how to make yours the best there is.

♦ **Western.** Usually found in paperback only, Westerns were once ruled by the legendary Zane Grey (who still manages to publish, even though he is dead). Larry McMurtry sometimes writes Westerns (when he isn't writing mainstream fiction).

♦ **Romance.** What was once a fairly easy category to describe (books with swooning women and bare-chested men on the cover) has morphed into a kaleidoscope of different styles. Chick lit books that feature spunky young single working women, romances that feature the second-time-around divorced woman, and the African American romance category is growing by leaps and bounds.

♦ **Mystery.** Alexander McCall Smith's best-selling *No. 1 Ladies Detective Agency* novels are mysteries, as are Sue Grafton's books. P. D. James mysteries that involve elderly women solving crimes are called "cozies." Why? Because they a re best read with a cup of tea at your side, with your tea pot snug in a tea cozy.

♦ **Historical.** Jeff Shaara's Civil War novels (following in his father's footsteps) are historical, as are novels like Gene Hackman's *Wake of the Perdido Star.* These books place invented characters into recognizable historic periods.

♦ **Science fiction.** The shelves are still jammed with Isaac Asimov and Philip K. Dick on the sci-fi shelf, so there is plenty of room for new blood here.

♦ **Fantasy.** Set in imaginary lands and far-off places, fantasy novels are still going strong, helped no doubt by the success of *The Lord of the Rings* on the big screen.

♦ **Suspense/thriller.** James Patterson keeps spinning tales in the suspense and thriller category. You know, the kinds of books that make you keep glancing back over your shoulder as you are reading, wondering what that noise was ….

♦ **Religious.** What was once an obscure backwater of the book world is now *huge.* Mega-bestsellers Tim LaHaye and Jerry Jenkins have opened up the market with their *Left Behind* series. Maybe you are publishing the next big success in this category!

♦ **Horror.** Stephen King still reigns in the horror category after all these years, as do Clive Barker and Dean Koontz. These books are different from suspense and thrillers, in that they include ghouls, ghosts, and otherworldly things that go bump in the night.

♦ **Young adult.** Fiction for the teen set, usually flip and irreverent in order to hit the right tone with the audience. Titles like *The Earth, My Butt, and Other Big Round Things* are popular with young adult (YA) readers right now.

♦ **Erotica/adult.** Yep, you can still find it on the bookstore shelves, usually tucked back in some obscure corner. One successful self-publisher of erotic fiction who goes by the name of Zane has sold 108,000 copies of *The Sex Chronicles* for $22 each.

If you are wondering whether new fiction categories ever arrive, the answer is, yes, they do. Just like the success of the *Left Behind* series pumped new life into the religious fiction category, Vickie Stringer has pretty much created a new one all by herself: hip hop lit. Vickie self-published her first novel, *Let That Be a Reason*, about her life as a madam and drug dealer. Her book was so successful (more than 100,000 copies sold in beauty salons, car washes, and other unorthodox outlets) that she now publishes other writers who write with similar styles and cover similar topics. Not only does she publish their books, but she now also acts as their agent now that New York is calling.

CAUTION **Cautionary Tales** _____

Yes, the book world is very rigid in the way books are categorized. But please do try to stick within the lines. Why? Because books are divvyed up not only on the bookstore shelves, but also by reviewers (most of whom stick to a particular genre and don't review outside of it) and bestseller lists, like the romance bestseller list, the how-to bestseller list, and the young adult bestseller list. If readers, bookstore employees, or reviewers can't easily tell what kind of a book you've published, it won't get very far.

Poetry

If you are writing and reading poetry on a regular basis, then you will agree with me that poetry is harder and harder to define nowadays! Generally, poetry is defined as free-flowing verse that focuses more on feelings and description than on story telling. Most poets still stick to some sort of stanza form, but the length and arrangement of the stanzas vary wildly.

Do spend as much time as possible in a bookstore, making the acquaintance of the different types of fiction that are out there. Sure, it can feel like goofing off to spend hours in the bookstore, but all of your observation will pay off in the end.

The more you understand what other books in the same category look and feel like, the better you can package and position your self-published book. If you are working on an espionage thriller set in Washington D.C., you might notice that many (if not all) of the covers feature the White House. If you want potential readers to connect your book with that genre, well, you will probably have to feature it on your cover as well! Is yours a romance novel? Stay out of the thriller aisles and acquaint yourself with the look and feel of those books. You will soon pick up a pattern in that genre as well.

Pro Style

Writer Sharon Boorstin had done it all—screenwriting, journalism, food writing, and novel publishing. But she just couldn't get anyone in New York publishing interested in her book *Cooking for Love.* A romance novel for middle-aged women? Publishers wondered how that would work. But Sharon knew that there was an audience for her story and put her own money behind it. She self-published her novel with the help of the iUniverse POD company and proved herself right. *Cooking for Love* has been so successful, in fact, that Sharon herself is now a poster child for the iUniverse company and was recently featured in a full-page ad in *The New York Times Book Review*—advertising that any author would die for!

Types of Nonfiction Books

Again, within the broad category of nonfiction, there are many, many subcategories that help readers, bookstore buyers, and reviewers understand what they are looking at.

What follows are broad definitions of the various categories. I'm also including a quick realistic comment or two on how easy the road is for a self-published book in that category. Some are easier than others ....

◆ **Autobiography/biography.** This is the story of a life, whether you are writing about yourself (autobiography) or someone else (biography). Personal memoirs fall into this category. After coming in second on *American Idol,* Clay Aiken quickly published his autobiography, *Learning to Sing;* John Cornwell's book *The Pontiff in Winter,* about the life and legacy of Pope John Paul II, is a biography.

◆ **Travel book.** Travel books can either cover specific destinations and offer practical info on hotels and so forth, or take a more literary approach to describing a region and its people. There have been many wonderful self-published travel books; this is a category that is easy to promote to interested readers. Many recent travel hits have focused on living abroad, like *Under the Tuscan Sun.*

◆ **Self-help book.** A broad category, this one includes self-improvement, relationship books, and even parenting. Peter McWilliams succeeded as a self-published author in the self-help psychology genre with titles like *Life 101.*

◆ **Cookbook.** Books of recipes, what better way to spend your time than in the kitchen? Cookbooks are a great topic for self-publishers. *The Joy of Cooking* started out as a self-published project from a plucky housewife (who couldn't really cook!). *The Wall Street Journal* recently reported that cookbooks remain a strong book category.

◆ **Health book.** Health books can range from heavy medical texts on a particular illness or affliction, to books written by the patients themselves about how to cope with a long-term condition. For many years, there has been a strong alternative health category devoted to herbs and other forms of healing; many alternative health titles come from self-publishers or small publishers.

◆ **Business or financial book.** Many self-published business books have been created to promote a speaking career, a consulting career, or a retail establishment. Robert Kiyasaki is one self-publisher whom we all hope to emulate. His *Rich Dad, Poor Dad* book not only became a huge bestseller, but also spawned an entire line of related books.

◆ **Humor book.** George Carlin and his *When Will Jesus Bring the Pork Chops?* isn't the only humorous guy around. Self-published humor books are a tough sell, though, unless you have a local following or plan to tour comedy clubs and sell books in the back of the room.

◆ **Political controversy/current events.** The ads that Authorhouse (a print-on-demand business) runs in *The New York Times Book Review* feature many politically tinged self-published books. In our hot political times, many of us are moved to put our political feelings into print!

◆ **History.** History books sound dull as a category, but they have been strong sellers recently. Think about the books on Benjamin Franklin and Thomas Jefferson.

Family genealogy and memoirs could fall into the history category. Also, regional history books might be sold at small state parks and other tourist attractions.

♦ **Inspirational.** Feel-good books like the *Chicken Soup for the Soul* series are inspirational books. Always a good category for self-publishers.

♦ **True crime.** Anne Rule is the queen of this category, but there is always room for more. Perhaps you will have an inside perspective on a true crime that happened in your town that will make your self-published version pop.

♦ **Reference.** Another of the huge book categories, reference includes dictionaries, foreign-language books, test-prep books, books about words and writing, and even this book, *The Complete Idiot's Guide to Self-Publishing.*

Are these categories coming into focus for you? Some categories are broken up into smaller, sub categories, like the children's book world.

Children's Books

Children's books are highly specialized, and if you are planning to self-publish in this category, you need to spend many hours familiarizing yourself with the ways in which the books are categorized. No doubt you have a groaning bookshelf or two filled with kid's books at home, but I'd also encourage you to make the acquaintance of a children's librarian as well as the buyer or manager of the children's book section at your local bookstore. They have amazing knowledge.

Adult books are written for anyone who can read the language, but children's books are broken up by age and skill level.

Picture Books

Picture books are the first books any child "reads." These are usually large books, filled with large and colorful illustrations and little actual writing. Self-publishing an effective children's picture book is a costly undertaking due to the size of the book and the production costs involved in working with color and pictures.

Children's Fiction

Also known as "chapter books," children's fiction targets grade-school children who have begun to read. Study the age appropriate breakdowns on the backs of existing books to get a feel for how these books are divided. Typical age categories are 8–12, 10–14, 10–up, and 14–up, but unless this is your professional expertise, you will need the assistance of a children's librarian or book buyer to determine where your work falls.

Children's Nonfiction

This is a big category, one that includes science, biographies of historical figures that are of interest to children, and activity books. My own son Julian is hoping to achieve success in this category with his compilation of news stories for kids called *The Gross News*.

If your plans include publishing for the children's market, I recommend buying *The Complete Idiot's Guide to Publishing Children's Books,* by Harold Underdown. It is jam-packed with specific information that will make you a more effective self-publisher.

Why Are You Writing and Publishing?

Now that you are thoroughly steeped in the different types of books, I hope an idea is forming in your head about just what type of book you are planning to publish. Let's examine another type of category, though—writers. I'd like you to categorize yourself and your reasons for writing and publishing.

Every writer, every self-publisher, has a different reason or motivation for making a book. And depending on just what your hopes and dreams are, self-publishing a book can be a success all around.

Cautionary Tales _____

"I want my life to change." That is the response I heard not long ago from a writer who had just finished her first book. She wanted her life to change because she had published a book. Well, it might, but chances are, it won't. The morning after you publish your book, you will probably wake up to the same old life. By publishing your book, you will have achieved a big personal success, but not always a life-altering one. I'm the author of 30 books, some self-published, some not. Am I mobbed by fans as I walk down the street? No. Is my bank account overflowing? No. Does the phone ring off the hook with calls from the press? Seldom. It is what you do *after* your book is published that might change your life—you might build a speaking career that you didn't have before, or you might enjoy the process so much that you publish book after book.

But many self-publishers fall prey to unrealistic expectations, and I would be derelict not to warn you here about what some of the common pitfalls are. I am not trying to deflate your balloon; I am merely offering observations gained from 20 years in the book business. If I can spare you a tiny bit of heartache, I will.

We are all motivated by different desires. Let's examine a few different results that self-publishers might be seeking: money, fame, personal satisfactions, a family project, or the hopes of selling out to a big publisher.

Money?

Some of you may harbor dreams of striking it rich with your book. If this is your goal, you need to pay very serious attention in this chapter. Publishers with financial motivations above all others need to evaluate their book idea thoroughly and approach the entire self-publishing process in as businesslike a manner as possible.

As we've wandered through the various categories, I've mentioned a financially successful self-publisher or two. Zane and her erotic fiction. Robert Kiyasaki and his personal finance book. Peter McWilliams and his self-help books. In some categories, it is entirely possible to not only cover your expenses while self-publishing your work, but to actually make money. As a general rule, those book categories are as follows:

- Business and personal finance
- Inspirational
- Cookbooks
- Regional travel or history

Categories of self-published books that seldom make money are these:

- Poetry
- Memoirs

If you plan to publish your own poetry or your own life story and hope to make money doing it, please understand that the chances are very slim.

Fame?

Money and fame are often linked but do not always appear together. The kinds of books that can steadily make money might not be the kinds of books that will lead to actual fame. To achieve fame, you *really* have to work at it. Constant publicity is needed for lasting fame, and constant publicity is time-consuming and costly.

What kinds of books might lead to fame? Controversial books, like Amy Fisher's recently released memoir of her troubled past. Remember that she was already infamous and that the media was happy to shine the spotlight on her again. Any book that succeeds on a large enough scale to draw the attention of the media will get some publicity, of course, but it will not really make you a public figure. If fame is your goal, if you are writing a book that you hope will rocket you into the spotlight, spend a great deal of time working on your marketing and publicity plans while publishing your book, and be prepared to spend for the help of a skilled publicist.

Personal Satisfaction?

Yes! Yes, yes, yes! The personal satisfaction you feel when you hold that finished book in your hand will be indescribable. A feeling of personal satisfaction is one that I can confidently promise you as the outcome of self-publishing your work. It might be the satisfaction that comes from knowing that you have faithfully transcribed the words and history of your family and now have a document that can be handed down for generations. Or perhaps the satisfaction that comes from knowing that you tackled a difficult creative project and saw it through to the end. Or even the satisfaction of knowing that you have successfully achieved something—a printed book with your name on it—that so few people on Earth ever get to do.

A Family Project?

Proudly displayed on my shelf at home is a copy of *The Basye Family in the United States*, researched and self-published in the 1950s by my distant relative Otto Basye. Imagine how time-consuming this would have been in the pre-Internet genealogy days. In his introduction, Otto Basye reveals that this family history project was started by his own father, Isaac Basye, in 1880. A multigeneration, multicentury project that filled many a fascinating hour in these men's lives. Is that what is driving your book project? If so, your work will be of great meaning and value to future generations of your family. Your market is your immediate family and other interested relatives. Other than trying to recoup some of your costs and hoping to break even, this kind of project should not be considered to have profit potential. Family history projects do not have a place in the general book market (unless you are Kitty Kelly writing about the Bush family!).

Researching and writing a family history is a tremendous way for an entire family to work together. Retired engineer John Amneus of Roseburg, Oregon, spent countless hours and many years on researching and constructing the Amneus family history and family tree in Sweden and the United States. In the course of his research, he solidified relations between cousins in both countries and also enjoyed working closely with his own brothers to check family history facts and involve them in the editing process.

Families also work together on other kinds of self-published projects. My husband, Peter, and I greatly enjoy the time we spend with our oldest son, Julian, to produce his own compilation of news stories that he thinks will interest other kids his age, *The Gross News*. Do we think about making money from this project someday? Sure, but we also think about how lucky we are to spend time with our children working toward a family goal.

Hopes of Selling Out to a Big Publisher?

Is selling out to a big publisher your secret hope? Your stated goal? The world of self-publishing is certainly full of examples where this has worked in a big, big way. Richard Paul Evans self-published his book *The Christmas Box* and quickly sold the hardcover rights to Simon and Schuster for many millions of dollars. Young writer and self-publisher Christopher Paolini of Eragon fame sold his fantasy novel to Random House for a substantial sum. But more common are the tales of self-publishers who invested thousands of dollars in a book and sold it successfully to the point that a major publisher noticed them and came around and made them an offer of thousands of dollars.

Selling out to a big publisher is a goal that can be achieved in many cases. You might find, though, that once your book is up and selling, you might decide not to sell out to a large publisher. You are just having too dang much fun!

Is There an Audience Out There?

Let's get down to the brass business tacks. If your goal in writing and self-publishing your book is money, achieve fame, or be picked up by another publisher, you need to make sure there is a big enough audience for this to work.

Robert Kiyasaki's self-published book *Rich Dad, Poor Dad* worked in a big way because there is a large audience for financial improvement books. A more specialized book on a topic like left-handed fly fishing, for instance, won't have that same built-in large audience. Are you being clear-eyed about how many potential readers are out there for your work?

In the same way that a major food franchise would first test a neighborhood to determine whether there are enough bodies to justify locating there, you need to test the size of your audience.

Pro Style _____

One thing that helped *Rich Dad, Poor Dad* on the way to the bestseller list is that it was embraced in a big way by Amway distributors. The authors of the *Chicken Soup for the Soul* books also credit much of their early success to Amway. Network marketers are always on the lookout for inspirational books that will help them recruit and also stay focused on success. Does your book have the potential to do that?

Who Are They?

Can you name your audience? "Concerned parents of toddlers." "Fans of midcentury architecture." This needs to be clear in your mind. My two self-published books were meant to appeal to "women who wanted to support businesses owned by other women" and "budget-minded travelers." Who is your audience? Can you quickly and easily explain just who you hope will buy your book? And I don't want to hear you say this: "Everyone is interested in this topic." Sorry, but everyone isn't interested, and you need to be more specific than that.

How Many?

Quantity is important. Size matters, so to speak. If the audience is too small, your book might not be financially viable. And if your goals include money or fame, chances are, it will elude you. When I published books that I thought would appeal to "women who wanted to support businesses owned by other women" and "budget-minded travelers," both of these were sufficiently large enough groups for me to feel confident going forward.

If you are publishing a book on a very specialized topic that appeals to a very specific but small group, antique watch collectors or some such, your small group might well be enough to justify going ahead if you know exactly how to get the word out to this small but interested group of people.

Can You Find Them?

Is there a magazine that caters to your group of potential readers and book buyers? Is there an organization to which they all belong? What about a website they frequent?

To sell *The Air Courier's Handbook*, I sent out press releases to travel editors of magazines and newspapers, who, in turn, printed mentions of the book in their publications. It was easy to find my readers and to identify the media that served them.

Don't count on the mainstream media—newspapers, magazines, radio, and television—to cover your book if the topic is too small.

Where Will You Sell Your Book?

Once you have a finished product, no doubt you plan to sell it. But how? And where? The answers to these critical questions can determine success or failure for self-publishers. Don't gloss over these questions, please. Even if you are 100 percent certain there is indeed a market for your book, take the time to calmly think this through.

I will explain how to set up distribution systems in Chapter 16, but for now, consider the context of where and how many outlets there will be for your book.

Friends and Family

Your friends and family love you—of course, they do. But will they really want to buy your book? Or are you expecting too much support from that one area? Ask now before you spend your money and your time; don't wait until you have a garage full of books. If your book is about you or about your family, realistically, friends and family will be your largest outlet.

Again, I don't mean to squelch artistic impulse, but you need to be clear-eyed about the actual market for a book before you invest your money and your time.

> **CAUTION**
>
> **Cautionary Tales**
>
> You've heard the stories, about self-published authors who end up with a garage full of books. Well, it really is true—I've seen it. Boxes and boxes of unsold books, tall stacks of dusty poetry chapbooks, and crates of shrink-wrapped cookbooks. It's not a pretty sight. Don't let your dreams gather dust in your garage, be clear-eyed and realistic throughout this process.

Bookstore Distribution

This can be a tough area for self-publishers. Chances are, you will have greater luck with your local independent bookstore than trying to get into the national chains from the get-go, but even small bookstores are not a given. Understand that you will need to drive sales into the bookstore to request your book and that the bookstore will expect you to do it. To sell in a bookstore, your book must have a very professional look to it; you cannot skimp on appearances. Sadly, more than one self-published book with an amateurish look and a too specialized focus has gathered dust on the bookstore shelf.

Bill Senecal, the manager of Beers Books in downtown Sacramento, has seen this happen over and over again. "I've stopped carrying most self-published books. It's a black hole. You hate to tell an author that, but only one out of a hundred self-published books will ever work. The other ones just sit there. We just moved locations recently, and I packed up six boxes of self-published books on consignment. I called the authors to come and pick them up, and no one ever did. I guess they just got discouraged and moved on in their lives."

"Any self-published poetry book just makes my heart sink," said one experienced bookseller. More than any other kind of book, poetry books have a tendency to gather dust unless the author is very active giving readings and making sure that the book is discovered by the public. Remember, I don't mean to hurt your feelings or squash your dreams of seeing your work in print. I just want you to be aware of the situation you are confronting and make your plans accordingly.

Online Bookstores

Unless you've been under a rock for the past 10 years, you know the power and presence of bookselling online. It is also a critical element in the recent success of many self-published books. I'll explain later how to actually establish these kinds of relationships, but think now: do you plan to have your book carried in online bookstores? How do you plan to drive sales there?

Unlike a real-life bookstore in which customers browse and look at books and sometimes stumble across an impulse item—your book, perhaps—online book sales are almost entirely dependent on someone driving the sales to that sight. Few web surfers really browse and click through different screens at an online bookstore. They read about a book, decide they want it, and go online to buy. So once your book is available online, it will be up to you to drive those folks toward it.

When asked about how they plan to sell the books they've just published, I've heard this from self-publishers: "Well, I plan to have my book available on Amazon." Okay, that's nice. But passive. Just being listed and available with the online bookstores won't actually sell any copies of your books. Chapter 17 walks you through the process of hooking up with online booksellers and also teaches you how to drive customers to those sites to buy your book.

Giveaways and Promotions

Are you writing and publishing a book as a way to market another business? It's not a bad idea, not a bad idea at all. Self-publishing a restaurant cookbook that is then sold at your cash register as customers leave can be very effective, as can writing a book to share your business philosophy and giving it to clients. Black pearl jewelry store owner Mary Kelly wrote a book, *The Path of the Pearl*, that could be sold in bookstores and also that she could stock on the jewelry counter of all of her stores. She now has a retail product that adds to what she can offer her customers (and it also encourages them to buy!). You have a clear path to your potential readers.

Will your book tie in with a product that is already out there? Perhaps you've written a book on collecting cars and plan to approach high-end car dealers to carry it. If so, understand that your finished book will have to be of the utmost quality. Trying to arrange for third-party sales will depend a great deal on the look and feel of your product.

> **Pro Style**
>
> If your book really takes off you could be asked to be an official spokesperson for a corporation. It happened to me ... my book *Wear More Cashmere* is now promoted on the Milano cookie bag and I'm the official spokesperson for these indulgent treats. Go for a high quality finished book product and it can really open doors.

Back-of-the-Room Sales

Can you make money selling books at the end of a speech? Can you ever! I have watched in silent awe as the supreme master of back-of-the-room sales, Mark Victor Hansen, rings up thousands and thousands of dollars to the audience members who flock to the sales tables. No, he isn't actually ringing up the sales himself; always try to bring someone else with you because you will need to be free to talk to customers and sign books.

If you regularly address large groups of people, you will have a ready and enthusiastic audience to whom you can sell your self-published books. I routinely make several book sales after I give talks to women's groups. If you are writing and publishing a book that you plan to sell this way, you have a solid chance of success.

Dedicated Website

Do you plan to put up a website to promote your book? This is another topic that I will explain in detail later in this book, but for now, let me state that, like sales at an online bookstore, any sales from your website will depend on you driving people to your website. Just putting up a website that you expect folks to find is not a viable plan to move books.

Other Nonbookstore Retail

Often bookstores are the worst place to try to sell your book. Just look back at the discouraging comments of the bookstore manager, about how slow moving self-published books are. But what if your book is the only book in a store? A store that sells something that complements your book and its topic? A self-published regional history book could sell well at the gift shop of a state park or tourist attraction. A self-published book filled with cutting-edge beauty hints could sell well at a beauty shop. Think long and hard about nonbookstore retail places that might be right for you.

Will This Book Really Work?

I've been waving a few red flags in this chapter, asking you to stop and think before plunging ahead with your checkbook and your credit card to publish the book of your dreams. Have any of these questions made you pause and consider your strategy?

The editorial meetings at commercial publishing houses are a time when the different divisions (sales, marketing, publicity, editorial, production) get together to discuss a potential book. It sometimes happens that a book seems like a good idea, but with a bit of tweaking, it could have greater sales potential. A roomful of creative folks discussing how to reposition a book can sometimes be what it takes to succeed on a bigger sale. Let's have an imaginary editorial meeting in which I share some of the ways that you might be able to increase the sales potential of your book.

If making money is not your goal, if you just want the satisfaction of seeing your name in print and sharing your story with a few friends and family, go ahead and skip over to the next chapter. If you are in this to make a buck, though, sit back with a cup of coffee and consider these questions.

Tweaking Your Idea

Sometimes the seeds of greatness are there in a book idea but just need a tiny bit of tweaking to adjust the focus and increase the sales potential. If you plan to publish a collection of your family's favorite home-cooked recipes, why not try to tie it into a larger idea?

Here is an imaginary project—*Three Generations of Sander Family Recipes: Midwestern Favorites for Any Occasion*, based on favorite meals from my husband's family. Sounds a bit limited right now, but can I change it to increase the appeal?

Linking it to the popularity of "comfort food," perhaps, or targeting stressed-out parents who want to gather their kids around the dinner table. Here are two new ways to publish the same book:

- *Comfort Food from Our Kitchen: A Midwestern Family Shares Its Crowd-Pleasing Secrets*

- *Sunday Suppers Your Family Won't Miss! Tried and True Midwestern Recipes from the Sander Family*

See how the emphasis has shifted from the Sander family recipe collection to an enticing-sounding book with greater appeal outside the small circle of our friends and family? Take a close look at your book—can it be tweaked to appeal to a larger audience?

Narrow Your Focus

Sometimes the audience is too broad, and you might be better off narrowing your focus and choosing a more committed part of the crowd. Change a basic travel tour guide of Utah to a tour guide targeting the mountain bike set, for instance. I once encouraged a writer to shift the emphasis of her book from a basic guide to Disney World to a book catering to parents bringing their kids to Disney World. The book hasn't stopped selling since!

Broaden Your Focus

The reverse can also be true, that the audience you are targeting is just too darn small to justify publishing a book with limited appeal. Perhaps by slightly increasing your approach, you can greatly increase your potential book sales. Instead of a house design book for people in wheelchairs, for instance, open it up a bit more to a house design book for people with any kind of physical challenge. You will still be able to address the topic that is close to you, and help more people in the process.

Cautionary Tales

It is also possible to confuse readers with a focus that is too broad. You might also confuse another important person—the bookstore clerk who is in charge of shelving your title. Too broad, and who knows where it might end up on the bookstore shelf!

Mulling It Over

Take all of these ideas and questions into consideration, please, before truly committing yourself to the expense of self-publishing. I want you to succeed and be satisfied with your self-publishing experience. Anything I can do to help you avoid the disappointment of not reaching the goals you had for self-publishing—even by asking you uncomfortable business questions—is worth it.

Remember, your project should match your goals. If you simply want to share your story with the world and are not concerned with the financial returns, go for it. If you plan to self-publish for reasons that involve money, ego, or business, then take the time to clearly evaluate your idea. The time is well spent, believe me.

The Least You Need to Know

- The book world is divided into categories, and you need to make sure your book fits into one.

- It is easier to achieve financial success with some book categories (cookbooks) than others (poetry).

- Make sure your reasons for self-publishing match the expectations of your book.

- Evaluate the size of your book's potential audience to help you determine its potential.

- Adjust your book idea as needed to attract a broader audience.

Chapter 4

Nonbook Ways to Self-Publish

In This Chapter

- Is your book idea better suited to e-book format?
- The emerging market—who buys e-books and why
- Turning e-books into printed books
- E-book production basics
- Producing CDs, online courses, teleseminars, and other nonbook media

Five short years ago, tech industry pundits predicted that *e-books* would quickly replace books printed on paper. "Dead-tree books," the futurists snickered, would soon fade away and be a distant memory as old-fashioned and quaint as silent movies. Did it happen? No. Dead-tree books still rule. But take a look at these statistics as reported in a recent essay in *The New York Times Books Review:*

- The e-book industry posted record sales the first quarter of 2004, a 46 percent increase compared with the same period last year.

◆ Between 2002 and 2003, the number of e-books sold rose 71 percent.

◆ The total sales of downloadable books in 2003 was 1.4 million units.

At this point I'd like to step back and ask you to consider yet another question: Do you really need to publish a traditional book? Would your idea work better as an e-book? A teleseminar? A CD? In this chapter, you'll learn some of the exciting new ways to publish your material that just might fit your needs better than a printed book.

Electronic Books

In the midst of the late 1990s techno frenzy, one man stepped out of the shadows and into the fray—Stephen King. Deciding to give the idea of electronic books a try while sidestepping his usual publishers, King made his latest work available chapter by chapter online, allowing readers to download and pay online. And that, as you well know, is called self-publishing.

Wise Words

An **e-book** is an electronic book. It's information that can be downloaded and read later on a computer screen or hand-held device like a cellular phone, personal digital assistant, or electronic reader.

Many lesser-known names have offered their words to the public in electronic book form. An e-book can be as simple as a Word file that you send out to an interested reader, or as fancy as an encrypted, compressed, virus-protected executable file. It is up to you how fancy you make it and whether you include high-tech bells and whistles.

Who is buying e-books, and why? The audience varies. For fiction, the audience has been dominated by young fans of science fiction. A recent swing in the market, though, shows that women are now stepping into the e-book world and purchasing e-book romance novels and erotic novels. In nonfiction, e-books run heavily toward the how-to topics. A recent bestseller list on www.booklocker.com, an e-book retailer, showed that these were among its top titles:

◆ *Play Piano in a Flash!*

◆ *The Ultimate Basic Training Guidebook*

◆ *The ADHD E-Book: Living As If There Is No Tomorrow*

Do these titles have anything in common? They are all topics that someone could have an overwhelming need to know right that minute. "Gee, I sure wish I knew how to play the piano well enough to pick out a tune at the party on Saturday night ...." And there it is, a book you can download and begin learning from right away. "Man, I'm thinking about joining the military but I'm not sure what basic training will be like ... " Oh, look, a book (linked from the recruiting site www.military.com) that will tell me exactly what to expect. I'll buy it right this second—don't even have to run out to the store. "My hyperactive child is driving me up a wall! I need help right this second!" Calm down, there is a book you can download now to help.

See how all of these popular e-books might work? People want them, right then and there. Are you writing a book that might fill a similar need? Is there a compelling reason for your book to be available in e-book format? If there isn't, you might want to go ahead and proceed with your plans to print. But if there is, why not go ahead and get an e-book version available for sale quickly? A few years ago, I made the decision to rush out an e-book ahead of a printed book.

> **By the Way**
>
> Libraries are now starting to offer e-books to their patrons. The New York Public Library now has 3,000 e-book titles available. One hot title has been the classic Indian sex manual *Kama Sutra*. At other libraries, the hot topics run closer to computer technology, health and fitness, and romance.

A Glimpse of Heavenly Miracles

For several months during the summer of 2000, I was the co-author of the number one best-selling e-book in the country, *A Glimpse of Heavenly Miracles*. It was an excerpt of five stories from a book called *Heavenly Miracles*, which was scheduled to release in early November 2000. Thrilling as it was to be number one, it was not without sadness that we had chosen to go the e-book route.

Laura Lewis, my co-author and best friend, had been struggling with cancer for years and was not expected to live to see the actual book published, so arranging for this five-story collection to be released as an e-book was a way for her to be involved in the experience. It was also a way to raise funds for her family, as 100 percent of the proceeds went to them.

There was world-wide publicity surrounding the e-book, and Laura was featured on Japanese TV, in the pages of *USA Today*, and in *The New York Post*. A moving sales letter about Laura and the e-book circulated through millions of e-mail boxes as readers sent it to friends who sent it to other friends, and so on. The letter included a link to purchase the e-book, so we were able to track sales daily and let Laura know how well it was doing, and also pass along the prayers and kind thoughts that the letter generated.

From the minute I had the idea until it was available online, the *A Glimpse of Heavenly Miracles* e-book took a few weeks to produce. I used a professional book designer and a professional cover designer to make sure it had the right look.

The Perfect Reason

If time is of the essence, publishing your material as an e-book is an excellent approach. If holding a printed book in your hands isn't as important to you as making your material available to the world instantly, then consider an electronic book.

E-book buyers are tech-savvy folks, so this is not the route to take if you are publishing a collection of nostalgic stories that will appeal to the Greatest Generation, say, or a regional cookbook that you think will appeal to tourists. Buyers can't see an e-book; they don't hold it in their hands and consider the purchase.

> ### Pro Style
>
> Tom Antion, an e-book master, makes my project look downright pokey. "One e-book I did went from concept to one sale in eight hours, and it now brings in a couple of hundred bucks a month." Is Tom a computer whiz? Nope. "All I know is where to click to make money," he likes to say. He specializes in creating what he calls "low-cost, no-cost" websites that sell e-books on topics that, like the folks thinking about entering the military or needing to cope with their kids, have a compelling reason behind them. His top-selling e-books are on eulogies and wedding toasts. Both the kinds of last-minute speeches that most of us don't look forward to and need help writing. You can learn more about Tom at www.antion.com.

Self-Publishing an E-Book

When I did my e-book, I used a professional book designer to make the interior as lovely as possible. After all, this was an excerpt from a book that I wanted people to buy. I didn't want them to buy a shabby-looking e-book online and then give the real book a pass. Do all e-books have to be beautiful, though? Not if it is strictly information that readers want—and want right away.

To publish a basic electronic book, make it available to your readers in an Adobe Acrobat PDF. PDFs run on most computers and operating systems. If you don't own a copy of Adobe Acrobat, go to the website http://createpdf.adobe.com and sign up for a free test version. Using Adobe Acrobat will also give you options regarding built-in security for your e-book file. You'll be able to add options like requiring a password (which you share with paying customers), specifying No Printing, or No Changes so that no one can alter the document after purchasing it.

It really is that simple. Once you have your manuscript in a PDF file, you have an e-book ready to sell.

Jim Edwards and Joe Vitale have both written and sold successful e-books. They have much to say about what a successful e-book should look like. Here are their ideas about e-book design:

- Use lots of white space
- Use lots of bullets
- Use a type size of at least 10 points or higher
- Skip the cute clip art
- Always use headers and footers

In other words, a readable book is a useable book. Learn more about what Jim and Joe recommend at their website, 7DayeBook.com.

CAUTION

Cautionary Tales _____

There are some topics that really should be instant e-books, that are so timely that the wait for a printed book might make you lose your inside edge. Two examples are the e-books that Cindy Cashman produced to capitalize on the popularity of the TV show *The Apprentice*. Turning her observations into unofficial books, *You're Hired: Unofficial Lessons from the Apprentice* and *You're Fired: 17 Things You Can Do to Help Speed Up the Process,* Cindy knew that time was of the essence.

Can I Turn It into a Printed Book Later?

If you do go the e-book route, you are well positioned to pursue your vision of a printed book at a later date. Just think, you will have used an e-book version of your work to …

- Generate revenue.
- Work out the kinks.

◆ Get feedback from readers.

◆ Test market viability.

Much of your work is already done, and the money and sales have already started. You could take the proceeds from your e-book and use them to offset the cost of printing a book.

Another idea that is much used nowadays is to release a chapter of your forthcoming book as an e-book in order to generate interest or press attention. Seth Godin has used this method successfully on more than one occasion. He actually gave away his entire book *Unleashing the Idea Virus* as an e-book download for several months before publishing it in hardcover. Did it hamper sales? Not at all. He firmly believes that the free e-book version created most of the sales.

> **By the Way**
>
> To produce your e-book, start with the Word file for your manuscript. Carefully proof and edit it thoroughly. Create an Adobe Acrobat PDF file with simple formatting. Get ready to sell!

With a solid e-book history under your belt, you might also have a chance to interest a commercial publisher in picking up the project. Once Joe Vitale's book *Spiritual Marketing* started to make waves as an e-book, editors started calling him with offers. I know because I was one of them! When I worked for an imprint of Random House, I paid very close attention to what kinds of e-books seemed to be working.

E-Book Sales Methods

Unlike a printed book, an e-book can't be stumbled upon by a bookstore browser. Every single sale of an e-book will need to be generated by you. To create interest in *A Glimpse of Heavenly Miracles*, I wrote a moving story about Laura and sent it out to a few hundred friends, who sent it out to a few hundred of their friends, and on it went. This is called viral marketing, a technique much used online. Write a compelling sales letter for your e-book and send it out to any mailing list that you might already have, of friends, colleagues, and clients. Make sure that you include an easy way for them to purchase your book, preferably a simple one-step click!

Other Nonbook Ways to Self-Publish

If the idea of quickly publishing an e-book appeals to you, consider these other nonbook media ideas as well. Many professional speakers sell their materials in the back of the room and on their websites in CD format. They hire professional recording engineers to record their speeches, press CDs, and sell the same speech to the folks who just heard it live!

Teleseminars are another popular way to market your information, to sell either the books you plan to publish, or the CDs of your speeches, or your professional expertise and knowledge. Fox TV producer and media trainer Jess Todtfeld maintains an active teleseminar schedule in which he lectures on how to get booked; the phone calls are "attended" by hundreds of listeners around the country who are anxious to learn from Jess. Can he charge those folks to listen in? Yes. Can he sell them his self-published CDs and tapes? Yes.

Similar to teleseminars are online courses, in which a large number of people are learning or listening at the same time to an expert instructor. Online courses are typically marketed like e-books, through a sales letter that is sent out to a large pool of interested folks. Once again, this is a method that will not only prepare you for greater sales success once your printed materials are available, but also give you a chance to refine your material before you do publish it.

> **By the Way**
>
> Why just publish in one format? Put your knowledge out in multiple formats, e-books, teleseminars, web-based courses, and more. Write it once and get paid over and over again.

Can I Carry Your Binder?

Susan Harrow, the author of *Sell Yourself Without Selling Your Soul* and a publicity coach based in Oakland, California, has been asked over and over, "How do I get booked on Oprah?" Sensing a business opportunity, Susan sat down and wrote out everything that she knew on the topic. Did she try to make it a book? No. Having already been through that process once before Susan decided to try something different. She printed the pages, used a three-hole punch, and put it all in a large binder. She markets this binder of information in the same way a book is sold, through her online newsletter (sign up at www.prsecrets.com), through speeches and appearances, and by participating in teleseminars with other media speakers.

The beauty of making your information available in a binder is that the price perception is different. Rather than a book that a reader might size up and decide, "It looks like a $15 book," this information is marketed as "professional information" that will make a dramatic difference in your life. The buyer's perception of price goes up along with the idea of how valuable the information will be. The binder format works best for selling "inside information" to professionals in a competitive field. This is not a method to use for a novel or a family cookbook.

Pro Style

Mark Victor Hanson, the co-author of the phenomenal best-selling *Chicken Soup for the Soul* series, wants to teach other writers how to make money in this business. Several times a year, he hosts Mega Book Marketing University, where he gathers together industry experts who share their knowledge. I confess, I am on occasion one of those experts, but that really isn't why I'm such a big fan of these events. Every time I go, I pick up new ideas and strategies about making money in this business. E-books, websites, CD courses, teleseminars—you'll learn it all in just two days. Check out his website for the latest dates and places, www.megabookmarketing.com.

I hope I've given you some new ways to think about self-publishing in this chapter. You just might put your printed book dreams on a temporary hold and pursue some of these fast methods to see your work in print.

The Least You Need to Know

- E-books are a faster self-publishing alternative to printed books.
- Not all topics sell well as e-books; make sure your topic is right.
- The best way to self-publish an e-book is with an Adobe Acrobat PDF file.
- Generate sales of e-books with online letters to interested mailing lists.
- Other nonbook ways to release material include CDs, teleseminars, and online courses.

Part 2

Getting Started

You have a book idea, and you might even have a manuscript, but now what do you do with it? How will you know what goes where and when? Are all books put together the same way? These questions and more will be answered as we examine the insides of a book and how your work will ultimately be put together in the pages of a finished product.

When you understand the physical book process, do you know about all of the extra questions that go along with it? Setting a price, choosing a printer, and figuring out all of the various extra publishing players—you'll get the inside scoop on all of these matters. An overview of legal questions that self-publishers should understand will help round out your understanding.

Chapter 5

Build a Book

In This Chapter

- Making your first decisions about your book
- Is it a hardcover or softcover?
- Will you include pictures?
- Should you use colored ink or basic black?
- A big book or a little book?

You are well on your way to self-publishing your book. You've put time and effort into planning what you will write, and you know who you think your reading audience is. The next step is to begin to visualize just what kind of a book your potential customer will want. You need to start building a book, but how?

The philosophical answer is "carefully." You want to be sure that all of your hard work will result in a book that is suitable to the marketplace. If you had a great idea for a new toaster, would you go directly into your garage and begin tinkering until you developed a toasting machine? Of course not! You'd buy a book that teaches you how to build a toaster and understand the toaster industry. What do toasters do? What do they look like? How are they built? What do consumers want from a toaster? How and where are they sold? And what do wholesalers and retailers look for in a toaster when making toaster-buying decisions? While building a book won't electrocute you, you will get burned if you create the wrong kind of book for your marketplace. Your dream of being a successful published author will be toast.

What Kind of Book Do You Envision?

The first thing you can do to create a book that is right for the market is to close your eyes and relax. Imagine your book in the marketplace …. Pretend you are browsing in a bookstore (with your latté from the bookstore café) and you are looking for a book on your particular subject. Ah! There it is … can you see it? Let me guide you …. What section of the store are you in? What does the book look like? What do the other books that surround your book look like? How much would you be willing to pay for this fine book? How does the content seem to serve your needs as you are browsing the pages? Is the book next to yours better? Not if you can help it! And you can.

Books come in all shapes, sizes, and colors—some are even scratch and sniff! Each genre of book has its own standards and characteristics. In order for your book to be taken seriously by your readers, it is important that it looks, feels, and smells like other books within its own genre. Readers have come to expect common traits for books in certain genres, for example: scholarly history books are hardcover, with a cover illustration that echoes the topic, poetry books are arty or evocative, and health books look serious.

Book designers have carefully developed formulas for visual communication that work very well for certain types of books. As a result, those visual and tactile characteristics are imposed upon and expected within the book trade. In other words, your cookbook should probably not be straight text with a dust jacketed cover, and your business book should probably not be full color and spiral bound with pictures of pies.

Four Major Types of Books and Their Attributes

Wait! Didn't you just wade through a whole big section on book types and categories in Chapter 3? Yes, I wanted you to have a better sense of just what kind of a book you were writing and how it fell into the major categories of books. Now I'd like you to look once again at books categorized in a slightly different way, for a slightly different reason.

By looking at just the major categories of books, you will be able to determine where your book fits and then select the book traits that are right for your book. For purposes of studying how to "build a book," we will now put all of those smaller categories into four main categories of books:

- ◆ Fiction

- ◆ Gift books

- ◆ Children's books (illustrated and nonillustrated)

- ◆ Nonfiction books, including cookbooks, manuals, handbooks, craft books, travel guides, how-to, biographies, history, business, philosophy, inspirational, and more!

That last category contains a wide variety of books in many subject areas, doesn't it? Each genre has its own peculiarities. Books come in many different formats—especially nonfiction. Some should be hardback, some should be soft, some should be both; some should be illustrated, and some should not; some should be printed on white paper while others should be off-white. These things are true for all genres within all four categories. It will help to look at specific types of books within each category.

A Table for You

Each category has a table to which you can refer that will assist you in making primary decisions about the attributes of a particular genre in that category. As we explore each category, eliminate the types of books that do not match your book. You'll be able to synthesize what type of book yours should be and what it should look like.

Because they are so specialized, I've moved the children's book and the gift book categories to their own chapter, which follows right after this. I'd like you to go ahead and read through this chapter, though, even if you are planning a children's book or a gift book. So first let's concentrate on building a nonfiction book.

The Truth About Nonfiction

Producing any one of these books is a lot of work. Each subject category has its own peculiarities. There are many issues to consider when communicating the widely different topics of how-to, history, finance, health, religion, and so on. We will address some of the key issues for specific types of nonfiction and explore what the user and market expectations are so that you can plan a better book for your reader.

With a nonfiction book, as with any book, keep your readers and their needs foremost in your mind at all times. Think long and hard about what *they* need, not what you need.

Usability = Profitability

For instance, if your nonfiction book is a cookbook, then think about what it is like to try to hold a book open as you measure and mix ingredients. How do you feel when it keeps flipping closed at a critical moment in the cooking process? Arrgh! Your cookbook—or any how-to or hobby book used for reference in a working environment—could be bound in a way that allows it to lay flat when open. You might also want it to be stain resistant, have handy diagrams of complicated tasks, and be logically organized for quick comprehension. A usable book will be a hit in the marketplace. The easier the use, the greater the chance of lasting success.

> **Pro Style** _____
>
> If you just can't get enough on this technical topic, Pneuma Books, an award-winning book producer, has a whole bunch of free and inexpensive instruction on nonfiction book development. Get free downloads from their website at www.pneumabooks.com.

You Got the Look!

Commonly, nonfiction books are seen as functional rather than beautiful. That does not mean that they have to be ogres. Nonfiction books should be delightful to use and pleasing to look at.

For any book, determining purpose is the key to deciding whether a book needs pictures, diagrams, extracts, applications, or any other feature. Here are some considerations:

- ◆ **Photos.** If a picture can truly help your reader comprehend your material either literally or abstractly, then that picture is worth a thousand words. If you use a picture simply because you want to share a moment (with your family, your children, or just plain you), then that is not a good enough reason to use that photo. Using elements in that fashion will cheapen your book and make it appear not only self-published, but also self-indulgent.

- ◆ *Epigraphs*, **quotes, and extracts.** If you are an old softie, you will probably want to reprint common anecdotes like *Footprints*. If you are a bookish academic, you might want to employ clips of literature, research, or Bible scripture. But you'd better have a very good reason for doing so or your book might feel trite or commonplace. If the extract you want communicates an idea that cannot be expressed through your own writing, then it is appropriate to use it. However, it is much more rewarding to find a

> **Wise Words** _____
>
> An **epigraph** is a motto or quotation, as at the beginning of a literary composition, setting forth a theme.

unique way to convey your thoughts and theories rather than recycling familiar words and ideas.

♦ **Illustration.** Amateur illustrations are often not appropriate for nonfiction books. For some reason, many authors see self-publishing as an opportunity to display their fine art talent. No commercial publisher would use elements in that fashion. You might want to gather objective critiques of the artwork you want to use to determine whether it is good enough for publication and to determine if it serves the content. In other words, don't just ask your friends and family.

♦ **Icons and clip art.** Clip art should never be used unless it is very high quality. If graphics can truly benefit the reader by visually communicating an idea your writing cannot, then you should contract a professional illustrator to render them. Unique graphics and icons build a brand look for your book. Icons add greater usability to nonfiction books and can guide the reader through your information.

♦ **Extra features.** I have always encouraged authors to build bulleted lists, tables, sidebars, and other features into their manuscripts because these extra items can be used in book promotions. A list can be excerpted and submitted to newsletters, newspapers, magazines, and websites as sidebar material; they're always looking for filler. Your bulleted list or table can be reprinted with credit to accompany an article, and that's a sure shot for your book.

♦ **Practical application.** If you are writing a self-help book, you should consider whether creating questions or exercises for the user would add value to the book. But be careful because certain sales channels such as libraries do not want to buy books that encourage readers to write in them. Work out your exercises in a way that instructs the reader to use a separate sheet of paper. Or you might consider creating a companion workbook or journal as a derivative product that will increase your sales.

I gave you this advice in Chapter 3, and I will no doubt repeat it yet again elsewhere. Spend as much time as possible looking at other books in your category. That analysis is critical to successful book development. See how they do it, and then do it better.

Choose a Binding—Hard or Soft

Since we're covering the outside of the book (pun intended), let's uncover the truth about the benefits of hard versus soft. Let's look at two nonfiction genres of books. How about business books and trade books that might be used in academic channels ....

What type of binding is best for those? In my experience, the best books in those genres are initially released in hardcover, otherwise known as *case bound*, with sewn bindings. But why? There is a different answer for each.

For many business books, it is a matter of prestige. A hardcover book is more attractive and more authoritative in the marketplace. The information is thus perceived as more persuasive—and that can position a book on the top of the heap.

For other types of books that might be used as supplemental curriculum or that may be purchased by libraries—books on sociology, trade practices, economics, history, and so on—durability is a huge issue. Those books should be case-bound hardcovers so that they can be used and abused by the masses. How long would a glue-bound soft-cover last in a frat house? Maybe longer than a student's beer-soaked college career, but not long enough to be resold 10 times in the college's used bookstore.

Most nonfiction hardback books will want to have a *smythe sewn* binding. That is when the pages are sewn together underneath the casing. The reason for this is the durability that sewing provides. In fact, libraries and the education market will often reject hardcover books that have glue-bound, otherwise known as *perfect bound*, pages rather than sewn pages underneath the casing.

Wise Words

Case binding is the process of combining paperboard, glued or sewn gathered pages, and covering papers or cloth to form a hardback book. **Perfect binding** is the process of gluing gathered pages to form the interior of a book. A hardcover case or paper cover (softcover) may cover the pages to form the completed book. **Printed case** is covering the paper boards of a book casing with printed papers rather than cloth, like a textbook cover. **Smythe sewn** binding is when the pages are sewn together underneath the casing for durability.

You and Your Binding

The National Information Standards Organization (NISO) and the American National Standards Institute (ANSI) publish whitepapers on requirements and benchmarks for various industries. The Library Binding Institute has provided the preferred standards for book binding in the book trade. Those standards are compiled in a report (ISSN 1041-5653) that NISO makes available online free of charge. This document is full of wonderfully boring information about sewn and reinforced book bindings. It is helpful to understand what a library binding is. But if you enjoy this report, you might even qualify as an antiquarian curmudgeon! Visit the website www. niso.org/standards/resources and download the PDF document titled *Z39-78.pdf.*

The Money Thing

Cost should be a big consideration when deciding which binding route to choose. Hardcovers are 20 to 35 percent more expensive to print. You should have a good reason to do it. One good reason is that books released in hardcover are more impressive to the book trade. Also, you should know that, while it is more costly to manufacture a case-bound book, it will increase the list price of your book significantly, resulting in a stronger return on your unit cost.

Not every book should be a hardcover. Sometimes a hardcover book is like a tux at a picnic. Appropriateness is everything.

These are some of the nonfiction books that benefit from having hardcovers:

- Biographies
- Business
- History
- Specialty or professional trade (psychology and so on)
- Textbooks
- Reference
- Inspirational
- Religious

Softcovers are bound with glue. That process is called perfect binding. Some of these nonfiction books are typically perfect-bound softcovers:

- Business
- History
- Specialty or professional trade (psychology and so on)
- Inspirational
- Religious

Yes, much of the second list resembles the first list. My point is that, with these books, it could go either way. It is entirely up to you and your reasons for publishing. Was it to impress your clients? Then go with the hardcover. To attract new business? Hardcover. To give away free in large quantities? Choose softcover!

Some of the nonfiction books that a commercial publisher would typically release as perfect-bound softcovers are as follows:

- ◆ Self-help
- ◆ How-to
- ◆ Manuals
- ◆ Workbooks
- ◆ Guidebooks
- ◆ Handbooks

The decision to manufacture a hardcover or softcover book should be made according to the marketplace expectations for a given genre. What is the competition doing? Learn that, and your decision will be made for you.

If you print in hardcover, you will have to decide whether you want a *printed case* or a dust jacketed cloth cover on the boards of the book. Chapter 8 further explains the hardcover terminology and options.

One last note: if you plan to do a hardcover, you might want to do a split run. Often books are released in hardcover as first editions and then in softcover post-release or second edition. A split run will give you inventory for that second run, while saving you money by printing in greater bulk. Of course, it is more costly to print and warehouse more books, but the savings on unit cost may be worth it down the road.

Get a Spine!

Let's really wind this toy up and talk about coil bindings, otherwise known as spiral bindings. Coil binding is a great way to get a book to lay flat. Cookbooks, gardening books, corporate manuals, and task planners all love to have these types of bindings. Retailers hate them. They hate them because they like to shelve most books spine out in the bookstore. If your coil-bound gardening book is spine out, no one will ever see the title and your publishing dream will wither for lack of sunlight. Any book intended for retail should have a printed spine. If you must have a coil binding, then you have three alternatives to strengthening your spine:

- ◆ **Concealed binding.** This is a coil binding that is hidden with a cover-weight paper or board (sometimes called a cased-in wire binding). The outer cover is glued to the outside of secondary underneath covers and wrapped around the outside of the coiled spine to conceal the wire. Most book printers do not do this type of binding in house; they will send it out for you. For more information on this, see http://eckhartandco.com/html/casedin.html.

- **Lay-flat binding.** This is a glue binding that enables the book to lie flat when open. This is more attractive to bookstores and is an economical alternative to concealed binding. Whitehall Printing offers an OpenBAK binding. This is my preference. See www.whitehallprinting.com/binding.html.

- **Slipcase.** This is a specially designed vertical box with an open end, into which you slide a book. (Think of a set of books, although even just one book can go into a case.) This is perfect for a spiral-bound book. The printed side would be shelved outward. Amica in Seattle manufactures all manner of casings. See www.amicaint.com/printing1.html.

- **Saddle stitching.** This is nothing more than an old-fashioned binding of staples. It is a common binding for pamphlets, poetry, chapbooks, and booklets. My little self-published travel pamphlet, *The Air Courier's Handbook*, was saddle stitched. I made the decision to sell mine that way because it was easy to ship in a small envelope, since all of my business was mail order. Binding technologies available today can perfect-bind as few as 12 pages, so there is no really good reason to use saddle stitching do it. For more information on casing and binding, see Chapter 7.

Booksellers have their likes and dislikes when it comes to bindings, and for good reasons. Hardcover books are easy to display, you can shelve them face out, and you can put them in the window without a book display stand and they won't fall down. Trade paperbacks are okay with booksellers, but here is what they actively dislike: comb bindings, spiral bindings, and saddle stitching. A saddle-stitched binding is so small and has no spine; comb and spiral bindings both are hard to shelve and tend to get snagged on each other. Think about where your book will be displayed and sold before you make your final binding decision.

Did You See the Paper?

Here is the plain truth: white paper looks cheap and is tough to read. Most large trade publishing houses of nonfiction books select an off-white or natural paper. Why does it matter?

The fact is, trade publishers print nonfiction books on natural paper because it is easier on the eyes. Your eyes will become more tired when reading text printed on stark, white paper. Most folks assume bright white paper is better for reading. The experts disagree.

The only nonfiction books you might want to print on white paper are: workbooks and activity books.

Whoa! That was a short list! Notice that the criteria is whether a user might write in the book. Be careful though … you don't want to select white paper for a journal or a daily devotional. Those types of write-in books should appear more like nice gift books. White paper is not as classy as off-white. There is usually a higher-quality finish to off-white paper. Always look for a vellum paper, the kind that is smooth to the touch.

If you intend to use white paper, try to use 60# paper. 50# paper will render bad show-through (that is when you can see shadows of the text coming through from the reverse side of the sheet). A 55# natural paper offers acceptable show-through prevention.

On the Other Hand …

Now, after all that complaining about white paper, there is a type of white paper that should be used for books that have high-quality photos or a wide-use of color. A coated 80# or 100# whiter paper is suitable for those kinds of books. Just ensure that the coating on the paper is a dull, matte, or satin finish. A gloss, even a semigloss, can create a bad glare that can destroy color and legibility. Another consideration is durability. If your book is a cookbook or nature guide—any book that is used often for reference in the field—then coated pages are stronger and can be cleaned. Books that benefit from coated paper include these:

- Guides (travel, nature, how-to, cookbook)
- Books with lots of photos (picture books, photo essays, yearbooks)
- Full-color books (coffee table books, manuals, children's books)

For more information on papers, see Chapter 7.

Just the Facts, Ma'am

The following table will guide you in making primary decisions about your nonfiction book in light of the previous information. Here is a key to the abbreviations:

PB = Perfect bound (Glue)
CB = Case bound
SS = Smythe-sewn case
LF = Lay-flat (Glue)

W = Coil
DJ = Dust jacket
PC = Printed case
CC = Cloth- (or paper-) covered case
SC = Softcover

BW = Black and white
1C = One PMS spot color
2C = Two color (BW + 1C)
FC = Full color
Note: All covers should be full color.

+ = Preferred attribute
– = Not preferred but acceptable
? = May or may not include this feature
* = May or may not include this feature

Genre	Sizes (w×h)	Binding/ Cover	Interior Features	Interior Color*	Paper
Autobiography Biography	5.5×8.5, 6×9	SS/DJ CC SS/DJ PC PB/SC -	Straight text, photos, timeline ?, maps ?, index, suggested reading ?	BW	55# natural
Business	5.5×8.5, 6×9	SS/DJ CC SS/DJ PC PB/SC -	Multilevel text, sidebars ?, tables ?, charts ?, application ?, index, suggested reading, resource appendixes	BW	55# natural
How-to (home and garden, craft and hobby, maintenance, sports, cookbooks, professional, personal)	4×9 (pocket), 5.5×8.5, 6×9, 7.5×9, 8×10, 9×12, any oversize	LF/SC + PB/SC CB W/SC W/SC - SS/PC (larger size)	Multilevel text, sidebars, tables, charts ?, diagrams, photos ?, application ?, index, suggested reading, resource appendixes	BW, FC, 2C	55# natural, 80# coated white
Personal finance	5.5×8.5, 6×9	LF/SC + PB/SC	Multilevel text, side-bars, tables, charts, application, index, suggested reading, resource appendixes	BW	55# natural
Health and fitness	4×9 (pocket), 5.5×8.5, 6×9, 7.5×9	PB/SC LF/SC CB W/SC W/SC -	Multilevel text, side-bars, tables, charts, photos, diagrams, app-lication, index, suggested reading, resource appendixes	BW, 1C, 2C, FC (for beauty)	55# natural, 80# coated white

Genre	Sizes (w×h)	Binding/ Cover	Interior Features	Interior Color*	Paper
Personal growth and self-help	5.5×8.5, 6×9	PB/SC	Multilevel text, side-bars, tables ?, charts ?, application, index, suggested reading, resource appendixes	BW	55# natural
Academic (psy-chology, sociology, history, political, religious, commen-tary, economic)	5.5×8.5, 6×9	SS/DJ CC SS/DJ PC + LF/SC - PB/SC -	Multilevel text, side-bars ?, tables ?, charts ?, photos ?, diagrams ?, maps ?, application ?, index, suggested reading, resource appendixes	BW, FC (for photos)	55# natural, 80# coated white
Guides (travel nature)	4×7, 4×9 (pocket), 5.5×8.5, 6×9, 8×10	PB/SC LF/SC + CB W/SC W/SC - SS/PC (larger size)	Multilevel text, side-bars, tables, charts, photos, diagrams, maps, application ?, index, suggested reading, resource appendixes	BW, FC (for photos) + 2C	55# natural, 80# coated white +
Textbooks (student texts) Student workbooks and teacher guides are 8.5 ×11, LF/SC or PB/SC with BW on 60# white	7.5×9, 7×10, 8×10, 8.5×11	SS/PC + LF/PC LF/SC PB/SC	Multilevel text, side-bars, tables, charts, photos, diagrams, maps, application, index, suggested reading, resource appendixes	BW, FC (for photos) + 2C	55# natural, 80# coated white +

Remember that not all interior features are recommended. Only the ones that will truly benefit your content should be used. In Chapter 11, I will give you a complete understanding of the different parts of a book, from the preface through to the glossary and everything in between—what they do and where exactly they fall.

Fiction—What's the Story with These Books?

Different standards govern fiction. The differences have to do with the expectations of consumers and of the book trade. It is important to pay attention to what the requirements are from various channels for particular audiences. There are basically two different buying channels for fiction—mass market and trade.

Mass-Market Fiction

This type of book is colloquially known as the dime-store novel. Generally, these books are known as paperbacks and are printed on *groundwood* (cheap) paper in one common size, w4.125 × h6.75. You will find these books in the bargain book market-place—drugstores, grocery stores, superstores, magazine stands, airport stores, and so on. You will also find larger hardback books in these outlets, but those books were typically released to bookstores first and then sold at bulk discount to those outlets.

Here's the deal: you probably don't want to release a new title as a mass-market novel. Working on your own as a self-publisher, it is almost impossible. Some subsidy presses, sci-fi, action/adventure, and romance publishers are able to do that because nonbookstore retail consumers are their primary marketplace. As a self-publisher with a book produced in a mass-market format—or any format—you will find that chain very difficult to break into. What do you do? You will want to release your novel to the bookstore trade first as a hardcover, establish strong sales, then approach a commercial publisher with your sales record and marketing plan, and finally reprint the book in a mass-market format once you have a deal.

> **Wise Words** _____
> **Groundwood** is an inferior-quality printing paper used for mass-market books, marked by its course texture. Generally, this is not an acid-free paper; it has a life expectancy of under 25 years.

Trade Fiction

You'll find this type of book in your local Barnes & Noble. *Trade* is short for the book trade (or carriage trade, depending on how far back you want to go in publishing history). First editions of these novels and novellas are released to the bookstores most commonly as w6 × h9 dust jacketed hardback. Other common sizes are w5.5 × h8, w5 × h7.5, and w5 × h7. After a year or so, another edition of the same book is released as a softcover version of the same size or the next size down. These are known as quality trade paperbacks (that is true for nonfiction, also).

By the Way
Take a look at the inside front cover of any mass-market paperback, and you will see a barcode printed there. This barcode is an EAN 13 Bookland Barcode. In older books, it was a UPC code. This convention comes from the days when books used to have a nine-digit EAN code on the back of the book. Supermarkets and drugstores could scan only the UPC code. So publishers would print, label, or stamp the inside front cover with a UPC code so the book could gain access to those retail channels. These days, the EAN 13 is the code that should be used on the back of the book. It can be read by all retail stores. But you should still print it on the inside front also, to conform to convention.

Casing the Store Under Cover

Take a look at the cover casings for new fiction releases in your local bookstore. You will notice some common traits. Fiction hardcover books are usually dust jacketed. Typically, the casing is not a printed case. The casing boards are usually covered with a vinyl-impregnated cloth. Kivar and Arrestox are two brand names of cloth covers. Or, for a classier look, high-calendared colored papers from the Rainbow collection can be used. They are not as durable, but that is okay for fiction. These papers can be stamped with a texture to look like leather, wood, grass, canvas, pebbles, and more. You want to make sure you put some effort into casing choices. Don't just choose black or blue Kivar cloth, or your sales might get black and blue and end up in the red! Look at other books in the bookstore, and you will notice that many casings have two different-colored papers on the outside and a colored or printed endsheet for the interior of the case. This is called a *three-piece case*. Do this, and you will have dressed your book up professionally, all set and ready to go to market!

Wise Words

Three-piece case is the three cloths or papers that cover a book casing. These papers are not printed. The first is a back, or spine strip, the second consists of the outside front and back panel covers, and the third is the interior front and back paper that is glued to the board, along with the book pages (called an endsheet.) All three can be different colors.

Also note that book titles are often imprinted on the front and spine of book casings. Some-times they are debossed, or pressed, into the board. Sometimes a gold foil is used. Some-times both. Foils come in red, green, pink, blue, and other pretty colors. All shine brightly when used properly. They will make your book far more appealing to buyers. Make sure the foil color you select works well with the colored casing papers and the dust jacket design. These treatments can be expensive, so determine whether your story is the type that should be represented by this type of finishing.

They Won't Let You in Without a Jacket

When you plan your dust jacket, don't go get a cheap coat. Plan to get a jacket that fits your style of book. Get one that projects personality, fashion, sophistication, professionalism, or an air of intrigue. There are jacket treatments you can select that will certainly get you into the party. Embossing, debossing, stepback die cuts, foils, and spot varnishes are all design choices that will put you in with the in crowd. Take a look at dust jackets from major publishers in the big show. You'll see that many of them are decked out with shiny or velvety accessories and revealing see-throughs. Just like at the movies, these costumes are the handiwork of experienced designers.

Pulp Fiction—the Paper Fiction Is Printed On

Not much needs to be said here except that most quality trade paperbacks are printed on 55# natural paper. Never print a novel on white paper. As we said before, mass-market paperbacks are printed on groundwood, which is a course, dark, stinky paper that is made from a lower-grade pulp. That is where the term "pulp fiction" comes from.

Should fiction be printed in color? No. The only time color should be used in fiction is in children's picture books, which we will cover in depth along with gift books in the next chapter.

Below is a table to help you understand the typical elements in the major genres. Here is a key to the abbreviations:

PB = Perfect bound (glue)
SS = Smythe-sewn case
LF = Lay-flat (glue)
W = Coil
DJ = Dustjacket
PC = Printed case
CC = Cloth- (or paper-) covered case
SC = Softcover

BW = Black and white
1C = One PMS spot color
2C = Two color (BW + 1C)
FC = Full color
Note: All covers should be full color.

+ = Preferred attribute
– = Not preferred but acceptable
? = May or may not include this feature
* = May or may not include this feature

Genre	Sizes (w×h)	Binding/ Cover	Interior Features	Interior Color*	Paper
Mass market	4.125×6.75	PB/SC	Straight text	BW	Groundwood
Trade fiction	5×7, 5×7.5, 5.5×8.5, 6×9	SS/DJ CC + SS/DJ PC PB/DJ CC PB/DJ PC PB/SC	Straight text, reading group, discussion questions	BW	55# natural

Are you still with me? That was quite a bit of information, wasn't it? Who knew that publishing a book would include so many different decisions? The next chapter covers children's books and gift books in detail.

The Least You Need to Know

- Study similar books to understand the general look and feel of your category.
- Make sure your readers will find your book both usable and practical.
- Not every book needs to be published in hardcover.
- Off-white paper is easier on the eye; stay away from printing on stark white paper.
- Booksellers find comb- or spiral-bound books difficult to display.

Chapter 6

Build Children's Books and Gift Books

In This Chapter

- ◆ Gift books—what the marketplace expects
- ◆ When and how to use color
- ◆ Choosing the proper paper
- ◆ Children's books—what the market expects
- ◆ Are you a writer/illustrator?
- ◆ Working with an illustrator

Now that you've waded through some of the early publishing decisions that nonfiction and fiction books need in order to be up to snuff, let's take a look at two entirely different types of books. Children's books and gift books are both quite different from your basic novel or travel book and, frankly, are a bit more complicated. The design elements to be considered can seem overwhelming—one-color, two-color, or four-color process? Fancy paper or plain? When done right, these two book categories are not cheap to produce. I want you to know that up front. With the proper information to guide you, and with all of the facts in hand, you should be able to make the right decisions and avoid costly errors.

A Present for Me?

How nice! What could be more thoughtful than a beautifully wrapped gift? And how delightful when inside the wrapping you discover a book that looks and feels like a gift. You've given books as gifts to many friends and family, I'm sure, and you've received them more than once. Perhaps it was the gift of a book that inspired you to think, "Hey, I could do something like this …."

The term "gift book" is a catchall phrase. Here are the kinds of books that are typically considered gift books:

- Journals and blank books

- Miniature and small novelty books

- Nonfiction inspirational and devotional books

- Photo-essay books

- Oversize display (coffee-table) books

- Books of verse, poetry, or prose

- Joke books

Are those the only kinds of gift books? No. Almost any type of book can be designed in such a way that it looks like a gift book. Before you dress up your book as a gift, though, please consider whether it really needs to be that way. A health book? Producing it like it was a gift book would be odd. A business book? Maybe. If it is a gift you plan to give your high-end clients, go ahead and emboss everything in gold!

We've all heard the expression "You can't judge a book by its cover." Well, when it comes to gift books, they are judged by their covers indeed. The cover, the look, the feel of the whole book are instantly judged by a potential buyer. How a gift book *looks* means everything. If it doesn't look great, you won't get a second glance.

Almost all gift books other than joke books and small poetry books should be hardcover. Gift books should always be as dressy as your budget can afford. Bookstores and gift stores let only the best-dressed gift books into their elite clubs. A dust jacketed printed case or nice cloth cover is your best bet.

When publishing a book that you plan to sell in the gift market, it is important that you think in terms of "product" rather than a book. For example, in 1987, entrepreneur Cindy Cashman left her real estate career and launched her own line of gift books whose sales now exceed one million copies. Her bestseller? A blank book titled *Everything Men Know About Women.* Her advice: "Think of your book as a 'gift item.' See it as a product because that's what gift stores sell. They don't carry books—they carry product."

You need to make sure that the product you are producing will look right on their shelves.

All Dressed Up As a Gift

In the last chapter, you learned about some of the different binding options and learned that hardcover books are often printed on the case. If you do a hardcover gift book and you don't have the case printed, you have the opportunity to select special *finishing* treatments for the casing cover, such as embossing, foil stamping, texture stamping, and special endsheets. One of the most delightful treats is a texture treatment on colored paper that covers the boards used for the casing. These are the elements that will elevate your book to the next commercial level. Book manufacturers will have many color, foil, texture, and paper samples. Request them when you call your printer to obtain a print estimate.

> **Wise Words**
>
> **Finishing** is the process of applying foil stamps, die cuts, embossing, debossing, varnishes, and so on to the dust jacket, book casing, or softcover. Finishing may also include insertions, stickering, wrapping, and anything else after printing.

While most nonfiction hardback books will want to have a sewn binding, gift books do not have to be as durable. It is less costly to perfect-bind the pages underneath the casing. You will find that most hardback gift books that are not large coffee-table books will have glued pages.

Color My World

Whereas nonfiction trade books do not ordinarily require any interior color, gift books are intended to transport their readers into worlds of colorful happiness. Color moves us. If you want to produce a book that stirs the emotions, then it makes sense to use color interiors for certain gift books.

Color should not be used for all gift books, however. Color does not make sense for long text. Often overwhelming color can be distracting and reduces the effectiveness of the writing. It is best to let the words instead of the color do the talking. Use color for the graphical elements, design, illustration, and photos. Special text, like epigraphs, might also be set in color.

These are some gift books that might benefit from full-color interiors:

♦ Small novelty books

♦ Nonfiction inspirational and devotional books

♦ Photo-essay books

♦ Oversize display (coffee-table) books

Some gift books that might benefit from one or two *PMS spot colors* include these:

♦ Journals and blank books

♦ Small novelty books

♦ Nonfiction inspirational and devotional books

♦ Photo-essay books

Wise Words

A **spot color** is one specified ink that is used instead of or in addition to black or standard four-color printing. **PMS** is an acronym for Pantone Matching System, a set of numbered inks that are used for spot color. **High-bulk paper/PPI** is a slightly thicker paper that increases the thickness (or bulk) of the overall book. A high-bulk paper will decrease the pages per inch, or PPI.

How do you use color in gift books? The trick is to not overuse it. If full color is used, it is best to create a standard color palette that can be used throughout the whole book for common elements. That palette should be drawn from the full-color elements, such as photos or illustrations. For one- or two-color books, it is important to use those colors as accent colors only. It can be hard to read long text in color, and red is always a no-no. Be careful not to flood your book paper with heavy colors; it can get very muddy, and you might get stuck.

Printing color is costly, so make sure you are using it wisely. How do you know when and how to use it? A day trip to your local bookstore will help you decide. The repeating theme of this book is, know your competition. Understand the marketplace. And that knowledge is particularly critical when it comes to producing gift books or the next category we'll examine, children's books.

Time to Take Stock!

Though your beautiful book will eventually be gift-wrapped, your current decision is what type of interior paper (stock) to use. As we discussed previously, if you are using lots of color, you will want to use a coated stock. And if not, you will use the same off-white stock you might use for nonfiction books. You never want to use uncoated white paper. Gift books other than coffee-table books tend to be short in length. A thin gift book is not as appealing as a thicker one, unless it is intended as a premium or impulse buy. You might check with your book printer to see if they have a *high-bulk paper* to fatten up your book. Using high-bulk paper will decrease the pages per inch, or *PPI*.

What's in the Bag?

When it comes to gift books, people expect something a little special. This means that your gift book should not be just straight text. The cover and the interior should be designed and typeset elegantly or with flair so that the overall package is a joy to receive. The trick is to not overdo it.

Obviously, photo-essay books and coffee-table books should have lots of pictures and visual elements. But what about inspirational gift books or small novelty books? How can those gift books be made more visual? It depends on the content. Consider adding emotional photos or little designs at the beginning of each chapter to communicate the sentiment of your ideas. Would sophisticated or wacky designs add to the page presentation without overdoing it? Or what about adding quotations from famous people in each chapter? Adding that something extra just might make your book that special gift for that special someone.

Cautionary Tales

Gift books can be very expensive to produce and manufacture. It is critical to your return on investment (ROI) that you explore the competitive gift book market. Because gift books are often purchased as impulse buys, they are priced a bit lower than nonfiction books. You must realize that major publishers attempt to profit on gift books from using an economy of scale. They saturate the marketplace with a giant quantity of lavish gift books priced to sell. Yes, they cost a bundle to create, but when the publisher sells 15,000 of them during the holidays and then sells the rest in bulk to the bargain book market, they are able to make a healthy ROI. Can you compete at that level? If you decide to publish a gift book, be prepared for the expense. Build a strong marketing plan that is based on a clear understanding of the gift book industry.

Gifts Big and Small

Special packages come in all shapes and sizes. Spend a day at the bookstore and size up the gift books that you like. As long as the content of the books you prefer falls into your genre, then you can imitate the size.

That Something Extra Special Counts

Gift books are all about creating something special. If you intend to do a gift book, do it right. Spend the extra money to create a luxurious book that buyers cannot resist. If you go only halfway, you won't sell as many and you may lose your investment.

I really can't stress this highly enough—a gift book sells because it looks beautiful. Produce an object of beauty, then, one that you will be proud to see displayed on the shelf of a gift store or bookstore.

Confused? Don't be. Following is a table to help you better understand the typical elements found in each type of gift book. Here is a key to the abbreviations:

PB = Perfect bound (glue)
SS = Smythe-sewn case
LF = Lay-flat (glue)
W = Coil
DJ = Dust jacket
PC = Printed case
CC = Cloth- (or paper-) covered case
SC = Softcover

BW = Black and white
1C = One color
2C = Two color (BW + 1C)
FC = Full color

* = May or may not include this feature

Genre	Sizes (w×h)	Binding/ Cover	Interior Features	Interior Color*	Paper
Miniature	Very tiny to 2×3	PB/SC (for tiny) PB/PC for 2×3	Decorative, illustrated*	BW	55# natural, 50# white
Small novelty	3.5×5, 4.125× 5.75	PB/PC	Decorative, illustrated*	BW, 1C, 2C	55# natural

Genre	Sizes (w×h)	Binding/ Cover	Interior Features	Interior Color*	Paper
Inspirational, devotional	5×7, 5.5×8.5, 6×9	PB or SS/DJ, PC or CC	Decorative, quality typeset, application*, graphics*	BW, 1C, 2C	55# natural
Blank book, journal	5×7, 5.5×8.5, 6×9, 7.5×9	LF, PB, or SS/DJ, CC LF, PB, or W/SC	Decorative, quality typeset, lines*, graphics*	BW, 1C, 2C	55# natural
Photo essay, coffee table	8×8, 10×10, 8×10 or 10×8, 8.5×11 or 11×8.5, 9×12 or 12×9, 10×12 or 12×10, 12×12, 11×12 or 12×11, 12×15	SS/DJ, CC	Whitespace, quality typeset, photos, illustrations*	BW, FC, 1C, 2C	80# coated white, 100# coated white
Poetry	5×7, 5.5×8.5, 6×9	PB/SC SS or PB/DJ, CC	Decorative, quality typeset	BW, 2C	55# natural
Joke	5.5×8.5, 6×9	PB/SC	Quality typeset, graphics	BW	55# natural

On to our next tricky category—children's books!

The ABCs of Children's Books

Like the other three genres we've discussed, children's books have standards—many of them. And even though children's books are child's play, they're not all fun and games.

Let's examine the different types of children's books:

- ◆ **Board books.** Illustrated picture books on heavy cardboard for babies, like *Goodnight Moon*.

- ◆ **Children's picture books.** Larger-size illustrated stories that focus heavily on illustration, like *The Maestro Plays*.

- ◆ **Beginning and early readers.** Illustrated books that focus more on reading, like the works of Dr. Seuss.

- ◆ **Children's chapter books.** Longer texts with chapter illustrations, like *The Hardy Boys* series.

Wise Words

A **board book** is a book that has pages of thick, stiff paperboard. The printed papers are glued to the boards.

◆ **Youth.** Small novels, biographies, or history, like *The Island of the Blue Dolphins*.

◆ **Juvenile.** Adult-length novels geared toward adolescents, like *A Wrinkle in Time*.

Each of these categories of books includes both fiction and nonfiction. Sizes, shapes, and bindings vary widely in the first three categories but become more standard in the latter three.

By the Way

Some children's books—especially board books for babies and toddlers—can benefit from special cover and interior treatments. Windows, pop-ups, ribbons, car shapes with wheels, squeakies, scratch 'n' sniff, bath time books … all the fun stuff. Be very careful about choking hazards on books intended for small children. For book manufacturing like this, you will most likely have to use an offshore printer that specializes in "handwork." Obviously, chapter books for fifth-graders don't require these elements. But if you're a baby, then you're gonna love this! For an example of these covers and interiors, see www.leo.com.hk/main.htm.

The very first thing you should do is learn everything you can about children's books. Personally, I think the best classroom is the children's book section of Barnes & Noble. To successfully publish a children's book, you will want to become like a child, act like a child, think like a child, read like a child. Pore through every children's book in the store. Note the illustration styles, quality, and usage. Note the size, length, and binding. Note the rhythm, rhyme, and reason. Note the clever copywriting. If you are not willing to spend three full days in the children's book section of a bookstore, then you should not be publishing children's books. The competition is tight and the market is saturated.

Harsh Reality Check

Okay, I confess. I've thought about writing a children's book someday, too. Over the years of being in and around the publishing business, I've learned it isn't nearly as easy as it seems when we, as parents, sit reading aloud to our children. Many other writers I know dream of writing a children's picture book. There is something heroic in the idea that you can create imagery that inspires a child. And many illustrators feel that illustrating a children's book is the apex of their commercial art career.

Here is the harsh truth, though: many writers can't draw, and many artists cannot tell a story.

When working with self-published materials, too many times I have read a good children's story that was hampered by poor illustrations, and I've seen beautiful drawings that were saddled by bad writing. Clearly, if you cannot draw or write, you should be collaborating with a professional, talented counterpart with commercial skills. If you need to hire an illustrator, please do not decide to work with an amateur artist just because he or she is a friend, brother, mother, or someone to whom you owe a favor or to whom you want to give a chance. The stakes are too high, and the money (your money) too great, to rely on less than professional work.

If you are considering working with an amateur, compare that person's work side by side with books from major trade publishers. Ask an objective third party to critique the illustrator's work—who better than a retail book buyer or a children's book reviewer?

Commercial publishers of children's books seldom allow the author to illustrate their own books. Famous examples do exist, like the works of Maurice Sendak, but more often the publisher assigns an illustrator to work with a writer.

On the Other Hand ...

Now that I've been stern with you, I will modify my stance somewhat. If what you are publishing is a family project that you don't have commercial plans for, then by all means go ahead and use whomever you want. My young son Julian gets enormous satisfaction from drawing the illustrations for his book project, *The Gross News*. For a 10-year-old, he is darn good. But I've warned him that if it is sold to a commercial publisher, he might well lose his job as staff artist! But for now, when it is being circulated only to his friends and family, of course, his own drawings are a major part of it. Be realistic, though, that the marketplace will not be kind to the artwork you feel so sentimental about.

One of the most expensive things you can do is to retrofit a story to the illustrations or, worse, redo illustrations to fit a story. Some children's book writers who are just starting out will write a story in Word and create page breaks, and then commission an illustrator to begin the drawings. But then when the story and pictures come together in the layout, they might not fit! If the story needs to be edited, that may necessitate a change in content of the illustration.

Sometimes a story is too long for the proper number of pages, and that will affect the illustration. The best thing to do is to compile a team of pros—a children's book editor, a creative director, and the illustrator to refine the story and plan it out page by page. This is called *storyboarding*. Editing, *copyfitting* (making sure the copy fits the page), type size and style, and illustrative concepts should be discussed page by page. You might then want to go get the storyboards critiqued. Once the storyboards are set and the text is final, the illustrations can be started. Imagine realizing in the layout stage that there is too much text for a given page to fit over top of an illustration.

Wise Words

A **storyboard** is a rough draft of one-page or a two-page spread in a children's book. This type of draft helps you plan for spatial planning and artistic concept in the early stages, prior to illustrating the story. This provides an opportunity to budget pages, **copyfit** the story, and ensure that the page-by-page visual concept is logical and contiguous.

Grow Up! Publishing Books for Older Kids

When we think about children's books, we tend to think of full-color picture books. Let's get the story straight here: there are many more types of children's books, including textbooks, readers, activity books, and more. Let's make some distinctions about color and various elements on the interior for some of these books.

Some folks think that children's novels should be illustrated with full color. Not likely. It's too expensive. Some of the classics for kids—Milne's Pooh books, for example—feature black-and-white line drawings with an occasional full-color plate. But the majority of youth and juvenile fiction features only black-and-white line drawings. For an example, look at *Mrs. Frisby and the Rats of NIMH*. A recently released joint project from best-selling authors Dave Barry and Ridley Pearson, *Peter and the Starcatchers*, has lovely etched dry point illustrations in black ink. Ridley Pearson joked at an author's luncheon that the publisher budgeted for only nine illustrations, but when they saw the artist's work, the budget shot right up and more were included.

However, you may be publishing nonfiction for kids. If you are doing biographies or history, then you will probably just stick with black-and-white illustrations. But if you are doing science or nature books, most of your competition uses full color, like the Grolier *Getting to Know Nature's Children* series.

Hitting the Books

Textbooks are a whole other story. Textbooks employ full color. In addition, you will probably want to create diagrams, charts, maps, puzzles, graphical icons, and more. Remember that you don't want to foster writing in a textbook, so you'll have to construct your exercises in a way that prohibits kids from writing in answers. This is a difficult equation to solve because instructors prefer complete solutions that are easy to implement. You will want to consider creating a three-part curriculum.

For instance, you might want to show some example exercises or study questions in each chapter of your full-color textbook. Then you can develop a separate one-color activity book or student workbook (called a consumable) that includes exercises or homework with write-in spaces, games, puzzles, coloring pages, and so on. The third component is the one-color teacher's guide and answer key.

By the Way

If you are intending to publish youth or young adult fiction, then you will want to know all about the educational market for schools. Many programs, like Scholastic, distribute books to school libraries, teachers, and parents of school kids. The paperbacks in this genre are usually printed in a w5.2 × h7.6 size. You will want your youth fiction book to conform to these standards. Books in this format are also acceptable to the book trade. You might want to do a split run in this size, with some smythe-sewn hardbacks and some paperbacks.

Yes, three books are more costly to produce, but you have just increased your product line threefold, and your consumable will be sold over and over again even if your textbook ends up in the used bookstore. Go back to school and check out the textbook curriculum from Pearson Education, Henry Holt, and McGraw-Hill. It is tough to make the dean's list in the textbook market. But if you build your books right, you'll go to the head of the class.

The Home School Market

Home schooling is exploding onto the educational scene. Every year it becomes more popular. Because it is a grass-roots industry, many of the materials are not very sophisticated. And neither are the distribution channels. Website communities, inexpensive catalogs, and word-of-mouth are the ways home schoolers find out about the next great set of books for educating their kids. Families often buy kitchen table curriculum from other home-schooling peers rather than buy the high-priced textbooks schools are using. Of course, that is an overgeneralization, and many mainstream textbooks from trade publishers are sold through home school catalogs. But this is a ripe market for well-built, commercially produced educational books.

If you can create a set of books that is better than your average homemade prairie primer, and sell it at a lower price than the expensive textbook market, then buyers will line up at your door. Once you begin to sell lots of books, you can cross over into mainstream educational markets. Prove that your books work and are popular for home schoolers, and acquisitions educators may buy your books for public and private schools.

Building a Web to Catch Your Readers

One last comment about building children's books: the children's marketplace is all about creating an experience for kids. All you have to do is go to www.nickjr.com or http://pbskids.org to know what I am talking about. The Internet is a place kids, parents, teachers, and librarians can go to immerse themselves in the experience of your story and learn more about your books.

I firmly believe that every children's book publisher must build an interactive website concurrently—or before—building a book. A commercially fun website will foster book sales and brand loyalty better than any ad, marketing piece, bookstore reading, book review, or any other medium for promotion. Offer free downloads, puzzles, games, links, educational information for parents and teachers, and discounts. You can build a community around your story or nonfiction topic through message boards, FAQs, and e-mail signups to which you broadcast newsletters. You will even collect new ideas for derivative products and *merchandising*. If you are thinking like a commercial publisher, then you will realize that your book is just the beginning of a long, prosperous relationship with the world that can be developed primarily through an effective website. Visit the websites I mentioned and get some great ideas.

> **Wise Words**
>
> **Merchandising** is the promotion of merchandise sales by coordinating production and marketing, and developing advertising, display, and sales strategies.

Here is a table to help you visualize the different ways these books are created and the typical elements used. Here is a key to the abbreviations:

PB = Perfect bound (glue)
SS = Smythe-sewn case

LF = Lay-flat (glue)
W = Coil
DJ = Dust jacket
PC = Printed case
CC = Cloth- (or paper-) covered case
SC = Softcover

BW = Black and white
1C = One PMS spot color
2C = Two color (BW + 1C)
FC = Full color
Note: All covers should be full color.

+ = Preferred attribute
- = Not preferred but acceptable
? = May or may not include this feature.
* = May or may not include this feature

Genre	Sizes (w×h)	Binding/ Cover	Interior Features	Interior Color*	Paper
Board books	Up to 8.5×11 binding/	Special self-cover	Illustrated ?	FC	Paper-covered stiff cardboard
Picture books	Square up to 12, 8×10 or 10×8, 8.5×11 or 11×8.5, 9×12 or 12×9, or any combo up to 12	SS/DJ, PC + SS/PC PB/DJ, PC PB/PC PB/SC -	Illustrated	FC	80# coated white; 60# white -
Early readers	5.5×8.5	SS/PC PB/PC PB/SC	Illustrated, for parents and teachers	FC, 2C	60# white
Youth fiction	5.125×7.625	SS/DJ, PC (for retail) SS/PC PB/DJ, PC (for retail) PB/PC PB/SC	Straight text, Illustrated per chapter	BW	55# natural, groundwood
Juvenile fiction	5.125×7.625	SS/DJ, PC (for retail) SS/PC PB/DJ, PC (for retail) PB/PC PB/SC	Straight text	BW	55# natural, groundwood

continues

continued

Genre	Sizes (w×h)	Binding/ Cover	Interior Features	Interior Color*	Paper
Nonfiction	5.125×7.625 (for bio), 5.5×8.5, 6×9, 7.5×9, 8×10, 8.5×11	SS/PC PB/PC PB/SC	Multilevel text, side-bars, tables, charts, photos, diagrams, maps, application ?, index, suggested reading, resource appendixes	BW	55# natural, groundwood
Textbooks (student texts) Student work-books and teacher guides are 8.5 ×11, LF/SC or PB/SC with BW on 60# white.	7.5×9, 7×10, 8×10, 8.5×11	SS/PC + LF/PC LF/SC PB/SC	Multilevel text, side-bars, tables, charts, photos, diagrams, maps, application, index, suggested reading, resource appendixes	BW, FC (for photos) + 2C	55# natural, 80# coated white +

We have discussed many different types of books and scenarios. It is time to get a warm-up on that latte and take some more deep breaths. This is a whole lot to digest. Close your eyes for a moment and imagine yourself succeeding in the areas we discussed that apply to your publishing dream. I hope it is becoming clearer and clearer.

I sound like such a broken record—the number one thing you need to do to succeed in any kind of self-publishing is to investigate the marketplace for the type of book you want to publish. Find out what type of book it should be, where it is sold, and how it is promoted and distributed to that sales channel. Begin to collect books you like, hang out in bookstores, explore the ins and outs of the book trade, and make your plans.

The Least You Need to Know

- Both children's books and gift books can be costly to produce.
- Gift books really are judged by their covers.
- Think of your gift book as a "product" rather than a book.
- Children's books should be professionally illustrated if you plan to sell them in the bookstore market.
- Make sure your story and your illustrations fit together nicely.
- Books for older children use less color and fewer illustrations.

7

Who Are All These People?

In This Chapter

- ◆ Editorial and production players
- ◆ Hiring freelancers to help you
- ◆ Cover copy and design
- ◆ Interior layout and design
- ◆ All about indexers

The moment has finally arrived—you've completed an entire manuscript. It was a long and lonely endeavor, and now it is over. Give yourself a big pat on the back and crack open a bottle of champagne. So many people talk about "wanting to write a book someday," and you have now joined the few folks who have actually accomplished that. Your manuscript is done, and you are now ready to begin putting the pages into book form. Uh, how exactly does that happen, anyway? How does a manuscript, that stack of pages that has steadily been growing under your diligent work, end up as a finished book?

Nothing goes straight to the printer, of course. Nor should it. The process of getting books into finished form involves a fairly large cast of characters. In this chapter, you meet them, one by one.

Pro Style _____

The words on the page of your manuscript are referred to as **text** or copy in the editing process, as opposed to illustrations. Your manuscript is your book before production. And production is the process by which your manuscript becomes a published title—a book!

Are these all folks that you will need to get involved in your project? Not necessarily, but you need to understand what they do and how it fits into the overall process. For you to publish the best book possible, though, you're going to need to acquire these skills yourself or hire out aspects of the editorial and design production of your book.

Let's peek inside a commercial publishing house to see what these folks do, the ones who work on one author's *text* to create a book—people who include developmental editors, copyeditors, cover designers, and more.

Meet the Players

You're here to learn about self-publishing, and to self-publish a quality title, you must operate like a professional publishing company. In a professional publishing company, many people polish the writer's work in the production of the book. Understanding what they do will give you a more complete understanding of the process and help you visualize all the roles you might be playing yourself. Meet the players:

- ◆ Developmental editor
- ◆ Production editor
- ◆ Copyeditor
- ◆ Proofreader
- ◆ Interior designer
- ◆ Cover designer
- ◆ Copywriter
- ◆ Indexer

Quite a long list, eh? For many years I worked as an acquisitions editor at a midsize publishing company. Acquisitions editors are the folks involved in signing up authors and helping decide what gets published. Once a book was signed, there was always that exciting day when the final manuscript arrived (on time, hopefully). I'd read it, and then it was sent on to the printer. No, just joking. I'd read it, add my comments and suggestions to the manuscript, and then pass it on to a production editor, who would be responsible for seeing the project through to a finished book. Behind the doors of a publishing company are a vast horde of eager folk who all have a big hand in the process.

> **By the Way**
>
> I tell people I'm an editor, and they assume I sit at a desk with a green eye shade on and a red pencil in my hand, carefully fixing up someone's text. Well, no. I hardly ever do that and, in fact, am not very good at it. Different editors have different skills. Acquisitions editors shop for a living; they look for projects to publish. Copyeditors comb through manuscripts carefully and clean up errors of spelling and grammar. Developmental editors help authors develop their book into a better work by suggesting ways to improve or expand in some sections, or cut in others. A managing editor is the person who is responsible for running the production end of things.

Who Knew There Were So Many?

Most people assume that the writer writes his tome and the printer prints it—but so many other people have a hand in the production. It's a daunting task to take on all roles, but many self-published authors choose to do so, whether because of budget constraints or control. The thing to consider is whether you have the skills (or the interest and personality) to professionally complete all the jobs in the production of the book yourself. In most cases, the author will need to hire freelancers. There are just some people who are literally born to be an indexer or a production editor, for example. These attention-to-detail types thrive with the cataloguing or copyediting of every word, whereas their beloved job would drive someone like a publicist or even a writer crazy.

Let's begin navigating the production team by taking a closer look at all the editors and designers.

How Many Editors Does It Take to Screw in a Light Bulb (or Publish a Book)?

When an author completes his manuscript, the work is handed over to a host of editors. But the title "editor" means different things, depending upon the type of editor with whom one is dealing. As I said a few paragraphs back, as an acquisitions editor, I was more involved in acquiring new titles than in the finer points of editing a manuscript. Publishing houses have editors up and down the aisles, each of whom does something slightly different. They all work to make books better, though.

Developmental Editor

A developmental editor works on content and helps you improve and refine the substance of your work. This editor is the "big picture" person for the storyline and themes within fiction works, and the purpose/intent within nonfiction works. The developmental editor looks at overall style and continuity of the work.

Ask yourself this: can I objectively look at my writing and unearth any developmental inconsistencies? Most writers believe that an unbiased opinion of their work can only help develop it. If you choose not to hire a developmental editor to look over your manuscript, at the least, pass on the work to a trusted friend, fellow writer, mentor, or astute relative to read and offer comments.

Pro Style

Writers write. Editors edit. Don't expect an editor to actually write anything in your manuscript, but instead to suggest ways in which you yourself can improve it. The best editors steer you gently toward producing your own best work.

Production Editor

Think of a production editor as the manager of the editorial team—or project manager. A production editor might follow the manuscript from copyediting to final page proofs and ensure that the work meets deadlines and stays on schedule; this editor may also have a hand in the content editing. The roles of developmental editor and production editor often merge. Alas, the production editor may also wear the hat of copyeditor. Let's look at what a copyeditor does.

By the Way

Andi Reese-Brady, longtime project editor for Prima Publishing and now a freelance editor, has embraced the meticulous world of editing. Why ever did she devote her career to edit marks, pagination, punctuation, and every nit-picky style element within book publishing? "I had a college professor who had a position open for an editorial assistant. He handed me *The Chicago Manual of Style* and said, 'Read it.' I did." Anyone who has perused the more than 900-page reference book will attest that the Reese-Bradys of the world are few. It takes another breed of human to pore over paragraphs explaining when and where to italicize words, how to document "papers read at meetings," the precise formatting of the colophon, and other intricacies of publishing.

Copyeditors

Copyeditors are the high school English teachers of the publishing arena. They mark up your work and correct every error. They also look for anachronisms, continuity flaws, and ambiguities. The copyeditor is to your book what a mechanic is to a car. I strongly urge you to hire a freelance copyeditor. The eyes of the copyeditor are essential in producing a professional and polished book. Unless you are confident that you are an expert in the written language (and perhaps have memorized *The Chicago Manual of Style*), you should find and hire a freelance copyeditor. (For more information, see the section "The Legionnaires: Hiring a Freelancer.")

Proofreaders

Proofreaders aren't actually trying to prove anything, so where did the name come from? The final stage in printing is called a "proof," and that is your last chance to look for errors before the presses start rolling and there is no turning back. A proofreader was the last pair of sharp eyes, making sure that what was about to be printed was as perfect as humanly possible.

John Clare, the nineteenth-century poet, wrote in a letter to a friend, "If life had a second edition, how I would correct the proofs." He'd have corrected all the egregious or ridiculous mistakes that made his days more difficult, right? And if you've ever purchased a new home, you're familiar with the "walkthrough." It's your last chance before moving in to find any glaring problems with the house. Are all the doors on their hinges? The rooms painted the correct color? The molding finished? Proofreaders, like the homeowners on a "walkthrough," check for conspicuous mistakes or subtle errors so they don't bemoan those mistakes later, as the poet Clare did. Again, proofreaders are the last-chance people for typos, paragraph or page problems, formatting inconsistencies, and more.

Although you may certainly hire a proofreader, this is one of the editorial jobs that you can—with a keen and discerning eye—do yourself. I highly recommend that you also give the page proofs to another set of eyes within your home or writing circle. When you've reviewed something over and over, you're likely to skip over and miss even the most obvious problems.

Book Designer

Book designers design the interiors of books (and sometimes, but not always, the covers). It is a specialized skill, not one that any graphic designer is going to have. Books have certain specific design needs, such as the minimum depth of the gutter required so that the type on the pages doesn't disappear into the spine.

The presentation of your text is an important component to the production and sale of your book. Unless you are a skilled graphic designer or art director, you will need to find professionals to handle most of the design elements of your title. We examine the basics of book design in Chapter 13.

The interior designer "lays out" your text, and the complexity of the interior designer's work depends upon the title. In a novel that is primarily text, the design elements are straightforward and generally rely upon a simple interior design. But with nonfiction books or heavily illustrated books, the interior design may prove more complex. Consider a book with annotations, pictures, or a stylized format (such as this book, with its many sidebars). The interior designer formats all the intricacies of each page—from shading, to icons, to artwork, to ink colors, and everything else that has to do with the interior layout. Once they have the "sample" design created, the interior designer writes a detailed description of the type specifications for the typesetter, who will actually lay out the final book pages.

> **Cautionary Tales**
>
> "Bill Gates is a very smart guy," says Ron Pramschufer of BooksJustBooks.com, "but he isn't a printer. Microsoft Word wasn't designed to be used as a page design, and books that are sent to the printer laid out in Microsoft Word never turn out well." Spend the money on a real compositor and book designer.

Cover Designers

Cover designers design book covers. It is as simple as that. They don't design logos, letterhead, billboards, or business cards. It is a specialized design skill involving type, color, and graphics.

Doctoral theses have been written on book cover design, no doubt. That's because many books sell by the merits of their cover. The first thing a prospective reader sees is the front and back cover and/or the spine of a book. The title and artwork had better grab buyers, or they won't delve any further into the pages. The cover of your book also should wrench the reader away from other like titles.

Interestingly, what began as a way to protect the precious pages of a book morphed into a modern-day marketing tool of paramount importance. In most cases, it is essential that you hire a cover designer. Unless you are a graphic designer with expertise in books, you'll need a highly trained professional who works with the computer programs necessary to create a printer-ready version of your cover.

So instead of merely hiring an artist to provide you with a few ideas for the cover and choosing one, research cover designs of best-selling books in your genre. Peruse bookstore shelves. What book covers stand out? Why? What artistic feel appeals to you and translates well to your book? Then share your discoveries and your ideas with the designer. In the final analysis, you either accept or reject the designer's product. That's another good reason to provide input from the beginning. You don't want to waste production time going back to the proverbial—and, in this case, literal—drawing board.

Book covers are in important step on your road to success. Coming up soon is an entire chapter devoted to the science of book covers.

Copywriters

The copywriter provides the text that appears on your front and back cover and inside flaps. The copy here must work with the cover to entice the buyer. Don't mistake this copy with your inside text. The copy written for the covers and flaps is marketing copy—not literary or journalistic text. Think advertising copy here.

A good copywriter is a highly paid professional with the ability to make your book sound like the greatest thing since sliced bread. Following is an example of how copywriting can make a difference:

> *The Rainy Day Rescue Book*
>
> You'll find 250 ways to keep your children occupied and entertained when they can't go outside.
>
> *The Rainy Day Rescue Book*
>
> "Mom, I'm bored!" Tired of hearing your children whine on a rainy day? Out of ideas on how to keep them amused? *The Rainy Day Rescue Book* is here to help! Inside you'll find endless ideas for how to turn rainy days into treasured memories.

See how one bit of copy sounds so much more appealing than the other? Copywriters know how to quickly grab the attention of a reader and keep them looking at your book.

Indexers

Categorizing and detailing every topic and substantive word in your manuscript—that is the job of the indexer. The indexer organizes and then alphabetizes everything within your book. *The Chicago Manual of Style* even describes attributes of the "ideal indexer." "The ideal indexer sees the book as a whole, both in scope and in arbitrary limits; understands the emphasis of the various parts and their relation to the whole; and, perhaps most important of all, clearly pictures potential readers and anticipates their special needs."

Although an author may know his work best and, therefore, provide the most thorough indexing of the book, more often, a professional indexer should be called in for this grueling, tedious affair. Concentration and the attention to minutia make up the indexer's day.

Some computer programs can create an index for you, but nothing beats a skilled indexer. Not every book needs an index, but if yours does and you are aiming for a polished product, use a pro.

Is There a Doctor in the House?

The term *book doctor* conjures up all kinds of images—that of a pile of manuscript on a gurney and anxious-looking professionals dressed in white coats bending over it, wondering whether there is still time to save it …. I've wondered that myself a few times when manuscripts arrived from authors in an unpublishable condition.

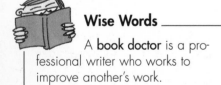

Wise Words

A **book doctor** is a professional writer who works to improve another's work.

A book doctor is a special kind of writer, the kind that can come in and work over someone else's material to improve it without losing the real author's voice. A book doctor is different from a developmental editor, though. A developmental editor suggests ways in which to improve your book, and then you do the work yourself. A book doctor actually sits at the computer and personally works over your manuscript.

Finding a Primary Care Physician

How are you going to find a book doctor? I've included a few I've worked with in the resource section. Book doctors do advertise in most of the major magazines for writers, but how do you know who to work with? Take your time getting to know candidates on the phone, and ask them for samples of their work. You'll want to see two things—what the original manuscript looked like, and what it looked like after they doctored it.

Paying Your Medical Insurer

The cost of a book doctor is subject to negotiation. I've paid doctors as little as $3,000 to whip a business book into shape, but the costs can also run much higher. Like the cost of real health care, the costs of hiring someone else to patch up your book can add up to $10,000 or more. But you won't know until you ask, and feel free to bargain away.

Do you really need to do this? Once again, I will ask you to examine your own reasons for publishing. Are you writing your own story just to share with your family and friends? Then your own writing should suffice. There is no need to drop big sums of money to fix up a manuscript that will be shared with people who will happily read it any way you wrote it and not expect professional-quality prose. Your life story sounds better in your own words, anyway.

Are you publishing a book that you hope will serve as a fancy calling card and help you ramp up your business and attract new clients? Then perhaps you should involve a book doctor if you sense that your own writing isn't polished enough.

Book doctor Melanie Votan suggests that, before hiring a book doctor or a developmental editor to help your work, you first spend time in writers' workshops and critique groups. "Book doctors charge by the hour, and it can quickly become expensive." Make sure you've got your work to the point that the professionals are doing real work to improve it, not just the basics that you should have been able to improve on your own.

 **Pro Style**

If you hire a book doctor or a ghostwriter, make sure you use the right agreements. Both a work-for-hire agreement and a nondisclosure agreement are perfectly proper. Agreements are covered in Chapter 10 and included in the appendixes.

The Legionnaires: Hiring a Freelancer

In the French Foreign Legion, professional soldiers make up the ranks. Mercenaries. Hired guns. Why are they hired to fight? Because they are experts in war. The term *freelancer* actually originates from medieval days and was a term used to designate a "lancer" or swordsman for hire—a soldier of fortune! Today freelance editors and designers comprise the "Legionnaires" of the book-publishing world, willing to put their skills to use for whomever pays them. Just how do you find these people if you need them?

Today finding a freelancer is relatively easy. A search of the Internet with the key words "freelance editor" will bring up myriad professional writer and editor sites, listing potential freelancers.

Another good way to glean a freelancer is by asking around in your local self-publishing or writing community. Get references from people you know and trust within the arena.

When you have a list of potential freelancers within the genres of work that you need (editorial, design, manufacturing), you'll want to gather bids and resumés from each. It's impossible to provide an accurate estimate of the charges you may accrue from freelancers. Each freelancer will cost the job according to the amount of work and his or her own rates, depending upon many things. One consideration is location. A freelancer in San Francisco, California, a major metropolis and competitive publishing city, is likely to charge more than a freelancer in Pocatello, Idaho.

Another consideration is experience. The resumé of the editor or designer affects the fee structure. You'll have to decide, based upon references, your budget, and the sample work you see from the freelancer, who to hire.

The Least You Need to Know

- When your book is written, there are still many steps to take in the production of a polished and professional book.

- The key players in the production of a book are the developmental editor, production editor, copyeditor, art director, interior designer, cover designer, copywriter, proofreader, and indexer.

- Everyone has their expertise. If you aren't an accomplished editor or designer, freelance the work out to a professional.

- You worked hard to write it, and you want your book to be a polished gem. Don't be afraid to spend money on diamond cutters such as developmental editors and proofreaders.

- Don't hire a book doctor or developmental editor until you have taken your manuscript to writers' workshops and critique groups.

Chapter 8

The Wide World of Printing

In This Chapter

- ◆ A little bit of history about printing
- ◆ The process of printing today for authors and timelines
- ◆ How to find a printer
- ◆ Reasons why print-on-demand might be a good choice
- ◆ Elements and options to consider in the printing of your book

The world generally considers the birth of modern printing to have arrived with Johannes Gutenberg's printing press. He was not the first ever printer, not by any means. What separated Gutenberg from other hip printers of 1440 Germany? His wooden press used movable type, cast in metal. Before Gutenberg's invention, most books were religious in nature, produced by monks with a lot of time on their hands, using a wood engraving process.

In wood engraving, the printing craftsman cut out the background, leaving the text and illustrations raised. The artisan literally sculpted the tablet to be printed. When each labor-intensive page was completed, it was inked and a page was pressed over it for the imprint. Because the wood was used over and over, naturally it deteriorated. The elements also caused a deterioration of the pages, limiting the lifespan of each wood block.

The advent of Gutenberg's press quickened the printing process—although not nearly as much as today's instant printing, of course. Consider that Gutenberg took two years to print his famous 42-line Bible. You are hoping to see your book finished much more quickly. Nevertheless, with his press, an industry was born. By 1499, more than 250 European cities used a metal press. A century later, in the 1580s, both Oxford and Cambridge universities began their printing publishing endeavors that continue to this day.

Baby, It's Hot in Here!

The next important step in the history of printing arrived with the linotype, or "hot lead" type. Introduced in 1886, linotypes were the first printing machines to produce a solid, straight line of type. Simply put, linotype operators set the brass matrices (or characters) for each line and then cast the lines with a molten metal pumped in from behind the cast. Just how hot was the casting metal? About 550°F. Linotype was used well into the twentieth century.

Although the linotype ushered in the era of even quicker printing than before, technology soon overcame the presses and words such as *platen press*, *xerography*, *silk screening*, and *inkjet* soon entered our vocabularies. With *The Sacramento Women's Yellow Pages*, my first self-published project, I made trip after trip to see Diane the typesetter; she had a large machine that she'd invested in quite heavily. Those days are gone, of course, and today *digital* is the word of the printing era.

As typesetting advanced throughout the ages, so did the printing presses. What you see in a printing plant today is a far cry from what Mr. Gutenberg proudly operated. As a self-publisher, you have four different types of printing press options available:

♦ **Digital printing.** Originally developed by Xerox, digital printing is used by the print-on-demand industry. Picture a big Xerox machine, a big copier that also trims and binds; that is what a digital press can do.

♦ **Short-run offset.** These presses print from paper plates that are made directly from your laser-printed text.

♦ **Traditional sheet-fed printing.** A sheet-fed printing press uses metal plates to print and is very good for books that use coated stock, which is paper that has a glossy finish to it.

♦ **Web offset.** A web press prints on large rolls of paper (not individual sheets) and prints very quickly.

What to choose? If you are going to do print-on-demand, you will, of course, go with a digital printer. But if you are going to plunge into the world of traditional printing and seek bids to find the best price for your project, you will soon learn that different printers have different equipment. Not everyone has a big manufacturing plant stocked with all the different types of printing presses.

As you collect your quotes, you will also learn what kind of equipment the printer you've approached will use for your book.

Pro Style _____

Printing comes with a jargon all its own—everything from grain to perfect bound, to "blue lines," to foil stamping, folding, scoring, and more. It's a whole new language to learn. The sooner you familiarize yourself with the jargon, the sooner you'll have a book on the presses. If you don't understand something thrown your way, look it up or just ask.

It's What's on the Inside That Counts

The bulk of printing, of course, is everything between the front and back covers. You'll need to consider several things about the paper on which the content is printed before even approaching a printer.

What factors go into the printing process of your book? Many things, most of which you were starting to consider back in the chapters on building a book. Remember these factors?

- Page count (How many pages is the book?)

- Size (What are the dimensions of the book? A huge coffee-table book or a small pocket-size book?)

- Paper (Where is it produced? What's the job stock? Weight? Color?)

- Binding (What type of binding? Stitched? Perfect?)

- Automated or a hand process (Can the machines do it all or must a human insert something in the book?)

- Print run (How many books will you print?)

- Color and type of ink (Will you be using color? What ink will you use?)

CAUTION   **Cautionary Tales** _____

Just because you are getting a lot of quotes doesn't mean you are getting the right quotes from the right printers. Most printers can print books, but most printers are not book printers. Stick with a printer that specializes in printing books.

You will need to have all these decisions made before you approach a printer and ask for a quote. All these factors will help your printing representative help *you* determine the best method to employ for the production of your book.

It's Magic

The actual printing process, after you've determined your options, goes something like this:

1. The printer photographs your laid-out pages.

2. The negatives are stripped into a flat.

3. Instead of hot molten metal, these days a bright light burns the thin printing plate through the flat.

4. Your pages are pressed from the plates and the ink.

We're more technologically savvy, but Gutenberg's basic premise is still at work in presses across the nation.

All Together Now: Binding

Remember all those factors I listed that determine the best printing process for your book (not to mention the items affecting expenses)? In Chapter 5, I touched on the different types of binding while helping you decide what kind of a book best suits your book's topic and needs. Because the binding process goes hand in glove with the printing process, here is an in-depth refresher. After you print those manuscript pages, you need a way to keep them all together. Your binding—like a cover—affects the marketing of your book. Think carefully about your binding choices. The most popular industry standards are these:

Wise Words

Books are divided into sets of folded pages, termed **signatures**. Industry standard for books usually runs 16, 32, or 24 page signatures, depending upon the press you use.

◆ **Perfect binding**—Pick up almost any trade paperback (softcover) book, and you'll see a perfect binding. With a perfect binding, the cover is glued around the content at the spine. But the pages aren't loose as they are glued. Instead, the book's content is folded into *signatures* first. The signatures are placed in order, and then the cover is glued at the spine to all signatures.

- **Saddle stitched.** You typically see saddle stitching in the catalogs that come in your mailbox. Saddle stitching can be used only with short books of about 32 pages. The book is stapled together at the center. It's probably not a good choice for most books, but it's an excellent and inexpensive route for short compilations of poetry and the like.

- **Stitched (cloth) binding.** Found in some hardcover books, the signatures are sewn together. Then the printed pages are glued and stitched to two hardcovers. By far the most durable binding method, cloth binding also allows for the title to be seen prominently on the spine.

- **Perfect bound case.** This binding is a hardcover cloth binding without the stitching. Instead, the signatures are glued together and then glued to the covers.

- **Spiral binding.** Think of your spiral notebook with the wires wound through the myriad holes at the spine of the book. Spiral binding is sometimes the best choice for authors who want to use their books as lecture tools—and also does not allow for a title on the spine. With spiral binding, you lose a valid marketing element. And remember how much booksellers dislike them.

Remember, consider your reader before choosing a binding. Think carefully about which binding will help sell your book.

Finding a Printer

At first, finding a book printer may seem like finding a needle in a haystack. Your job is to find a reasonably priced book printer that can print the number of books you want in your first print run and deliver a well-produced product in good condition.

Your first concern is finding a list of potential printers. Here are a few ways to accomplish this task:

- Navigate online, and in a search engine, type "book printers." More than likely, the search engine will suggest www.bookmarket.com/101print.html, an excellent resource for book printers around the world. I've also listed a number of well-known book printers in Appendix E. Don't be afraid to approach many printers at once. Remember, they each have specialties, and they each have different types of equipment.

- Ask a self-publisher who is pleased with the book he or she had done. Assuming that you are publishing a book of similar type (size, page count, binding, print run), that is a great place to start.

CAUTION

Cautionary Tales _____

Always request printed samples from the printers you are going to for quotes. These are the companies' resumés. Compare like works from each printer so you'll have a better understanding of the quality you will be getting. Then ask questions. The printer is there to help. The sales representative has designers, programmers, press workers, and myriad other people who can help with any questions you may have—and they all should be willing to answer your questions. If a printer won't answer your questions or at least lead you in the right direction, it's a red flag.

Make a List and Check It Twice

After you've networked and navigated your way to a list of potential printers, you'll need to provide all the printers with the same set of guidelines from which to quote the print job. You'll want a "quote," too, as opposed to an estimate. In printing, a quote is a firm commitment from the printer to hold to the price for a certain period of time—usually about one month. Fax or e-mail the sales representative these items for the quote:

- **Print run quantities.** Most printers start out at about 3,000 copies. Even if you plan on going for only one small run today, make sure you tell the sales rep to quote for runs with two other figures. For example, have the sales rep provide you with a quote for 3,000, 5,000, and 7,000 books.

- **Total number of pages.** The printer cannot accurately give you a quote unless you provide a page count. The cost of the paper greatly affects the pricing.

- **Trim size**—Provide the printer with the dimensions of your book. Printers usually specialize in certain trim sizes, so this is critical information.

- **The mode of copy and illustrations.** How will you send your work to the printer? Will you provide the printer with a disk, formatted by a designer? Printers today usually want secured PDF files of the typeset pages. Learn first what modes the printer uses and choose one. With illustrations, provide the printer with the number of illustrations and the format you will be sending them in (for example, 10 JPEG and 2 BMP).

- **Paper weight.** You'll need to feel the different paper weights and discuss with printers the best weights for your project. The weight of the paper also encompasses such elements as texture, opacity (will the type show through to the other side?), and bulking factor (pages per inch; heavier paper doesn't necessarily mean a bulkier book). Printers will have sample papers and printed book samples with different weights for you to compare. Choose the weight and reflect your choice in the request for a quote. Generally, the heavier the weight, the more expensive the print run. Most books, incidentally, are printed on 50- to 60-pound stock.

◆ **Ink color.** Most books use black ink for the text and four-color process for the cover. More about color processes in a bit. You've certainly researched why you'd want a different color than black for text—if that's the case—but, regardless, list your ink color. Be specific. It'll save you heartache and price fluctuations down the road if you are very specific now.

◆ **Proofs.** Specify that you must see the folded and trimmed proofs, or "bluelines," before your book goes on press. Bluelines show your book exactly as it will appear in its final form. The only difference is that proofing the bluelines is your last chance to make changes, but not without a steep cost. Find out what the printer charges for blueline changes.

◆ **Deadline.** Tell the printer when you need finished books. Understand that most standard printing jobs are not speedy, and the more rushed you are, the less likely you will get a quality product. Give yourself plenty of time with this phase. If your books are to be shipped somewhere be sure to allow for this in your schedule, and make sure the printer knows what you have in mind.

Mistakes to Avoid

Ron Pramschufer of BooksJustBooks.com has been in the book-printing business for a long, long time and has seen many a self-published author through the process. Here are his observations on the most common mistakes self-publishers make:

◆ **Printing too many books.** "Years ago, you had to print in large quantities to bring the costs down, but technology has really changed that." Ron says you should guard against a sales rep trying to convince you to print more books than you can reasonably sell.

◆ **Stay away from paper salesmen.** "Don't be dazzled by all the choices in paper. The consumer doesn't care what you spent on your paper, so don't overdo it. Stick with the standards; they're called standards for a reason."

Print-On-Demand Examined

Print-on-demand gets so darned much press nowadays, how do you know what it all means and whether it is right for your project? With the advances in technology, many self-publishers (and, indeed, publishing houses) are relying on print-on-demand (POD) for their book-publishing needs. The advantage of POD is that you aren't stuck with a huge overstock of your book—the stuff of bargain tables in bookstores everywhere (also known as remainder tables). You buy only the number you require.

Some POD entities use ink, like a traditional printer, but the POD company's equipment allows for a less expensive print run *for them*, not necessarily you. Other POD companies use digital printing—like a laser copy. Each page may be as crisp as the first, but the question remains whether toner used for your pages will hold up over time. POD allows for a quick turnaround—if you follow the company's guidelines for submission. But the process does not necessarily prove less expensive; it just allows for less waste in the end. Think very carefully about the number of books you plan to print with a POD company. Just as with a traditional printer, the more you buy, the bigger the cost break.

Pro Style

Digital technology has truly made it easier for self-publishers to go with print-on-demand and see their work out on book-shelves quickly. Consider that Lightning Source prints as many at 500,000 books a month with a 'round-the-clock printing operation.

Quote and Quote Again

Just as with buying a car, with printing, you need to get out there and ask around to get the best deal.

Dierdre Honnold, successful self-published author of *English with Ease* (two editions and selling widely abroad), *Sacramento with Kids*, and the novel *Gold Country*, says the best advice she can give anyone interested in embarking upon the printing part of publishing is to shop around and network. "I asked everyone I knew in the business who the best printers were and what their experiences were with printers," she says. "There are all kinds of deals you can make with printing. So definitely get bids but compare the company bids with what you learned from your research and talks with others in the business."

Another reason to seek out multiple quotes, as Ron Pramschufer points out, is that printing sales reps work on commission and want to sell you more, not less: "They can sell you only what fits on their equipment."

Pro Style

To shrink-wrap or not to shrink-wrap? That is the question! Unlike the shrink-wrapped products you see in the toy stores, this is an extra step in the process of printing and binding. The benefit of shrink-wrapping your book is protection against those glossy covers rubbing against each other and scratching or dulling. The shinier or glossier the paper, the more you'll want to shrink-wrap. The cost of shrink-wrapping depends upon the dimensions of the book but typically runs about 20¢ to 25¢ per book.

Navigational Help

Are you feeling overwhelmed by the idea of putting your project out for a bid to so many different companies? Of course, there is someone who'd like to help: a print broker.

A print broker works between a designer/client and the printer. The broker manages all the details of the print job—things such as budget, quality, and timeline. Brokers usually have relationships with a network of printers. Because of their good relationships, they can negotiate a slightly better price. Also, whereas you or I wouldn't necessarily know what to look for at a press check, a print broker will. Think of a print broker as the printing project manager. You don't have to deal with finding the most cost-effective printer for the quality job you want. You don't have to proof your book on the press or at the blueline proofing. The broker does it for you. From formatted file to hot off the presses, the broker takes care of everything.

How much is this going to cost? Print brokers make their money from the printer, not you. How? Well, you don't pay the printer directly; instead, the broker pays the printer. You pay the broker for the print job and his services. If you know nothing about printing, don't necessarily want to learn, or just don't want to bother with all the specifics of printing, a print broker may be for you.

Another Bit of Help

You can also hand over the management of the printing process if you have been working with a book producer throughout your self-publishing process. Someone at a full-service book-production company, such as Brian Taylor of Pneuma Books, can deal with getting bids and working directly with the printer if you do not feel comfortable doing so. However, this is generally a service offered to clients who have been using them for book design and production.

Turnaround Time

Every author wants to see his or her book immediately after penning the last line, but several factors delay that moment. The turnaround time of your book—from ready-to-roll digital file to book—depends upon these factors:

- ◆ **Changes.** Are there changes to the proofs? Something to consider is that any changes affect deadlines.

- ◆ **The printer's schedule.** How busy is the printer? What kinds of jobs are they already working on? Are there previous print jobs on the presses?

- ◆ **The complexity of the job.** How many color presses are necessary? Is the paper difficult to work with? What sort of prep and finishing equipment is needed?

- ◆ **Actual printing time.** How long will it take the presses to run the job? Days? Weeks? The number of books you want printed probably most affects your timeline.

- ◆ **Drying time.** How long will the ink take to dry?

- ◆ **Binding time.** How long will it take to bind the pages after they've dried?

The best thing to do is ask the printers at quote time what the estimated print time will be. You should probably be researching printers as you're writing the book, especially if you have put yourself under a tight deadline. You need to consider that the printer can't work miracles; it can go only as fast as the process allows. As designer Chris Hayes says with a chuckle, "They don't have magic leprechauns at the presses."

Printing with Color

Printing with color is merely creating screens with dots of color. When the dots of color cross at slightly different angles, new colors emerge. The degree of offset affects the color. When you put a magnifying glass up to a printed document, you can see the dot patterns.

The industry standard for covers and colored illustrations seems to be the four-color process. Interestingly, printing presses can print only a small part of what the human eye can see. The more "color processes," as in 8-color process or 10-color process, the more nuances there are in the color that our eyes can detect. As you go up in number, you widen the range of colors.

Unfortunately, the higher the color process number is, the more color plates are used and the more labor intensive and the more expensive it gets to be. But with titles such as an illustrated picture book or a beautifully illustrated cookbook, you need the color process. And chances are, you won't be using an American printer for the job.

Offshore Color Printing

Much of four-color printing is contracted offshore. The term *offshore* sounds like you are describing a boat on the horizon, but is a catchall industry term that means any non-U.S. printer (even Canadian printers are referred to as offshore). You'll need to work with printers primarily in Asia. Unfortunately, printers in the United States and other countries cannot compete with the Asian market. Several factors contribute to the break in cost when working with an offshore printer. Without going into a whole lecture about globalization and outsourcing of manufacturing jobs, suffice it to say that overhead is much less, labor prices are lower, and many of the Asian countries, including Singapore, Thailand, and China, just don't have the stringent environmental impact laws that we have. Thus, they can produce the product for less and charge you less.

Although the cost is an advantage, you will need to consider aspects of offshore printing:

- **Communication.** Can you or the print broker communicate well enough in the language to properly handle the deal?

- **Shipping time and cost.** The shipping will add time to your delivery timetable, and the cost to ship from Asia to the United States adds to your budget.

- **Customs.** You'll need to check into the import regulations of the United States before you cut any offshore deals. What good is it if your books are stuck in a Singapore warehouse or even at a Customs depot?

How do you find an offshore printer? The same way you find a U.S. printer. Start by asking other self-publishers who might have sent their children's books or gift books to offshore printers. Then start researching online for book printers with color capabilities. I've listed a few in Appendix E to get you started.

Paying the Bill

Chances are, the print bill for your book will be the biggest single expense you run into with your project. Gulp. As a part of the bid and quote process, be sure to ask each printer what its payment terms are. Take a good look at the fine print on the quote because you also need to know what "terms and conditions" means to each printer.

Printing is an odd business, one in which it is standard practice to either underdeliver, or overdeliver, and expect to be paid accordingly. Most printers guarantee a 10 percent overrun or underrun, which means that if you are expecting 4,000 books, it is well within reason that the publisher might deliver only 3,600 books. Huh? Or they might deliver 4,400 books to you. Because books can be damaged on the press or during the bindery process, you might well end up with fewer than what you wanted. If you get fewer books, you pay for fewer books, but if you get more, you will be expected to pay for that additional 10 percent, too.

The Least You Need to Know

- Before even approaching printers for bids, have a good idea of what you desire—everything from dimensions to page count and more.

- Know the differences in bindings, and ask yourself what the most effective binding is for the sale of your book.

- Find a list of potential printers through networking and online research. Know exactly what you want from the printer in the creation of your book, and detail it in a quote request.

- If you just don't want to be bothered by the whole printing process, consider hiring a print broker.

- If you choose to print offshore, make sure you can communicate with the foreign company, consider shipping costs and scheduling, and follow all import regulations.

Chapter 9

What Should You Charge?

In This Chapter

◆ What you should charge can depend on your goals

◆ Deciding what the market can bear

◆ Basic retail pricing strategies

◆ What the retail price really means to you

Fraught with romance, mystique, and poetry as books themselves are, the fact is that, as a self-publisher, the business you are in is the manufacturing business. Doesn't sound nearly as glamorous, does it? Well, get used to it, folks. As I mentioned many chapters ago, the people who end up with the title "publisher" at most commercial publishing companies are not editors who spot literary masterpieces and work with Pulitzer Prize–winning writers, but rather, the less-celebrated folks who work on the money side of the business.

As your own publisher, one of the most critical decisions you will ever make is how much to charge for your book. Take the time to read this chapter thoroughly and consider all of the questions, even the most unpleasant ones.

I could make this a very short chapter by immediately revealing the standard formula that commercial publishers use to arrive at the *retail price* for a book. If that is all you want to know, then skip ahead to the section

"Basic Price Formulas." I urge you to read all the elements of this chapter thoroughly, though, because once again we will circle back to fundamental questions of purpose to decide what works best for your project.

> **Wise Words** _____
>
> **Retail price** is the price at which a retail store sells products to its customers. Many bookstores discount off the retail price, but they do use it as a starting point. _Wholesale price_ is the discounted price needed by any reseller to make a profit when selling your book to its customers.

Back to Step One—What Is Your Goal?

In Chapter 3, I asked a critical question: why are you writing and publishing? I do hope that you have been examining your own motives carefully. What motivates you to self-publish is no doubt different from what motivates your neighbor. One of you might be setting your sights on fame and fortune, the other one on preserving a slice of family history. Down the block, another neighbor might be publishing a book to share her views on home schooling, while a fourth neighbor is planning to build her consulting career with a book meant to showcase her skills and knowledge.

In this chapter, we examine how to effectively price your book. You might find, however, that your pricing strategy can be affected by your reasons to publish. Remember the five major reasons we examined in Chapter 3: for money, for fame, for personal satisfaction, as a family project, and to sell out to a big publisher.

> **Wise Words** _____
>
> A **P&L** is a worksheet that takes into account all the aspects of a project and the costs attached, balanced against all the potential revenue sources, to determine whether a project is likely to achieve a profit or produce a loss.

But how do those reasons relate to the final price that you have printed on your finished book? Keep reading.

Money

This is pretty clear, I'd say. If your goal in self-publishing is to make money, then you need to be as businesslike as possible when setting the price for your product. When it comes to your _P&L_, you want only a profit.

Fame

Hmmmm, fame, eh? Well, then perhaps you are not looking at your book as the potential source of funds, but rather as the launching pad for notoriety. If this is the case, you might be giving it away free or inexpensively to stir up as much publicity as possible. Price won't be as big of an issue.

Personal Satisfaction

If your aim is to gain personal satisfaction from seeing your work in print, you might not need to see your project end up in the black.

Family Project

Family histories or other kinds of genealogical projects seldom carry a printed price on the book because they are distributed inside the confines of a family group. If you have taken the lead in having a family project published but really don't intend to underwrite the cost for all the copies, you will have to set a price that covers your production costs. Few family projects are intended to include a profit for the publisher. (And doing so might well discourage some of your family members from buying copies—relatives get so *touchy* about money!)

Sell Out to a Large Publisher

What makes a large publisher sit up and take notice of a self-published work is a solid sales record. In this case, you might well consider actually under pricing your book, to move more copies. Maybe taking a loss on your self-published book will get you into the position you really seek and, you hope, pay you back in the long run ....

Do you see how your personal publishing goals can affect how you price your book? A standard pricing strategy is used widely in the industry, and I'll explain it shortly. But deciding whether it is the formula that gets you to your goal, is up to you.

Different Goals, Different Prices

Kristine Taylor's son Martin is a dedicated artist and entomologist. When he was still in grade school, he wrote and illustrated a book, *The Story of Aphid City.* "We printed up 700 copies," Kristine remembers, "and we are now down to only 10 copies left after four years." The Taylor family spent $9,000 to produce those 700 copies, sold each copy for $17.95, and came close to breaking even. But was profit ever the goal? Not really. Some years earlier, the Taylors had self-published and sold more than 40,000 copies of a book about windsurfing and certainly knew how to make money with books. The point of *The Story of Aphid City*, though, was more to validate and celebrate Martin's talent and creativity. Not only did he get to experience the thrill of publishing a book, but he also got to do book signings in major stores. As part of a home-schooling project, Kristine also used the book to involve Martin in a real-world business situation. "He enjoyed it," she says, everything from opening orders they'd received in the mail and writing up bank deposits, to packaging books to be shipped. He enjoyed it so much that now, several years later, Martin is hard at work on his second book.

On the other hand, Jack Everett, an estate trust expert based in Granite Bay, California, wanted commercial success with his book *The Truth About Trusts: A Trustee's Survival Guide*. He knew that he would profit professionally from the increased exposure and speaking gigs that the book would bring him around the country, but he also thought that his book's image would benefit from the $27.95 price tag. "My readers are willing to pay the price because the information in the book has a financial impact," he told me. "They might be suspicious if a book on this topic had an unusually low price."

What Can the Market Bear?

Before setting the retail price on *The Truth about Trusts*, Jack did a fair amount of research into the pricing of other books on trusts. As he just pointed out, the audience for this information might well be suspicious if a book on such a high-level topic was priced like a cheap mystery novel.

Pro Style

According to Ipsos, a survey-based market-research company, American consumers spent an average of $22.95 for a new hardcover book in 2003 (the most recent data available). This represents a 4.1 percent decline of the average price since 1998. Why? Publishers aren't dropping their prices (because their costs sure aren't going down). The drop in price is a function of the discounts offered to customers by booksellers in an effort to compete.

Every few chapters, I've encouraged you to go and spend as much time in bookstores as you can allow yourself, browsing and looking at books in general, and examining the types of books similar to yours in particular. By now, you should have a good idea of how similar books are priced. Are you working on a cookbook? You should have spent enough time in the cookbook aisle at your local bookstore that you can easily tell me that trade paperback cookbooks sell in the range of $16.95 to $19.95, while hardcovers sell for as much as $35 or more. Is yours a book of financial advice? Trade paperbacks in that category run from $16.95 to $19.95, and hardcovers range from $22.95 up to almost $30. You should know this information like the back of your hand.

If you see seven competing books already available on the bookstore shelf where you're hoping to see yours, and the prices printed on the books run the gamut, how are you going to decide? Do you want to be the cheapest or the most costly? This is a marketing decision that you will have to make.

Just this morning, I talked to one of my consulting clients about his publishing project. After years in the radio industry, he is working on a book that shows industry executives and station managers how to meld the powers of radio and the Internet. His is a very interesting idea, but not one that will likely move many copies in a general bookstore. Instead, I recommended that he go ahead and self-publish it as a very high-priced industry-professional book, one for which he could charge $50 or $75 and market directly to the radio folks themselves in trade magazines. This is valuable information for a specialized audience, so price it accordingly.

Who wouldn't want to be in the business of selling a book for $50? Sadly, the instances in which a book will work at a very premium price are rare and involve situations such as the radio market expert. Most of us are left trying to figure out how to price our products to maximize sales.

As you work through the pricing formula and fill out the profit and loss worksheet later in this chapter, you might suddenly realize that the market price for a book in your category won't be enough to recoup your investment. Are you sunk completely? No. When you have all of the financial facts in front of you, you will be able to see just where you can make changes to shave costs and move your project closer to the break-even point.

Cautionary Tales

Do your research on what the market can bear for your book before you set any of your production plans in stone. Do this before you order a fancy gold-stamped cover, or a photo insert, or deckle-edged handmade papers that will run up your production costs and require you to set your retail price way above similar books to avoid losing your shirt.

Books are one of the few retail products on the market that arrive at a retail store with the price already affixed to the item—printed on the item itself, in fact. Bookstores are free to sell the book for whatever price they want, of course, and they usually do so by discounting the printed price.

Profit vs. Break-Even

Is this your first attempt at manufacturing? If so, it is worth familiarizing yourself with the difference between making a profit on your product and merely breaking even. To break even is to generate enough revenue to cover the amount you spent creating it. This does not include your time spent writing the book, or the time and energy (or money) spent promoting it. The break-even point takes into account only the fixed costs to produce it. Add up the bills you've paid to your designers, printers, binders, and so on, and when you've generated revenue in an equal amount—bingo! You just broke even on the project!

Congratulations are in order when and if you do hit break-even—this is a very significant milestone for self-publishers. Anything over and above your break-even point represents a profit, also a significant accomplishment in the self-publishing world.

What if you don't break even, though? What if you don't even come close to breaking even?

Pro Style _____

Most commercial publishers will tell you that they expect their first print run of a book to only break even, at best. Traditionally, the profit comes in the second printing and other printings thereafter. Why? Because you have already paid for all your fixed costs with the first printing. Your cover designer, layout person, copyeditor—all those bills have been paid. Now every time you order up a print run, the only bill you have to pay is the printer's.

Can You Afford to Lose Money?

I have to ask this grim and unpleasant question: what will happen if you lose money on your self-published book? If your goal is to create a money-making product and that goal is not met, then what? Please do think this scenario through with respect to your own project. Are you placing your family home in jeopardy by borrowing against it to publish your novel? Are you borrowing from your children's college account to finance your literary dreams? I recommend strongly against it.

Can you afford to consider the money that you are spending on your book as money that might never be recouped?

Some books that do earn back the money spent on them and then go on to earn an actual profit take years to reach that point. Can you afford to let your money be tied up for that long? It might also happen that you lose interest in publicizing, marketing, distributing, and selling your book before you've sold enough copies to recoup your investment. Publishing can be a time-consuming process; selling several thousand copies of a book seldom happens overnight. Make sure you have the stamina to see your project through to a profit.

Basic Price Formulas

Okay, are you still with me after all those unpleasant questions about money? Your patience is now rewarded. Here is how commercial publishers set the retail prices on their books: Start with the individual printing price (the cost per book), and multiply it by either 8 or 10. It goes something like this:

> If your per-book printing cost is 1.80, you should charge at least $11.95 for your book ($8 \times 1.80 = \$11.60$). To give yourself a better chance of making money, you could charge $17.95 ($10 \times 1.80 = \$18$).

How do you decide? It gets back to that marketing question: where do you want to be price-wise compared to your competition? It is entirely up to you.

Why the 8 or 10 times formula? It gives you a big enough number not only to take into account your printing and production costs, but it also builds the retail price up to the point that you can start discounting it when you deal with wholesalers and booksellers. We'll examine that topic more fully in Chapter 16.

Print Costs Will Change

In the printing chapter, you learned another basic truth about manufacturing: the more of something you produce, the cheaper each individual item becomes. The bigger the print run is, the less each book will cost to produce. Please take this into account when you are setting your retail price.

If your first print run will be your biggest, remember that your per-book printing costs will be larger the next time you print. Sure, you could change the price on your book with every printing if you felt like it, but it wouldn't be your wisest move. It will confuse your distributors and make you look undecided. Set your initial price to reflect the fact that your future printings might cost a tad more per book.

What the Retail Price Really Means

Hey, that $27.95 price that Jack Everett charges for his hardcover book on trusts is looking pretty good, isn't it? What does that printed retail price on the book *really* mean to a self-publisher?

If Jack is giving talks on a cruise ship and his listeners are flocking to the back of the room after he finishes to buy copies, it means he is actually receiving $27.95. That must feel good! Most of his sales, though, occur through other venues—online bookstores, national chains such as Borders, and smaller stores serviced by wholesale distributors. I'll be covering these topics in greater depth in the chapters on dealing with booksellers and distributors, but it is important to talk about the discounts that you will have to give various folks along the way. Remembering what you have to give away to others will help you focus on what that retail price figure actually means to you.

When pricing *The Truth About Trusts*, Jack Everett told me that one of the reasons it never occurred to him to charge any less than the full 8x formula (the retail price on his book, $27.95, is roughly eight times his per-book printing cost) was that the other folks in line—the distributors, booksellers, and so on, wouldn't be lowering their percentages. "If they are going to be making full markup, then so am I!" he says.

Distributors' Percentage

Wholesale book distributors will want anywhere from a 55 percent to 67 percent discount to distribute your book. So if your retail price is $20, you would sell your product to a distributor for $9 or less.

Why such a big whack? Because they, in turn, are selling to bookstores at a roughly 40 percent discount, so they are making in the neighborhood of 15 percent for their efforts. That's not an unreasonable thing for anyone in business to expect.

Bookstore Discounts

If you are selling directly to bookstores, whether the corner bookstore in your neighborhood or the buying office of one of the big national chains, they will expect to receive a discount of roughly 40 percent. The $20 book you've published is being sold to them for $12.

The Gift Market

The gift market is somewhat different from the general bookstore market. If you are self-publishing a book that will fit well in the gift market, such as a cookbook that might be carried in the gift section of the Cracker Barrel restaurant chain, these markets expect a 50 percent discount. Wow! Sounds pretty big, doesn't it? Your $20 book is now selling for only $10. Yes, but what usually goes along with that 50 percent discount is the lovely word *nonreturnable*. It's also sometimes called a one-way sale.

I'm Back!

Yes, get used to the fact that books are returnable products. Not only are you paying the freight when you ship your products, but you might also some day see those same books again, along with paperwork asking to be refunded the money for the unsold books. Gulp. Yet one more thing to think about when pricing your books and working out your P&L.

Cautionary Tales

Geez, how does anyone make money in this crazy business? Now that you are working through the numbers, you should at least take comfort in the fact that, unlike a commercial publisher, at least you don't also have to pay royalties out of the price of your book. You are the author. But keep that in mind if you someday decide to publish other folks' books—it's one more item to factor into the equation.

Selling Direct?

What if you plan to sell most, if not all, of your books directly to your customers? Maybe through back-of-the-room sales after you've given a professional speech, or perhaps a mail order–only product such as my little pamphlet on traveling as an air courier? Because I got orders in the mail directly from folks who'd read about it in the newspaper, I made a huge profit. No money was lost to distributors or booksellers.

If this is your sales plan, does that affect how you might price your book? You bet. Here are a few strategies:

- ◆ Print a high price on the book, but then always tell your audience that they are receiving a special price for attending your event: "My book ordinarily sells for $30, but today for you folks I'm selling it for only $22!"

- Price your book to reflect the fact that you aren't paying any middlemen, and pass the savings on to your readers (make sure they know it!). "This book should cost $30, but I'm bypassing the middlemen so I can pass the savings on to you with a better price!"

- Price your book at the top end, sell it for full price, and get to a profit position more quickly.

Had enough of the money talk? You'd think I'd choose a lighthearted chapter subject to tackle next and give you a bit of a mental break. Alas, that is not to be. If you do need a break, then set the book aside and take one because our next item of business is … the law.

The Least You Need to Know

- If you plan to make a profit, your retail price is critical.

- Family legacy projects are seldom profit oriented.

- The more sought-after your information is, the more you can sell it for.

- Unless you sell directly to your customers, you will not receive the retail price for your book.

- Remember to figure in the discounts needed by distributors and bookstores.

Chapter 10

Legal Matters

In This Chapter

- ◆ Legal issues of concern to self-publishers
- ◆ Copyright laws and the fair use doctrine
- ◆ Libel and slander laws
- ◆ The importance of getting agreements in writing
- ◆ Agreements with freelancers and collaborators

Copyright law has made the news more than once in the past few years. The estate of Margaret Mitchell sued over a book that took characters and a splash of plot from *Gone with the Wind* and spun them into *The Wind Done Gone*. Historian and best-selling author Stephen Ambrose was accused of plagiarism, as was Doris Kearns Goodwin.

Many, if not most, of the legal issues that can arise in the course of self-publishing have to do with copyright law. In the process of selling and distributing a book, you might have a tangle or two over unpaid bills or disputed deliveries, but those would largely be related to business law.

Most of this chapter, then, is devoted to issues that flow from the concept of copyright. "Who owns what" is what it all comes down to. Some of you might be working with ghostwriters or collaborators, and you will definitely need to clarify who owns what. The old "I paid for the work, I own it," belief isn't true at all. I will address how those relationships can be structured toward the end of the chapter.

Let's remember that I'm not a lawyer and that what follows is not actual legal advice, but merely an attempt to familiarize you with some of the issues you should know about. If you have further questions or concerns, please do seek legal advice from a lawyer.

You might have a wonderful attorney who you've worked with successfully over the years, but chances are, he or she isn't familiar with intellectual property issues. If you decide at any point in this process that you need a lawyer, please seek out an attorney who has experience in intellectual property law.

The Main Legal Issues

There are several main issues with regard to copyright. The first is your own copyright to your work. You will need to establish the legal copyright on the work you have created. Once you control the copyright on something, that gives you the right to exploit the copyright in many different ways, including selling a book (and any other kind of derivative products) that might be created out of the book.

> **Wise Words**
>
> According to *The Associated Press Style Book and Briefing on Media Law*, a **copyright** is "the right of authors to control the reproduction and use of their creative expressions that have been fixed in a tangible form."

But often in the course of writing a book, even a highly original book, we might want to quote from the writings of someone else. Our own original book might have been strongly influenced by someone else's writing style or ideas, or we might have stumbled upon some long-forgotten work from years past that we feel needs to be brought back into the public view. All of those involve copyright issues. Let's tackle these three main points: *copyright*, fair use, and public domain.

Copyright—Yours and Theirs

Copyright law has to do with who owns and controls the right for profit from a creative work. A work is not covered by copyright forever, though—only for a defined period of time, which can change according to law. Here is a publishing geek factoid: the copyright law underwent a major change in 1976 (and went into effect in 1978). Before the change, all works were protected by copyright for 28 years, plus a renewal period of another 28 years, for a total of 56 years from the date of copyright. Skipping ahead over some tiny changes, the law now states that a copyright is good for the life of the author, plus 50 years. There is a slight variation having to do with works that have more than one author: those works are covered for 50 years beyond the life of the last author to die.

In the dusty days of yore, the law was quite particular about exactly where the copyright notice appeared in a book. Specifically, for books, it needed to be on either the title page or the page immediately following the title page. The updated law just states that it had be placed "as to give reasonable notice of the claim of copyright." Most publishers do still hew to tradition and place it following the title page.

The law requires owners to send copies of their work to the U.S. Copyright Office. You have three months to get this done. Should you worry in the meantime, though, that your work is unprotected? No. The fact is, any original work that you create is sort of instantly copyrighted by the mere fact that you created it. So even if your paperwork isn't done, don't panic.

Pro Style

You wrote it, you own it. Don't panic about showing your work to others before you have officially registered it with the U.S. Copyright Office. The very act of creating it means that it is protected under common law because you created it. If it makes you feel better, you can add this to your manuscript: Unpublished Work © 2004, Jane Doe.

Another method is to put a copy in an envelope and mail it to yourself. Leave it sealed in the envelope, and the date serves as proof that your work is yours at a particular time.

Here is a surprising fact: ideas and facts are never protected by copyright. So if you have uncovered a little-known historical fact in your research and include it in a book that brings the knowledge out into the public sphere, other writers, researchers, and historians will be able to write about the facts you discovered. They can't copy your words exactly, of course, because that is *plagiarism*. We'll get to plagiarism in a minute here.

Another thing that can come as a surprise to authors and self-publishers is that you cannot copyright a title. You might be able to trademark your title, but you can't actually copyright it.

According to the U.S. Copyright Office website, here are a few types of material that can't be copyrighted:

◆ Works consisting entirely of information that is common property and contains no original authorship (for example, standard calendars, height and weight charts, tape measurements and rulers, and lists of tables taken from public documents)

◆ Titles, names, short phrases, and slogans; familiar symbols or designs; mere variations of typographic ornamentation, lettering, or coloring; and mere listings of ingredients or contents

◆ Ideas, procedures, methods, systems, processes, concepts, principles, disclosures, or devices, as distinguished from a description, explanation, or illustration

All self-publishers should know that you cannot copyright a book title. I should know. I'm the author of a *New York Times* best-selling book called *Christmas Miracles*, which has been on the market every year since 1997 and sold over 100,000 copies. But that didn't stop another publishing company from publishing a book with the exact same title a few years ago. Sigh. The only way that I (or anyone else whose title gets used by someone else) would have a legal claim is if the other publisher or author intentionally tried to make readers believe that it was my book they were buying.

I'll go through this in greater detail in Chapter 15 on paperwork and registration, but let me briefly describe to you now what the copyright process entails.

Visit the Copyright Office website at www.copyright.gov and download the form. Click on the Current Fees link to see how different types of works are assessed. Enclose the completed form and a copy of your book or manuscript (and it must be a printed copy—no computer disks or CDs), and send it with a check to:

U.S. Copyright Office
101 Independence Ave S.E.
Washington, DC 20559-6000

Fair Use

Although your copyrighted material is now protected, there are instances in which someone else could use parts of it. There are also, of course, cases in which you might want to use someone else's copyrighted material in your work. These circumstances fall into a section of copyright law called *fair use* that dictates exactly how much copyrighted material can be used fairly. If you've overstepped the boundaries of fair use in the way you want to use someone else's copyrighted material, you will need to seek that person's permission. Likewise, if you feel that someone else has exceeded the fair use clause when it comes to your own copyrighted work, you should contact them about it.

According to *The Chicago Manual of Style*, fair use was originally developed by judges as an equitable limit on the absolutism of copyright. The current copyright law doesn't define fair use in a totally black-and-white way. It has always been understood to vary from circumstance to circumstance, below are the factors that come into play when deciding whether your use of someone else's material is fair use (or whether someone else's use of your work is):

◆ The percentage of material used in relation to the entire piece. For instance, using one line of a five-line poem is quite a large percentage of the whole piece; using one line of a 20-page article is not.

◆ Does your use take away the copyright owner's ability to profit from that person's work? Can the poet still sell his five-line poem to a literary magazine if you have already printed one line of it? Perhaps not. Can the author of the 20-page article still sell it to another magazine even though you've used one line from it? Probably.

> **Wise Words**
>
> Circumstances in which you may use a limited amount of copyrighted material without the owner's permission are considered **fair use**. According to the Modern Language Association, "to use another's ideas or expressions in your writing is **plagiarism**. Plagiarism, then, constitutes intellectual theft."

Fair use should be fair. Don't use large swathes of someone else's work in your own because you don't want anyone out there in the writing world to do it to you.

Public Domain

Once a creative work is no longer covered by copyright law, it is in the public domain and may be freely used by anyone. Remember, the copyright on anything eventually expires.

There are some instances in which material can't be copyrighted; we covered those a few pages back. Add to that list a big section of printed works—material published by our own U.S. government. There have been many successful self-publishers and small publishers who have taken advantage of this legal quirk to profitably publish government material. In the last decade, large publishers have gotten in on the act as well—think of the best-selling versions of the Starr Report and also the report from the 9/11 Commission. I could have published a version, you could have published a version—we all had the equal right to use this governmentally produced material.

Other works in public domain, like classic children's books, are up for grabs for publishers. I remember working in a bookstore during the year that the famous children's book *The Secret Garden* came into public domain because the copyright had expired. There must have been four or five different illustrated versions available from competing publishers, each hoping to make a bit of money from a work on which they didn't have to pay royalties! If you have a hankering to publish classic works, you could publish your own versions of Dickens' works, or Shakespeare's plays, or even Bram Stoker's *Dracula*.

Plagiarism

If, on the other hand, you typed up Stoker's *Dracula* into a new manuscript, slapped your name on it as the author, and then sent it out into the world, you would have just committed plagiarism. Plagiarism is the act of claiming authorship or taking credit for work that is not your own. You have the right to publish works in the public domain, but you never have the right to claim authorship of anything that you did not write yourself.

Okay, we do get a bit muddled nowadays, with the ease of Internet research and the incredible access we have to cut and paste on our computer screens. This excuse has been used by many who have lately been called plagiarists. "Oops, I forgot to take careful notes and mark down where it all came from, and I ended up including it in my manuscript thinking that I'd written it and …." To avoid charges of plagiarism, always carefully cite your sources. By way of example, I'll cite mine for this chapter: Sarah Harrison Smith's *The Fact Checker's Bible*, which, in turn, cites much of her information to the Modern Language Association.

The Air Courier's Handbook

Despite the fact that I spend a great deal of time reassuring authors not to worry that someone will steal their ideas, someone once stole mine. In the very first few months of marketing my little travel booklet, *The Air Courier's Handbook*, one of the first 35 people who bought it copied it word for word, changed the setting of my first-person travel tale from Indonesia to Germany, gave the book a slightly different name, printed up copies, and began to advertise them in the very same travel magazine where I was advertising!

I learned about it after a nice guy in Canada named Yuri bought a copy of mine and then the fake one, and alerted me to what was going on.

Did I hire an attorney and sue? No. At that point, I didn't have the money to pursue it legally.

What I did do, though, was talk to the publishers of the magazines where I had been advertising and where the idea thief had also been advertising, and told them what had happened. The magazines dropped his ads. I also went back through my sales records, found a name and address of someone in Florida in the very same ZIP code that the book was being marketed from, called, and got very huffy on the phone. "I don't know what you're talking about …," the fellow said, but the book disappeared not long after that.

Song Lyrics

Song lyrics are copyrighted and fiercely protected against casual use.

Just because you remember the words to the songs from your youth doesn't mean that you can sprinkle them throughout your memoir.

Years ago, I was the editor of a book about a football team, and the author felt strongly that he wanted to use a stanza from a Rolling Stones song to set the tone. Fine, but he was going to have to pick up the tab because we, the publishers, didn't think it was editorially necessary and didn't want to pay for the permissions. So he did, to the tune of $350. And mind you, that was for just one stanza, maybe 20 or so words, out of the entire song. I won't quote the lyrics here because I don't want to pay for them! My point is, buying permission to quote from song lyrics can add up quickly. Once you find out how much, you might change your mind about using them.

To find out who controls the rights to the lyrics of a song, check with the three major licensing agents:

- ◆ American Society of Composers, Authors, and Publishers
  ASCAP, 212-621-6000, www.ascap.com

- ◆ Broadcast Music Incorporated
  BMI, 212-586-2000, www.bmi.com

- ◆ Society of European Stage Authors and Composers
  SESAC, 1-800-826-9996, www.sesac.com

Permissions

Another type of creative work that you need to request permission to use is cartooning. Many self-publishers and commercial publishers like to sprinkle their text with amusing cartoons to set the mood and help readers understand a point. Great idea, but remember, unless you drew that picture yourself, you'll need to seek out permission.

"I used six or seven cartoons in my book *The Truth About Trusts*," self-publisher and tax-planning expert Jack Everett told me. "I enjoyed the process of finding these cartoonists and corresponding with them."

In my books *Wear More Cashmere* and *The Martini Diet*, I've included recipes. Most of them were my own developed over the years, but a few were from cookbooks that I enjoyed. I contacted the permissions department of the publishers and requested permission in writing. In most cases, it costs only $50 or $75 to get the okay, and you can rest easy knowing you've done the right thing.

How do you find cartoonists? If this is a cartoon that runs in your local newspaper, you can start by making a phone call there to find out who syndicates it. Check www.cartoonbank.com for cartoons and illustrations from *The New Yorker*.

Libel, Slander, and Defamation of Character

I can't possibly give you an entire legal lesson on what exactly constitutes *libel*, slander, or defamation of character within the confines of this chapter, nor do I want to. I will once again remind you that I am not an attorney. I can share with you some of the warnings that are commonly available to writers, but I will strongly urge you to seek out further information on this topic if you think you might be wandering at all close to it in your own writing and publishing.

The actual definition of libel varies somewhat from state to state. According to *The Associated Press Style Book and Briefing on Media Law*, in the state of Illinois, libel is defined as "the publication of anything injurious to the good name or reputation of another, or which tends to bring him into disrepute." In New York, though, a libelous statement is "one that exposes someone to hatred, contempt, or aversion or to induce an evil or unsavory opinion of him in the minds of a substantial number of people in the community." And the variations go on from there. You aren't intending to libel someone, but it wouldn't hurt to look into what the law is in your state, just to be better informed.

Working journalists know this truth: most libel claims spring up from terribly mundane news stories. What seems run-of-the-mill to you, a casual description of someone as a criminal or a disreputable person in some way, might well come back to haunt you.

Novelists, listen up. You can be sued for libel over a novel. On this I quote an expert source, *The Fact Checker's Bible:* "Just because an author thinks she's given a fictional name to a character doesn't mean that there isn't a real person with the same name, and if that person's life matches the character's in other details, such as the city he inhabits, or the company he works for, or his profession, the coincidence could result in unintentional libel."

Also be aware that a novelist was once successfully sued by an ex-boyfriend who believed that the unsavory main character in her book was based on him. It was. So if you are writing a novelized version of true events in your own life, you should be very, very careful. Do check into this legal matter further.

Wise Words

Libel is a published false statement that harms or injures the subject's reputation. "Words, pictures, cartoons, photo captions, and headlines can all give rise to a claim for libel," cautions *The Associated Press Style Book and Briefing on Media Law.*

Pro Style

You can't defame or libel the dead. There is no course of action for the defamation of the dead. This doesn't mean you should, of course. If someone is suing you and *then* they die, the case will probably proceed because the person wasn't dead when he thought you defamed him!

Are you protected if what you repeat has been printed elsewhere? No. If you pass on libelous allegations in your book that you heard somewhere else, you are still on the legal hook if someone is offended and comes after you.

Get It in Writing

Any time you involve someone else in your book project, from a tiny bit of work to a great deal of help, you need to protect yourself from a later claim that person might make upon your work. It all leads back to copyright issues.

If you plan to build your self-published book or books into a business, you need to have these legal issues taken care of clearly from the get-go. You do not want to be in the position of having to go back months or years from now to try to clear up who owns what and why. Keep it all out in the open to begin with, make sure everyone involved understands what you have in mind, and get it in writing in as tight a form as possible.

Here are some of the situations you will need to have documented with agreements:

- Legal agreements with freelancers

- Legal agreements with contributors

- Work done with collaborators

- Freedom of speech

Each is described in the sections that follow.

Legal Agreements with Freelancers

Ivan Hoffman, a longtime copyright and publishing attorney, believes that the single biggest mistake that self-publishers can make is to not establish a paper trail with all of the freelancers who might help on a book. "It's all about the documentation." If you are not the actual creator of all aspects of the work, you need to document your exclusive rights to the things you've paid for. If you've hired a copyeditor to copyedit your book, get that person to sign a document that affirms your sole ownership of the work. If you've hired a ghostwriter or developmental editor, get a signed document. And most important—the cover art.

"So many self-publishers fail to get contracts with the cover artist," Ivan says, "and without the exclusive rights to the cover art and image, that limits your entrepreneurial opportunities to just selling books. It eliminates the possibilities to market your book in other ways. What if someone approaches you and says, 'We love your book and we want to do a calendar based on it'? Well, unless you've already got a signed agreement with the cover designer you hired granting you the exclusive rights, you will have to go back and negotiate with them." And guess what? It will now cost you more!

"You have to think down the road," Ivan recommends. "Think backward. In five years, I want to make money from this book, so what can I do today to make sure I can make money then?" By having all of your freelancers sign documents attesting to your exclusive right to your project, you will be able to make money without worrying that anyone might someday emerge to make a claim to a part of your success. Yes, it can seem like a long shot, paying attorneys now to create agreements to ensure a success that may or may not happen, but as Ivan says, "If you aren't going to assume success, then why do it at all?"

According to Ivan, this is the *fundamental legal principle* under U.S. copyright law:

> If you are not the actual creator of copyrightable work, then the *only* way that you can acquire exclusive rights to the creator's copyrightable work is by having a valid, written, signed, and legally sufficient writing transferring some or all of those rights exclusively to you. (I am assuming that the creator is not a bona fide employee of yours acting within the course and scope of his or her employment; even then, it is always better to have such a thorough, written, and signed agreement.) If you see with vision (read the articles "The Need for Vision" and "What Business Are You In?"), you will understand that that writing should be a thorough, valid, written, and signed agreement covering the many, many issues involved in this sort of transaction. Thus, if you are a publisher, website owner, author, or any other noncreating party engaging the services of an independent contractor cover artist, illustrator, editor, ghostwriter, website designer, or any other independent contractor creating party, you *do not own* exclusive rights to that independent contractor party's copyrightable work unless you have such a valid, written, and signed writing. In the absence of such a writing, all such exclusive rights remain solely owned by the said creator.

Pro Style

Ivan Hoffman has a website jammed with important and useful information for self-publishers. Check it out at www.ivanhoffman.com.

Does it surprise you that I asked Ivan for permission to copy that whole piece off his website? It shouldn't!

Make sure you have a signed document that gives you exclusive rights to the work that the following folks have helped you with:

♦ Cover designer and the artwork on the cover

♦ Freelance editors, including developmental editors and copyeditors

♦ Any additional writing help you've used

Legal Agreements with Contributors

Planning to use stories and contributions from a number of writers in your book? Get ready to collect paperwork! I'm the co-author of several story collections and have been through this process many times. Each and every contributor to your book will need to sign a story release, giving you the right to include the story in your completed book. I've included a sample story release in the back of the book in Appendix D. The basic components are these: you'll need to state whether there is compensation involved, how the story will be used, whether you have the right to change it in any way, how long you have the right to use it, and what kinds of rights you will control (Do they have the right to sell it again elsewhere, or will you own it exclusively? What about movie and television rights?). Again, try to imagine all of the possible outcomes for your book, and cover those in the release. What about publicity? Will you have the right to use their name and picture for publicity purposes? Will they come along and help publicize the book for you?

Story contributors love to be involved, that has been my experience. Twice the *Christmas Miracles* collections were featured on the television show *The View*, and some of the contributors shared their own miracle experiences on camera. Two of our contributors actually ended up on *Oprah* to participate in shows about miracles. So anticipate that your book will be successful, and make sure those scenarios are covered.

Working with Collaborators

Get it in writing! Always, always. What if you break up? It has happened to me. Not every collaborative arrangement between writers really works. When you start down the rosy path of writing a book together, no one really thinks ahead to anticipate these situations:

♦ One of you might lose interest, move, change professions, or be incapacitated in some way and unable to fully participate.

- It could turn out that one of the partners is, well, lazy, and doesn't hold up their portion of the work.

- It could also turn out that one of the partners simply can't write.

- Perhaps you can't agree on the direction of the book.

I've included a sample collaborative agreement for writers working together on one book (also Appendix D). Be sure to think through any possible scenarios that might occur between you and your collaborator, and add those to the sample agreement found in the back of the book.

Freedom of Speech

In these rocky political times, who knows what kind of statement can get you into trouble? If you are not sure whether what you want to say in your book is protected by the U.S. Constitution, take a look at *The First Amendment Handbook*, published by the Reporters Committee for Freedom of the Press. It is available free online at www.rcfp.org/handbook.

I cannot stress the legal issues strongly enough. Please continue reading up on this topic to stay current with legal issues regarding publishing and copyright. It is a fascinating section of the law, one that contains many surprises and relevant topics to your life and the world around you.

The Least You Need to Know

- "Who owns what" is the single most important legal issue.

- You can quote from another's work, but how much you can use for free can vary from circumstance to circumstance.

- Get signed agreements with everyone who helps with your book—editors, designers, and so on—establishing that you have the exclusive rights to all aspects of the book and artwork.

- Writing partnerships and collaborations can start off well and end up poorly— get it all in writing.

- Always seek a license and permission to use any part of another's work, no matter how much or how little.

- Money spent on making sure you have your documents in order is money well spent.

Part

Getting Down to Business—How a Book Is Made

Moving further into the process will involve morphing your carefully polished manuscript into a finished book. Whether you work with book designers and cover designers or decide to do it all yourself, you will soon understand what it takes to produce a professional book that is pleasing to the reader.

Books intended for commercial sale need to have various registrations and numbers attached to them. What do you need, why do you need it, and where do you get it? Don't panic—all the paperwork and registrations are clearly explained.

The Parts of a Book

In This Chapter

- ◆ How books are put together
- ◆ Major parts of a nonfiction book
- ◆ Major parts of a novel
- ◆ Major parts of a poetry book
- ◆ When and why you need an index

As the author, you know what you mean to say to people, but unless you plan to sit on the couch next to each reader as they read, your information needs to be easily and quickly understandable to anyone who happens upon it. The structure and pieces become important and must unfold in a logical manner. Given time, any reader should be able to find what he or she is looking for pretty quickly.

Imagine how bewildering it would be to try to read a textbook without a table of contents, or a history book without a timeline or glossary of terms, or a novel written as one long, continuous chapter. While you might have a distinctive way you want to handle this, think through whether it will help the reader understand your message. If not, you probably want to stick to the tried-and-true way of pulling information together and presenting it to your reading public.

Why Books Are the Way They Are

Book editors through the ages have been sticklers for detail. They play the role of the "first reader" and understand that words have to be parceled out in a way that makes sense to the average person.

As books themselves evolved throughout printing history, so too did an editorial system of organizing the insides of books. And so the table of contents (TOC) was born, along with a standard organization in the first few pages.

The front pages in a book before the main body of text welcome the reader and introduce him or her to what lies in store. These pages are called *front matter*. Some pages explain what the book is called, who wrote it, who published it, and when. Other pages help the reader understand the structure of the book, provide pages numbers for references and might even list charts or tables to help give the reader a road map. Other sections also help the reader understand why the writer felt compelled to write the book and why the reader should be compelled to read it.

Every book, whether a textbook, a how-to manual, or a novel, is made up of several parts and is divided in some form or fashion. Nonfiction books are divided differently than novels. The divisions themselves might be identical, but the terms used to describe the parts vary. We'll go over the names of these book parts in a minute.

Many functional parts of standard book design also have to do with making the book easier on the eye. Look at an open book with two blank pages, where does your eye naturally fall? Over to the right- hand side, doesn't it? Therefore, it makes the most sense to always have important material like the table of contents, or the beginning of a chapter, start over on the right side. You will hear the terms *verso* and *recto*, or left and right, quite often as you begin to decide how the information in your book should be organized.

Wise Words _____

The Latin term for left pages is **verso**; right pages are **recto**. You can remember this by remembering that the recto is the right hand page (and both begin with the letter "r"). Recto page numbers are odd-numbered and verso page numbers are even-numbered because books start numbering pages on the first recto of the book. **Front matter** is everything that comes before the actual text of the book itself, including the half-title and title pages, copyright information, acknowledgments, dedication, table of contents, preface, introduction, foreword, and any other tables, charts, or introductory text.

Like so many building blocks can create a large structure, all of the parts of a book can create a large impression. The following nonfiction book style should be used for anything other than a novel—a business book, a family memoir, a cookbook, a travel book, any type of book that is based in fact. Let's see how it all breaks down.

Front Matter Elements

Front matter is an odd-sounding term to those new to publishing. This refers to anything that comes before the actual text of the book itself. Front matter also conforms to a strict and logical style about what comes first, what comes second, and so on.

You'll find that many books use a combination of all the possible front matter elements, but few use them all. Some specific elements are required for some types of publishing; look at other similar books to see what elements should be in your front matter.

> **By the Way**
>
> The cover of a book is not considered front matter. On the inside front section of a cover, there may be printed materials as well as a blank printed or textured page. These are called endpapers. They are not considered part of the book's front matter, but part of the cover. Endpapers, or endsheets, are only found in hardcover books.

Testimonials

You might have noticed that many recent best-selling business and motivational books have several pages of glowing testimonials in the front few pages. It is hoped that flipping through page after page of quotes and atta-boys from recognizable business leaders and thinkers will help the casual reader make up his mind to buy. If you have endorsements and testimonials from major names in your industry about yourself and your work, this is where they go.

Half-Title Page

The half-title page is always a recto (right) page on which only the title of your book appears, not the subtitle, your name, or any information other than the full title of your book. It is meant to have an elegantly spare look, and it often echoes the design of the cover itself. It is also the first page to be deleted if the pagination is too long for your signatures.

Frontispiece

Frontispiece is a fun word to say (try it). This used to be an elaborate page on which a gilded woodcut would appear to set the tone of your masterpiece. Now the frontispiece, a verso (left) page, either is blank or contains a list of other books you have written. It is seldom used nowadays.

Title Page

The title page is where your full title and subtitle, your name as the author, and, should you create a name for your publishing venture, and the name of your publishing company appear. It is always a recto page. Often the type style used here on the title page echoes the design from the front cover of the book (unlike the simplicity of the half-title page).

Copyright Page

The copyright page is on the back side of the title page (verso). This is where you list the copyright notice, Library of Congress *CIP*, ISBN, and additional copyright information. The name of your publishing company and contact information also go on the copyright page. You can also include permissions notifications, photo or art credits (if you don't run them with the photos or art), and other legalities such as disclaimers. Many publishers list the contact information for their publicity or foreign rights contacts, and some even list their staff. For more academic titles, you'll see a catalog card reproduced on this page.

> **Wise Words**
>
> **CIP, cataloging in publication,** is information you file with the Library of Congress, which then supplies back to you a formatted description and catalog number to help librarians catalog your work. It is always printed on the copyright page.

Dedication Page

The dedication page includes a brief sentence identifying the person or persons you want to dedicate your book to. *The Chicago Manual of Style* points out quite pithily that in a dedication, it is redundant to start your dedication off by saying, "Dedicated to Laura," and that you should instead get straight to the point with "to Laura." Your dedication can also be included at the top of the copyright page if you don't want to use an entire page on its own.

Epigraph Page

A not-often-used page is the epigraph page. An epigraph is a short quote or poem, and the page is, as it sounds, a place for you to include a quotation or poem to set the tone or prepare the reader for what follows. The epigraph is typically a recto page.

The Table of Contents

At last, your TOC is about to begin. Always start your TOC on the recto (right) page because it is where the eye falls naturally. The reader uses a table of contents to find page numbers, so listing the reference and where to find them in the book is critical. And always double-check the page numbers in the TOC against the final typeset book before it goes to the printer.

Your table of contents can include several elements, all of which together are still included in the front matter. The following sections will be listed in your book's table of contents, in this order:

◆ **List of illustrations.** If you include illustrations or plates in your book, it is helpful to the reader to have a complete list in the front of the book.

◆ **List of tables.** If your work is a scholarly one that includes tables, this list follows the list of illustrations.

◆ **List of abbreviations.** *The Chicago Manual of Style* notes that "in some heavily documented books … it might be a convenience to the reader to list abbreviations for these sources before the text rather than in back matter." A list that runs longer than one page, however, should be placed in back matter.

◆ **List of events.** Some history books might include a list of events that are covered in the book and the dates on which they occurred.

Foreword

A foreword is written by someone other than the author and is usually at least one page long. Forewords are typically from well-known names and are filled with praise for both the author and the book itself, as a way of encouraging readers (and book sales). At the end of the foreword, the name of the person who has written it appears. This is typically a recto page.

Preface

A preface is written by the author and is used to explain how the book came to be. It can also provide an overview of the book's content and the special features in the book. Some prefaces are chatty and personal in tone, and end with the author's printed signature to further personalize them. A sweetly pretentious touch is to also add the location where you have been writing. The preface to this book would then be signed by Jennifer Basye Sander, Granite Bay, California.

Acknowledgments

The acknowledgments section is where you list everyone you'd like to thank or everyone who helped you on your journey in writing the book. Please try to keep your acknowledgments short; if they run more than three pages, consider moving them to the back just before the index (perfectly proper). Some authors also like to keep it simple by acknowledging a few folks in their preface, thereby skipping the need for an extra section.

Introduction

The introduction allows you, as the author, to introduce your readers to the topic at hand and further explain what they will find therein. The introduction typically starts on a recto page.

Cautionary Tales

A common mistake in the self-publishing world is to use the word *forward* instead of the proper term of *foreword*. Is a reader likely to notice that you've made this mistake? Maybe not. But should you send a nice letter to an eminent expert asking them to write a "forward," the mistake will stand out.

Primary Text

What follows after all of this front matter run-up is the book itself. The basic chapters of your book are considered text, from beginning to end. When you were writing your book, you doubtless followed a structure, an outline, that made sense to you as the author. Now you need to order your chapters in a logical way that helps your reader understand your point. You can simply list the chapters one after the other in the table of contents. You might also want to further divide the chapters themselves into smaller parts that hold together and, once again, help the reader understand the point of the book. Confused? Don't be.

For instance, a historical book on a famous Civil War battle could simply list the text chapters in the TOC, or it might divide the chapters chronologically and add part titles, like this:

Part I The Build-Up

Chapter 1

Chapter 2

Chapter 3

Part II The Battle

Chapter 4

Chapter 5

Chapter 6

Chapter 7

Part III The Aftermath

Chapter 8

Chapter 9

Chapter 10

See how that helps the reader understand quickly how your book is divided? Readers who like the heavy battle scenes will know they can flip to Chapters 4–7 for their reading pleasure.

So, now that you have placed all of your front matter in the right order, what happens to these middle parts? Thankfully, it is quite simple.

Chapters

Chapters follow one after the other in numerical order. Each chapter should begin on the recto, or right, side of the book. Each chapter of a nonfiction work addresses an overall topic.

Parts

It may also make sense to divide your chapters into larger part groupings, once again to help the reader understand your work as a whole. A book of 12 chapters, for instance, might be divided into 3 large parts, each containing 4 chapters that work together as a group.

Afterword

Writers use the afterword to wrap up their thoughts outside of the final chapter. Why include an afterword? You might have discovered something after you finished writing the book, new information or new investigation that should be shared.

We've covered front matter and the main text. Now your book moves on toward the end with back matter. Everything that comes after the afterword is referred to as back matter.

Back Matter

Back matter contains important elements, particularly for a nonfiction book. This is where you can give your readers more information to supplement the points you've made in your book, to send them toward other places they can find more on the topic, or share your sources and research. The elements that make up back matter are described in the sections that follow.

Wise Words

Back matter is what comes after the final chapter of a book: the appendixes, glossary, bibliography, index, and so on.

Appendixes

An appendix, or appendixes, in the plural form, may include important information you'd like to share with readers, as well as other helpful resources. Most often, appendixes are in the form of lists, tables, or charts that help support the book's main purpose. In a book about self-publishing, for instance, you'll note that the appendixes contain lists of professional contacts and organizations, and websites for further information.

Glossary

This is the definition of terms that appear in the book. You can also include other important terms as needed, even if they don't appear in your text.

Bibliography

A comprehensive list of the books and materials you used to research.

Index

A list of the key terms, people, places, and other topics covered in the book, with page references. They should be clearly explained so that the layperson reader can understand them.

Order Forms and Marketing Materials

You should save your very last pages of back matter for sales opportunity. You might include blank order forms to help sell more copies of the book, or information about professional services you might offer.

About the Author

Many authors and publishers like this section to be at the very end of a book; it makes it easy for the casual browser to flip to the back of a book and learn more about the author. This section is also sometimes placed in front matter, you can choose where you want yours to appear.

Primary Parts of a Nonfiction Book

Are you in a fog about which parts you will need for the type of nonfiction book you are writing? Let's take a look at some of the types of books you might be preparing and which parts of the book you should make sure you include.

How-To

Most how-to books will be fairly straightforward and involve simply an introduction, a table of contents, and lists of illustrations, if they are to be included. No need for anything fancy here like an epigraph.

Pro Style _____

You might have noticed that this book, _The Complete Idiot's Guide to Self-Publishing_, has information printed on the inside of the cover. Although many paperback books have covers that are printed only on the outside (often an economic decision because to print on the inside of a cover, it has to go back through the press a second time), using that extra space can be a good technique. The insides of a book cover are called endsheets or endpapers. The folks who publish the _Idiot's Guides_ call them the inside front cover and inside back cover. They use the inside front cover for a note from the author to the reader, and the inside back cover for the "About the Author" section.

Memoirs, Letters, and Diaries

Most memoirs, letters, or diaries lend themselves to a strictly chronological approach. Begin at the beginning and end at the end. You should certainly set the stage for your reader with an introduction. Including a well-written chronology will also help your readers follow the material you've collected.

Cookbooks

Like how-to books, cookbooks should be fairly simple and straightforward. Include an introduction, a table of contents, and lists of illustrations and photographs, if included. To be useful to cooks, cookbooks must include a very detailed index that lists not only by recipe name, but also by major ingredient.

Encyclopedia or Other Reference Books

A reference book tends to be organized much differently than other types of nonfiction books. Alphabetical order rules, of course, for encyclopedias, so you will not need actual chapters. Other works of reference do require chapter divisions. The main difference is that reference books are heavily footnoted throughout (rather than putting all footnotes in the back as less scholarly books do).

Travel Books

Travel books are traditionally divided by city and by region, so you will use this formula when divvying up your chapters and parts. Travel book readers do expect a great deal of solid information to be included, which you will put into a well-crafted TOC.

By the Way

There is no difference in the interior of a hardcover book and a paperback book. Why? Traditional book design and layout was invented for hardcover books (paperbacks did not routinely appear until the later part of the 20th century), and so the paperback book started life as a hardcover book. The interior did not change when it went to print with a different cover.

Be sure to include a list of maps directly after the TOC. While literary travel books (like *Under the Tuscan Sun*) do not normally have an index, any other type of travel book will need a very good index to be of use to your readers.

Primary Parts of a Fiction Book

Now that you have been dazzled by the various and sundry parts that make up most nonfiction books, those of you who are planning to publish novels are in for a treat. Most novels have far fewer book parts to keep track of. What falls by the wayside pretty quickly are the pieces like a glossary (although, yes, some novels that are set in exotic places with exotic language sprinkled throughout might have a glossary), a bibliography (although some novelists might want to display the thorough research they put into their writing and share a bibliography), and a preface (because in a novel, it is usually called a prologue). Ah, well, perhaps we've been too hasty in discarding so many parts of the book. Let's take a closer look at the standard novel construction.

Much of the first few pages of your novel will look just like the style of a nonfiction book. Remember that there is no difference between how a paperback book is ordered and how a hardcover book is ordered. Your first few pages will include these elements:

- Half-title page
- Frontispiece
- Title page
- Copyright and other registry information
- Acknowledgments
- Dedication

- Epigraph
- Table of contents

Depending on the style and subject matter of your novel, many writers like to also include the following to help their readers:

- Chronology of events
- Cast of characters
- Maps of the area (either real or imagined)

The novelist might then choose to include a prologue or author's note, in which they address the reader directly.

- **Prologue.** A playwriting term that literally "sets the stage" so that everyone can understand what followed. In a play, a prologuist would come out from behind the curtain and stand before the audience to fill them in on action and events they needed to understand before the play began so they did not feel bewildered. In a novel, this serves the same function.

- **Primary text.** This is laid out in chapter form, from Chapter 1 through to the last chapter.

- **Epilogue.** The counterpart to the prologue, an epilogue is sometimes used in a novel to leave the reader with a hint of what might have happened to the characters after the close of the book, or to wrap up loose ends in the plot.

Primary Parts of a Poetry Book

In their strictest form, books of poetry are put together much like novels. Often there is an extended author's note that shares with the reader the author's artistic motivation and literary influences. Put your poetry book together in the following order:

- Half-title page
- Frontispiece
- Title page
- Copyright and other registry information
- Acknowledgments

- ◆ Dedication

- ◆ Epigraph

- ◆ Table of contents, or list of poems

- ◆ Introduction/author's note

Poetry books seldom have actual chapters, but there are ways to group poems by theme or location or chronology that might help you shape your material in a way that readers can understand.

Back matter in a poetry book is traditionally brief and may consist only of a short biography of the author.

Does My Book Really Need an Index?

Indexing is a tough task. There are computer programs to help you do it, and many writers have tried to make up their own system. Professional indexers are well worth the money, though, and if you can afford their prices, it is money well spent. An outside indexer will also bring a fresh perspective to your work and will include many concepts that you might have grown accustomed to and otherwise would not see as important.

The good news is that not every book really needs an index. How do you decide? Getting back to our overall focus that books need to be easy to understand and useful to the general reader (remember, you won't always be sitting there next to them on the couch as they read), you do need an index if your book is filled with information that a reader might want to quickly refer back to time and time again.

You certainly should include an index in a book that is historical, that deals with reference material, or that explains complicated theories. Cookbooks always need an index, lest an anxious cook suddenly not remember where to find that favorite cookie recipe. Does your family memoir need an index? Possibly, depending on how many generations you are trying to cover!

A good index seems to anticipate the kinds of questions readers might have and does a good job of selecting the key concepts of the book so that the reader can refer back to them at will. Most books have only one index that combines subjects and names, although highly specialized books might have a separate index for names and a separate index for subjects. While it is possible to do it yourself, indexing is a specialized skill, and it might be faster and easier if you hired a freelance indexer. The resource section lists several.

By the Way

Do you hope that a copy of your book will be found on the shelves of your local library? This may well affect your decision about indexes. In my 20 years in publishing, I have always been told that "libraries won't buy a nonfiction book unless it has an index." Bronwein Cancilla, the branch librarian at my local library, recently confirmed this. "Yes, indexes do affect our buying decisions. Does it have an index? Is it a good and useful index? Reviews in the trade magazine *Library Journal* actually include an opinion on whether the book has a good index."

Is My Book Overdressed?

All of these rules about the parts of a book and how to order them come to us from book-publishing tradition of hardcover books, with each new book treated as a small piece of art. If you are publishing your book as a paperback original, are all of these fancy frontispieces and epigraphs overkill? No, not at all. You still need to be able to clearly present your ideas in a way that the ordinary reader can follow. And you still want your chance to give it the personal touches—the dedication, acknowledgment, and preface—that we authors all crave. Go ahead, dress up your paperback to the hilt!

This is your chance to really shine and to put your personal stamp on what you have produced. Make sure that the book you plan to put your name on is an accurate portrayal of your personality, one you'd be proud to see on a bookstore shelf.

The Least You Need to Know

- Books are put together in a clear way to help the reader navigate the information.

- The basic parts of a book are fundamentally the same but are not all used in every book.

- Introductory material written by someone other than the author is called a foreword in the book world.

- The three basic sections of a book are as follows: front matter, text, and back matter.

- An index is not always required but is helpful in a book filled with a great deal of information and detail.

12

Everyone Needs an Editor

In This Chapter

- ◆ What an editor and copyeditor do
- ◆ Why you need to take ego out of writing
- ◆ How editing and revision can improve your work
- ◆ What it means to workshop your writing
- ◆ What is proofreading?
- ◆ Hiring an editor/copyeditor

It's natural for writers to be territorial about their work. Once they write it, no one better deign to change it! It's like a baby that you've given birth to and raised to adulthood. The book was your idea, after all; your creative energy and thoughts, not to mention time, all went into the book's advent, process, and ultimate completion.

But repeat after me: everyone needs an editor. There's a reason publishing companies, newspapers, magazines, journals, and other publications all retain editors, copyeditors, fact checkers, and proofreaders on their staffs. All writers can use constructive criticism and, well, a little feedback and help in the perfection of their "baby."

All writers need to check their ego at the door and listen to the experts in editorial when it comes to their work. Truly, editors are a different breed than writers. Sure, they can write—but they're more like the engineer to the architect. The writer is the architect; the editor is the engineer. The writer, like the architect, comes up with this amazing image, sees it in his head, and then draws it—every nook, cranny, window, hallway, molding, everything. But the engineer on the project needs to make sure the building won't come tumbling down.

In this chapter, you'll learn the different ways to receive relevant feedback on your work, what an editor can do for you, and how to hire an editor. You'll receive a solid overview of the editorial process necessary for all publishing endeavors. So before you put your work in print, read on and learn why the revered Roman Titus Maccius Plautus (254 B.C.E.) uttered, "No man is wise enough by himself."

Anything You Can Do, You Can Do Better

All writing can be improved. From Ernest Hemingway to John Grisham, all professional writers have submitted their work to polishing with the help of an editor, a proofreader, or a workshop. Just like a professional athlete surrounds himself with myriad professionals to improve his performance—from nutritionists to trainers, to coaches—a writer needs input from experts to hone his or her skills.

Good writers know that they must continue to work at their passion and seek the help of people like editors and proofreaders to perfect their manuscripts. More eyes are better. Often a writer can be too close to the work to notice imperfections. Luckily, there are many ways to approach the "proofing" of your book, from receiving content suggestions to having a copyeditor review your work for proper grammar.

> **By the Way**
>
> What is the difference between an editor and a copyeditor? Generally, an editor looks at the overall "style" or subject content and makes suggestions. A copyeditor, however, edits the manuscript for proper punctuation and grammar. In most cases, the copyeditor also formats the book for typesetting.

When self-publishing, you don't have the support of a team that a commercial publishing house offers a writer, such as a developmental editor, a copyeditor, or a fact checker. But that's okay. To create the best product possible, you'll just need to follow the same process as a publishing house would with your own manuscript by yourself and with a little help from an outside team of experts. But before hiring an editor, there are several things you can do to improve your book.

Pro Style

Lynne Rominger, an author and educator, insists that her high school students all follow three steps before turning in any paper. First, they must read it aloud to someone. "I don't care if they read it to their dog," emphasizes Rominger, "the act of hearing their own words usually helps the writer catch any choppy writing or grammar problems." Second, she puts her students in small groups and they exchange papers, correcting each other's work and providing comments to each other. "They workshop their paper with their classmates." Finally, all students go to a writing center on campus, where accomplished students provide help with papers. "In a sense, the writing center students act as editors," says Rominger. Although the kids all write their own works, they use an editorial process to complete their papers. As a journalist, Rominger recognizes the power of the editorial process both in teaching young writers and for professionals. In fact, she lets her students know that she relies upon a similar process before turning anything in to her editors at magazines and publishers.

Reference It

Several books exist on the market that all good writers use to improve their writing and to brush up on the latest literary guidelines. Whether you check them out or buy them for your personal library doesn't matter. Just get your hands on a copy of the following books:

- *The Chicago Manual of Style*
- *The Associated Press Stylebook and Briefing on Media Law*
- *Bartlett's Familiar Quotations*
- *A Handbook to Literature*
- Any one of many excellent grammar books
- A comprehensive dictionary
- A comprehensive thesaurus

You are your first editor. These books will help you check and double-check your work. Books like *Bartlett's Familiar Quotations* and *A Handbook to Literature* may also help bring fullness to your work, arming you with references to the important thoughts and words of previous great individuals and the tenets of literary endeavor.

May I Suggest a Class or Two?

Grammar and punctuation can be a lot like a foreign language; you lose it if you don't use it. Grammar and punctuation can also be a lot like calculus—especially technical. That is why the American Press Institute's website www.americanpressinstitute.org/content/3696.cfm, showcases copyediting help, one of which is Northwestern's Media School of Journalism's "100 Most Common Usage Errors." Language is ever changing, and so are the usage rules. Just because you have a good command of language and write well doesn't mean you couldn't benefit from an advanced grammar class. Many universities offer these courses that really dig into the mathematics of constructing prose and the usage of literary device, like allusion, alliteration, and metaphor, which can all bring fullness and expertise to your writing.

Pro Style

Screenplay and magazine writer Dawn Blunk encourages anyone to take an advanced grammar class. While working on her Master of Arts degree in English, she was required to take Dr. Marc Bertanasco's rigorous class at California State University, Sacramento. The mention of the course brought tears to the eyes of many. It is the equivalent of finite math within the English department, a course of survival of the fittest; by midterms, half the students have dropped. Already a seasoned journalist, Blunk was skeptical of the need for the course—but upon its completion, she realized how much her writing had improved. "By taking the class and really understanding the intricacies of grammar and punctuation, I absolutely improved my writing. I think it would be a good thing for any writer to audit an advanced grammar class every few years just to brush up on skills," offers Blunk.

Check out your local community college, Learning Annex, adult school, or university for advanced grammar classes in your area. Or if you're really feeling enthusiastic about the editing process, check into editing workshops. Many major universities with strong writing programs, like Stanford University in Palo Alto, California, and online institutions offer intensive seminars/courses in publication editing, where you'll learn things like editor's marks and fundamentals of style and punctuation in editing.

You might also check out www.writerstraining.com to find a multiplicity of online courses in writing, including "Editing Skills," which you may conveniently take from home. You might become so good at it that when you've finished self-publishing your book, you can hang out your shingle as an editor to help other writers improve their work.

Pro Style

The lauded American writer Raymond Carver admitted in his essay "John Gardner: The Writer as Teacher," how integral his former Chico State professor's editing was on his early development as a writer and how receptive Carver was to Gardner's strong advice in 1959–1960. Carver wrote, "Before our conference he would have marked up my story, crossing out unacceptable sentences, phrases, individual words, even some of the punctuation; and he gave me to understand that these deletions were not negotiable. In other cases, he would bracket sentences, phrases, or individual words, and these were items we'd talk about, these cases were negotiable."

Speak Loudly and Carry a Big Red Pen

Every aspiring fiction writer longs to belong to the elite club of tale weavers who attend the Iowa Writer's Workshop. What plenty of neophyte authors do not understand is the intensity of the "workshopping" that takes place at this and other writer's gatherings across the globe. Letting other writers review your work may seem out of the question right now. I'm sure several things are swimming in your head, like, "What if he steals my book idea?" and "What if she says my novel stinks?" Put those fears aside. Yes, you'll definitely feel competition at writer's seminars and workshops, but you'll also receive tremendous feedback from writers with a keen eye for good writing—just like you.

When you subject your work to a workshop, you do so with the intent of improving your piece. You may not see that something is ambiguous or confusing or grammatically imperfect within your manuscript because you've probably read it a thousand times and just aren't catching it. Give fresh thoughts to your work. Have an open mind and either join a writer's group in your area or attempt to gain access into a prominent writer's workshop. Writer's groups, defined by genre, proliferate most cities.

Good places to look for a group are bookstores and online. You might ask the English or journalism departments at nearby universities if they know of any upcoming writer's seminars.

Typically, writer's groups are less formal but do require your input in discussing works written by members. More academic organizations may insist that you come prepared with works you've written. Still other workshops expect you to write while at the seminar and receive your critique from attendees almost daily. It'll be up to you to determine what style of workshop you'd most benefit from.

What if you think your work, fiction or nonfiction, is already done? Should you still join writer's groups and seek feedback? Absolutely. You will still learn from the process. And maybe you'll learn that your book *isn't* done.

⚠ CAUTION **Cautionary Tales** _____

Zava Hart, a romance novelist, has belonged for several years to her local chapter of Romance Writers of America. When she first joined, she was an aspiring novelist. Now, with the publication of her first book last year and another manuscript completed, she's well on her way to writing success. But she still feels the need to receive critiques and suggestions related to her work. She craves feedback and wholly acknowledges that her growth as a writer is the result of "practice and listening to the advice of other writers." Unfortunately, she noticed that the writer's club to which she belonged wasn't providing her any feedback on her work, and that the same few writers spoke over and over at each meeting on the same few topics. "No fresh ideas or new blood were ever infused into our group," laments Hart. Frustrated with the lack of constructive criticism and the repetition of topics, she made a tough decision to leave the group. A writer's club is a great thing if the purpose is to workshop each other's writing and help improve skills. Wasting time when you could be writing is another issue.

Skip the Polite Pats on the Back

What exactly should you receive from a workshop? Feedback. Critique. Editorial suggestions on everything: diction, clarity, style, grammar, punctuation, spelling, organization, you name it. You want to expose yourself to writers who won't be afraid to tell you to use another word in place of the one you've written, or point out that you've misplaced a modifier. You want to see the red ink on your paper and, in turn, ink up someone else's manuscript. In short, you want to help improve someone's work, and hope someone will improve your writing, too.

Check Your Ego at the Door

I hope you feel comfortable with the idea that editing is a natural part of the manuscript process and is inevitable in every writer's work. In addition to talent, creativity, and perseverance, all writers need thick skin and humility. No egos allowed.

As a writer myself, I work often with co-authors. We'll exchange chapters and review them. Just last week a co-author sent me the introduction to a witty little book about everything any boyfriend ever taught us. I liked her chapter but suggested the lead would prove stronger if she moved her second paragraph up—just swapped the first and second paragraph. Did my co-author balk and fume over the suggestion? No. She considered it and took my advice. Likewise, a little later in our workshop, she suggested that I use a different word to better describe a scenario. Did I feel hurt and rejected that my co-author pulled a better word from her vocabulary archives? Not at all. Instead, I was thankful for the input. Together we are writing a better book than if we just each wrote the book individually and didn't rely on the other's participation.

The Three-Step Plan

When you've created something, it's hard to let go. Releasing to an editor what might be your life's ambition and letting that person change any part of it seems unreal. How could you possibly let someone change your work? Relax. A good editor won't change your work—just improve it and catch mistakes you might have made (and, trust me, we all make mistakes). A good editor will offer suggestions to improve the flow. Don't you want readers to readily grasp and embrace your work? Well, editors help you accomplish that goal.

Editors are a different breed. They are the attention-to-detail people, the minutia corps. They make sure every *i* is dotted and every *t* is crossed. Essentially, an editor protects you from future criticism and disdain. The drama critic Walter Kerr once adeptly expressed the role of an editor in describing *The New York Times* esteemed Arts Editor Seymour Peck. Kerr said, "[His] editorial hand ranged far, wide and deep, touching lightly but expertly. He seemed less an editor of any sort than the very best sort of guardian angel." Here are three steps to take mentally to prepare yourself for the editing process:

- **Step 1.** Revere your editor as your guardian angel, not the demon who will destroy your creation. Repeat the prayer: "My editor is my guardian angel. He/She will protect me from the slings and arrows of criticism and the brunt of bad writing jokes. My editor is my wall of defense." Next in your three-step plan?

- **Step 2.** Check your ego at the door and grow calluses. No writer gets very far by balking at the suggestions of other writers. Moreover, once your work is in published form, just accept the fact that someone won't like it. Writers, like artists, continually receive rejection and negative criticism. It's the nature of the beast. You need to accept it.

- **Step 3.** The editing process is tough. It's difficult to listen to someone tell you to change what you consider is just right as is, finished. But wouldn't you rather tweak a few things to make an amazing manuscript rather than publish something mediocre? Don't take it personally. Accept all suggestions, then consider them, and finally go with your gut when making changes. Realize that there are experts out there who know more than you do about style and grammar. Use them. Appreciate their forthright help.

Remember, all writers—Hemingway, Grisham, and everyone in between—see their work marked up by an editor. Best-selling author Pat Conroy endures a grueling editing process with each book. Over 300 pages were cut out of *Prince of Tides,* and about 600 pages were gleaned out of *Beach Music.* The author admits that once the editing is done, he doesn't look back. Although Conroy may be the man cutting away, he's doing so by the direction of his editor.

Believe in your work, but not to the detriment of ever seeing it in print. By all means, fight to keep lines in if you deem them necessary, but do not hold up production over insipid diction debacles or grammar gaffs. Just take the advice of the expert and move ahead. Decide you are going to learn something every day, and look forward to the criticism as a learning adventure.

> **Cautionary Tales**
>
> Don't depend upon spelling or grammar check on your computer as your sole editorial device. Often the programs are limited and also riddled with errors. Use the computer's checking systems, but don't rely on them. Get a human to look over your work. You'll be surprised at what the computer misses and an actual person will catch! I regularly type "form" instead of "from" and depend on others to help me catch that error.

Hiring an Editor

So now you've written your manuscript and had several eyes look it over. Now you're ready for the editor. Again, in self-publishing, you are working in the capacity of author, developmental editor, and production editor. And certainly, you've proofread your work. But now is the time to hire a bona fide, meticulous copyeditor and proofreader. Especially if you've never been exposed to the publishing world, you may not know where to begin.

Since in self-publishing you most likely wear the hat of several editors—the developmental editor, project editor, and production editor—here's the lowdown on what each editor typically does within a publishing house. We went over this in Chapter 6, but here is a reminder:

◆ The developmental editor "develops" a book idea and works to make the book stand out in the marketplace.

◆ The project editor coordinates the whole publishing processes—everything from hiring an indexer to supervising the editorial staff.

◆ The production editor (sometimes also called the managing editor, and also a print buyer) ensures the printing of the book, working with everyone from paper suppliers to printers and binders.

Some editors actually do all of these things, you won't know someone's specialty until you ask. All editors keep to stringent deadlines, to ensure that the book arrives on its publication date. In the self-publishing arena, all these editorial demands exist for the author—you!

Where's Waldo?

Now that you are ready to hire someone, where are you going to find that person? Sitting next to you at the table at Starbucks? Perhaps, but here are a few more great resources for finding a copyeditor or proofreader:

◆ **Writing organizations.** Look first to any groups to which you belong. Perhaps a person within your writing club moonlights as an editor.

◆ **Academic establishments.** Any university with a journalism department should be able to provide you with a list of either students or faculty who possess excellent editing skills and welcome the pay for the services.

◆ **Online.** Type "editor" or "proofreader" into any search engine, and a list of organizations and businesses offering these services will pop up. The Editorial Freelancers Association remains a good choice to begin your search. You may reach the EFA at www.the-efa.org. Once you access any directory of freelance editors, however, it's up to you to determine which editor to hire.

Certainly, the price sheet of each editor and your budget on the book will prove integral factors in determining just who to hire, but reputation and experience are also important facets to consider. Generally (and not to sound cliché, but …), you get what you pay for. And since you are paying for these services, be sure to ask every question on your mind. These are some things to consider:

- How long has the editor been in the profession?

- What academic history does the candidate hold?

- From what editing programs has he or she graduated?

- What else has he or she edited?

- Can the candidate offer you names and phone numbers of references, others who have used his or her services?

- What are his or her areas of expertise?

Not all editors work in all areas. Some editors focus entirely on fiction, for example, while others might work only on textbooks. My own sister, Anne Basye, is a developmental editor who works only with business books (do you get the sense that I come from a book-focused family?). Ask a few questions and get a feel for both the competency and the expertise of the editor before hiring.

Once you've found a few candidates, have them take a proofmarker's test and a grammar and punctuation test. You can find questions from any grammar textbook or within the pages of *The Chicago Manual of Style* (1993). Same goes for the proof marks. You'll be paying the editor, so you have every right to ensure that you're hiring an expert.

Show Them the Money

Freelance editorial rates fluctuate according to the economy, the location, and the expertise of the editor. The price of a copyeditor won't be the same in Wyoming as it will be in San Francisco, California. Supply and demand dictate price wars. Check with local writer's organizations to find out the going rates in your area.

Pro Style

Editors aren't cheap. Expect to pay between $25 and $50 per hour for a copyeditor. Developmental editors run closer to $100 an hour. Try to negotiate a price for the entire manuscript, to keep a tighter rein on the costs. My husband, Peter, a much-published personal finance and business writer, recently charged $2,000 to developmentally edit a money book that a self-publisher was readying for release.

Ouch! That Hurts

Don't expect your copyeditor to coddle you. Remember, you are paying this person to point out the flaws and inconsistencies in your work. The editor is there to make *you* look good. Look forward to the criticism; you'll grow as a writer. At the same time, if you find that your copyeditor has nothing critical to say at all about your work, know that that editor isn't working hard for his money. A good editor looks closely at the manuscript and finds the "needle in the haystack" problems along with the egregiously blatant errors. These editors possess an attention to detail unparalleled. In fact, if your editor doesn't ask you at least a couple of questions per page, move on to another editor. You want the editor who is asking, "Why did you name the protagonist Frank? What is the significance?" or "You're the queen of comma splice—lose the comma-happy pen!"

Once the editor receives the manuscript, relax. Now it's your time to let someone else do the work, but, at the same time, be prepared to answer any questions and provide any clarifications the editor may need.

Firing Your Editor

What do you do if you determine that your editor isn't helping improve your manuscript? What do you do if you feel like the editor is a detriment instead of an asset? You need to be a professional and fire the editor. A good, clean way to do this is by thinking of the possibility before hiring anyone and providing a contact for the business arrangement. After all, when you hire a freelance copyeditor, you are engaging in a contract. Why not spell out the details?

Basically, you should make sure that the pay and the deadline are agreed to in advance. You will want to retain complete control of your work, and you will want to have the freelancer sign a nondisclosure agreement (a standard NDA is included in the resource section), stating that he or she will not steal your work and ideas and use them as his or her own, or tell anyone else about the manuscript. You should probably also stipulate what will happen if the copyeditor's work isn't acceptable. No one wants to let someone go, but no one also wants to think "what if."

With proofing your manuscript yourself, getting other writers to look at it and provide suggestions, and, finally, hiring a true copyeditor, you should produce an excellent and cleanly written work.

Remember, the more eyes, the better—and check that ego at the door. These editors are here to make you look good. Let them. You want to publish the best book you can, a book that makes you proud to have written it. Working with an editor, any editor, will make sure that what you send out to the world is not only free of mistakes, but also polished to perfection.

The Least You Need to Know

◆ Have several people look over your work before sending it in for publication.

◆ Keep an arsenal of reference books on hand.

◆ Continue to work on your craft by attending classes, workshops, and seminars.

◆ Check your ego at the curb and view all criticism as positive.

◆ Hire an expert copyeditor to ensure that your book is perfect.

◆ You are your own publisher, which requires that you wear several editorial hats—but you can depend on experts for the tough questions.

Chapter 13

All Things Production

In This Chapter

- ◆ The pros and cons of doing your own production
- ◆ How to give your book a professional look
- ◆ Designing your book
- ◆ Working with photos and illustrations
- ◆ Learning the typesetting guidelines

Gentle reader, we now enter the world of Mr. Rogers. No, not the late Fred Rogers from children's TV, but rather Bruce Rogers, the famous book designer. You are ready to begin the process of book production. Perhaps you've heard that laying out the pages of a book is mere child's play …. Just fool around a bit in Microsoft Word or Adobe, and you can easily create your pages and send them off to the printer. What a great new world desktop publishing has given authors. Well, hold that imaginary trolley, please! Before you go off into the land of make believe, let's examine the reality of getting your book ready to print.

Avoiding Disaster

When you produce a book that is intended to compete with major trade publishers and to sit proudly alongside them on bookstore shelves, you want to be sure that your book looks good enough to compete with these major trade publishers. Additionally, good book design offers your reader maximum comprehension. Bad book design will adversely affect your book's success in book trade channels.

Easy, you say? No one knows your content better than you, right? So your Microsoft Word formatting is just the design your readers need, right? I need to disabuse you of that notion here in the first few paragraphs of this chapter. Perhaps your visual outline works well, but the layout may leave much to be desired by book reviewers, distributors, buyers, and readers.

Book trade professionals can spot an amateur design or layout a mile away. This is one of the main reasons that self-published books are disparaged in the book trade. It is a sad truth that poorly designed self-made books stereotype the lot and create a stigma for all self-publishers. Remember that, as a self-publisher, you are a part of a larger group of small presses. What you do and the book you create impact the whole independent publishing industry. In other words, you have a responsibility—to yourself and to the industry—to produce a book of the highest quality in both content and appearance.

> **CAUTION**
> **Cautionary Tales**
>
> Jan Nathan of Publisher's Marketing Association and Curt Matthews of Independent Publishers Group (a master book distributor) have publicly stated that amateur book designs and poor page layout are the top reasons they reject self-published books that are submitted for screening in PMA's Trade Distribution Program.

It takes great knowledge, skill, and talent to produce a book to those standards. And that is why major trade publishers invest in professional cover and interior book designs.

The Pros and Cons of Creating Your Own Layout

Yes, you can create your own page layout. Novels are particularly easy compared to most nonfiction books with lots of elements. The question is, should you? The obvious cost savings might be compelling, but hidden costs can be associated with producing your own book—financially and otherwise. The table that follows contains a short list of the biggest pros and cons to consider.

The Pros and Cons of Doing Your Own Production

Pros	Cons
Save money on not paying a	Hidden costs in fixing layout if not properly formatted for the printer.
	Cost to redo layout professionally if formatting becomes too difficult to complete on your own.
Save time not having to work with a designer or typesetter.	Time lost while learning how to operate software, understanding typesetting specifications, and learning proper page-makeup standards and procedures.
	Time lost having to fix or redo the layout.
Gain experience in working with software and formatting.	Missed opportunity to gain experience working with a professional book producer.
Get exactly what you envision for the cover and the interior formatting.	No benefit of professional development for content.
	Risk of creating an unattractive design or a confusing layout.
Satisfaction of doing it yourself.	Risk of rejection by reviewers, distributors, buyers, or consumers.
	Printing investment opened to rejection.
	Risk of ruining the book and the dream of being a successfully published author.

Planning Your Book

Whether or not you intend to do your own layout, you will want to plan your book so that it has a visual rhythm and so that the content is well presented for maximum comprehension. The following sections will enable you to ensure that the layout created for your book properly represents your content.

You worked through much of this in the chapters on building books, but I review them again here in the production chapter because these decisions are absolutely critical.

Before you jump into your layout, you need to understand what books similar to yours look like. The best thing to do is go to the bookstore or library and check out the books in your genre. Ask yourself, "How do other publishers treat their content?"

"What do their covers look like?" "What typefaces are used—and why?" "Are there multiple levels of text—heads and subheads, lists, boxed features, sidebars, photos, appendixes, and so on?" Make a list—or, better yet, buy the books—so you can consider applying the same attributes to your book. When you have an understanding of what the competing titles look like, you can better plan your book and determine how your book can outperform them.

Getting the Story Straight

After you have examined similar books, you can decide whether your text should be laid out in similar fashion. If heads and subheads and other multilevel text are required for your book, you'll want to ensure that your text is written in a way that will translate to that type of a visual layout. If your text is not hierarchically consistent, the layout will not be rhythmical or consistent. Clearly, it is better to resolve these textual inconsistencies prior to the layout stage. Retooling the layout can result in costly editorial changes.

One of the ways you can examine your text in preparation for page layout is to style-tag the paragraphs. This simply means that you enter a small code surrounded by brackets at the beginning of each paragraph to define its hierarchy. For example, insert [1H] next to the first-level heads and [1B] next to the text that follows them. If a subhead follows, you can insert a [2H] tag. Indented paragraphs, such as extracts, should get a [2B] or an [E] for extract tag. This process enables you to envision how the text will look when it is laid out. The point is to resolve any hierarchical inconsistencies. For instance, if you find that Chapter 2 has up to four levels of heads but the rest of your chapters have only two, close your eyes and imagine how that might look in the finished book. You can see that it might appear poorly planned and inconsistent. You should resolve that textual problem before layout.

Pro Style

Styletagging is a device used by professional editors to check hierarchy and by professional typesetters to lay out books. It is also called typecoding. For more information on using this simple method to prepare your text for layout, Pneuma Books has a comprehensive treatment at www.pneumabooks.com/style.htm.

Making a List and Checking It Twice

If you find that yours is the type of book that will have different text treatments—heads and lists and features and other bells and whistles—then let's take a moment to examine what these things are and how they can be used consistently in your layout.

This is known in the book trade as a "design memo" and will be useful to everyone involved in the production of your book.

Chapter Presentations and Sections

If the section or chapter titles include subtitles or epigraphs, be sure that all of your chapters have them. Check your titling to be sure that each title is generally the same length. If you intend for the breaks to feature photography or illustration, ensure that the quality and style is consistent throughout the book.

Introductions

Make sure your sections and chapters are set up thoughtfully. They may need introductions. Often intros serve as much of a visual purpose as they do an editorial purpose. When designed and formatted, intros function as a formal presentation of the text and make a book look more appealing.

Heads, Subheads, and Run-In Heads

If your book uses heads and subheads, ensure that you use them consistently as you introduce your thoughts throughout your manuscript. You may also want to use a *run-in head* to introduce paragraph lists.

Iconic System

If icons are planned as part of your design, ensure that their intended placement is consistent and that the art is of the highest quality. I don't recommend using clip art.

Lists

There are several different types of lists, and you will need to decide which best suits your

Wise Words

A **run-in head** is a word or phrase set in bold or italic that forms the beginning of a paragraph. It is used in lieu of subheads and is used primarily for paragraphs that are intended as lists. If this is used in your book, make sure you use it more than once or at least once in each chapter, or it may stick out like a sore thumb.

Cautionary Tales

Many word-processing programs have special bulleting or automatic numbering features. It is probably best not to use this feature. If the text is imported into page-layout software, the automatic numbering may be automatically stripped out, leaving the text unnumbered.

book's needs. Should you use a bulleted list, or numbered lists? Whatever you decide, employ your approach consistently throughout the manuscript.

Cautionary Tales _____

Here are some tips from the pros on formatting words (or not formatting them!):

◆ Never underline words. This is messy and unprofessional, and can lead to too much emphasis throughout the book.

◆ Bolding should be reserved for heads, subheads, or run-in heads. Rarely, if ever, use bolding to add emphasis. If your book has a glossary in the back matter, though, the terms should be set boldface in the text.

◆ Use italics *sparingly* for emphasis. Use italics for words you might otherwise put in quotes, otherwise known as *quotation marks*. Make sure that correct italicizing is used for titles of books and magazines.

◆ *Generally*, additional <u>emphasis</u> is RARELY beneficial for the reader. It *may* even <u>CONDESCEND</u> to the <u>READER</u> by *emphasizing* the <u>OBVIOUS</u>.

Supporting Content

Consider whether adding or developing supporting information will be beneficial to the reader. Supporting content refers to main ideas that are more fully developed and presented in a different format within the text. This can include the author's own content or the addition of third-party contributing content. Supporting content adds value to the existing idea by providing the following benefits:

◆ **Proofs.** Extracts from other texts, quotations, examples, statistics, and practical application support and help prove your ideas. These things are proof of good research. Keep permissions laws in mind when using the work of others.

◆ **Points of departure.** A "break" from the main text to explore an idea more fully or to illustrate a particular point that is not central to the main idea.

◆ **User-friendliness.** Consumers love a professionally developed product that packages solutions or applications with theory. Checklists, questions, journal entry prompts, or workbooks are favored in the marketplace because busy people want well-prepared and easy-to-use solutions.

◆ **Expanded viewpoints.** Instead of merely offering personal viewpoints, examples or stories support the main idea and expand inclusivity by offering common denominators or societal threads.

- **Stronger visual benefits.** If photos or visual data are presented, they increase the overall appearance of the design and, thus, its value on the shelf. However, photos can also replace the vivid imagination of the reader. Sometimes the writer's content is stronger if the reader is left alone to interpret it visually. On the other hand, tables, charts, and graphs used in exposés or guidebooks are always helpful.

- **A more interesting design.** Additional elements will always enhance a book design and make it a more attractive product on the shelf. Presentation of the elements should be expert, or the book could be quite ugly or confusing.

Here are some different types of supporting content:

- Extracts, quotations, and dialogue

- Sidebars or features: pull quotes, quotations, contributed content, in-depth development of main ideas, related ideas, current events or related stories, tip lists, resource lists

- Figures and statistics: flowcharts, graphs, stats, tables, diagrams

- Maps, photos, and illustrations

- Footnotes or endnotes

- Appendixes: bibliography, suggested readings, lists of resources, glossaries

- Indexes

- Applications: end-of-chapter questions, exercises and activities, journal entry prompts

After you have examined competing books and considered all the possible interior elements, you can pore over your manuscript to determine whether you need to restructure it.

Remember, it is less costly to revise and rewrite than to end up with a poorly planned book. Take the time to styletag your manuscript. You might want to share the final draft with a book designer to get feedback on its visual potential.

Designing Your Book

You don't have to go to art school to design a book. You have already seen my personal bias toward hiring a professional designer for a professional look, but I know that there are those among you who are determined to do it on your own. If you count yourself among these hardy souls, please do pause in your pursuit of a finished book and gain an understanding of the various elements of book design and typography.

I am a big believer in learning from books, and no doubt you, as an author, feel that way, too. There are many classic books about book design that, although they won't replace talent and a careful eye, will certainly give you an understanding of some of the finer points.

Here is a short list of books that will teach you the basics of type and book design:

◆ *The Non-Designer's Type Book*, by Robin Williams. This is a great little handbook that includes origins of type and current usage. In her humorous style, Williams educates the novice on the proper use of various typeforms and the correct implementation of them in the digital typesetting environment.

◆ *The Elements of Typographical Style*, by Robert Bringhurst. This is the Strunk and White of the world of typesetting. Bringhurst's classic examines various type styles, their histories, and their uses. It methodically imparts the fundamentals of correct typesetting and is lush with examples. A must.

◆ *Words into Type*, by Marjorie Skillin, et al. This is a critical manual for the correct style and formatting of special words, abbreviations, acronyms, phrases, and other special situations. A must for editors.

◆ *Bookmaking: Editing, Design, Production, Third Edition*, by Marshall Lee. This is a classic that has been updated to embrace the digital age. Perhaps it is a bit outdated, but the general information on page layout and design considerations will always be useful.

◆ *On Book Design*, by Richard Hendel. This is the best reference book out there. Its solid teaching based on classic fundamentals. It allows readers to think critically about book design so they can make informed choices about their books.

> **By the Way**
>
> Luc Devroye maintains a great website at McGill University in Canada for all things typography. The site includes a great reading list and resources for learning about fonts. Visit http://cgm.cs.mcgill.ca/~luc /typography.html.

Book Design Fundamentals

The best book design results in a layout that is not noticeable. In other words, a strong book design does one thing: serves the content without upstaging it. A good book design is well planned and functional, supports maximum comprehension of the material, and offers optimal readability. A good design has a bit of controlled flare or personality—but only when it promotes the book's content. A good design never shouts.

Many self-publishers do not realize how much the design and layout affect the success of the book. Many very well-written self-published books are never purchased because they appear just too difficult to read. Taking care in preparing a proper page grid, selecting appropriate fonts, planning the content for layout, judiciously using and formatting supporting material, and correctly typesetting the book will give your self-publishing a better chance in the book trade and with consumers.

I know that some of what follows will seem familiar, but it's very much worth reviewing at this stage of your production.

Common layout traits are found in every book. Generally, every book should have page numbers, headers or footers, consistent leading, and comfortable margins. The sections that follow detail some of the guidelines.

Page Size

Nonfiction books are generally w6×h9 or w5.5×h8.5. Some manuals are w7.5× h9. Inspirational nonfiction intended for the gift market will likely be smaller than w5.5× h8.5. Examine similar books in the marketplace and make the decision that best benefits your book. Check with your book printer to ensure that the intended size is an economical size for printing. Finalize your trim size with your printer before doing any actual layout and production.

Page Numbers

Every page should feature page numbers, except for decorative pages and section breaks. Normally, those pages have what are called blind *folios*.

Wise Words

Folio is another word for page number. A blind folio is a page in sequence that has no visible page number. It is interesting to note that the word *folio* can also be used for a group of pages in a signature. It is also used in reference to oversize books, and it can be used in reference to a group of 100 words.

Page Headers and Footers

These are the repeating titles at the top or bottom of each page, respectively, except for the decorative pages, section breaks, or chapter openers. If your book has lots of heads and varying types of information, you will want to use footers rather than headers; this will prevent your page content from appearing too busy as the reader flips through the pages. Traditionally, the book's title goes on the verso running head, and the chapter title goes on the recto.

Part Openers

Part openers are often spreads, with the titling on the right-side page. The left-hand page can include a decorative element. You might want to use an epigraph to inspire the reader. Consider using a graphic design derived from the overall creative direction to enhance the presentation.

Chapter Openers

The traditional convention is to begin each new chapter on a recto—a right-side page. Of course, this means that your facing verso—facing left page—should be decorative or functional, pertaining to the chapter start. For instance, you can place a "what you'll learn in this chapter" on that recto. Or you might want to have a repeating design that is in character with the overall creative design. Or it could be blank.

It is undesirable to sometimes have the previous chapter end on the verso opposite the chapter start and other times have it be blank, if the previous chapter ends on a recto. That is inconsistent and will make the entire book look poorly planned.

Pro Style

Blank versos are acceptable but can be avoided with skilled page makeup and sometimes content can also be added to avoid them.

If you are doing a nonfiction book, it is acceptable to begin chapters on either a verso or a recto, although the best book designs always have chapters begin on a recto. You will always want to start the very first chapter on a recto.

Chapter Endings

It will be difficult to end every chapter on a recto. So how do you remedy that? One tactic it to use a small decorative flourish, a simple graphic design that pertains to the content or overall creative direction, or a one-line quotation to end each chapter. If the chapter ends on a recto, place the small dingbat two or three lines below the end of the text for decoration. If the chapter ends on a verso, place the dingbat on the blank recto page all by itself in the middle of the page. This ensures that there is a consistent visual approach to the end of every chapter. It will also ensure that the ensuing chapters always begin on a two-page spread.

Front Matter

Here is a refresher course from Chapter 11 on the proper order for front matter. If you don't get this right, you'll look all wrong.

1. Page i—Endorsements

2. Page ii—Endorsements or blank

3. Page iii—Half-title page or *bastard page* (just the main title)

4. Page iv—Blank

5. Page v—Full-title page (including main title, subtitle, byline, edition, and publishing imprint)

6. Pave vi—Copyright page (including full title and author; publisher information; edition history; copyright, usage, and reprint information; legal disclaimer, CIP data; and printing history)

7. Page vii—Dedication

8. Page viii—Blank or list of illustrations

9. Page ix—TOC (table of contents)

10. Page x—TOC continued, or blank

11. Page xi—Publisher preface (the "why" of the book)

12. Page xii—Publisher preface continued, or blank

13. Page xiii—Foreword (written by a third party)

14. Page ixv—Foreword continued, or blank

15. Page 1 or xv—Introduction (the "how" of the book)

16. Page 2 or xvi—Introduction continued, or blank opposite Chapter 1

17. Page 3 or 1—Chapter 1 start

Wise Words

The **bastard title page,** otherwise known as the half-title page, is really just a front matter page that contains only the main title, nothing else.

You'll note that the front matter is always paginated using Roman numerals. The main text always begins with the Arabic number 1.

Photos and Illustrations

If you are producing a book that includes photos or illustrations, it is critical to the visual presentation that the photos are placed amid the running text rhythmically and consistently. Additionally, pictures and illustrations must be used judiciously and with purpose. Nothing disrupts comprehension more than images that do not support the content in a meaningful way.

One way to add photographs to your book and keep the cost down is to use a "photo insert." A photo insert groups all of the photos together in one place.

Children's books and gift books (coffee-table books) are especially subject to proper planning. That is called storyboarding, and I covered it in Chapter 6. The key is to ensure that all visual content is placed within the text at regular intervals so that the overall presentation flows.

If you are planning to use additional content to support your text, it is wise to format those features in the same creative style as the overall design. For instance, if you have a graph, you will want to use the same typeface for the labels as you are using in the book. If your book design is soft, you may want to use rounded-corner boxes. These simple design considerations can create a cohesive layout.

One thing you don't want to do is cut and paste or import your Microsoft Excel charts and graphs or PowerPoint flowcharts into your page-layout program. The native program language used for those applications may not print properly when ripped to Postscript in prepress. The best thing to do is to use an illustration program such as Adobe Illustrator to create the graphics. You may be able to cut and paste the graphics from Excel or PowerPoint into Illustrator and save the file as an EPS file. I'll talk more about file formats later in the chapter.

Sidebars and Features

When planning these, the key is to build them into the content at regular intervals. This creates a good visual rhythm. Try to make them consistent lengths. You may need to work with an editor to do this. The design treatment you give the sidebar should be based on the overall design. This is your opportunity to add some flare to the pages. But exercise restraint! Don't make your sidebar design too loud, or it will upstage your content.

Typeface

The type you choose for your book seems like such a small detail. Typefaces can look very similar to the nondesigner. But to the ordinary eye, the eye which your reader will be casting upon your work, the typeface will be critical. Choose the wrong type face, and you may well lose a reader to eyestrain and headaches. Choose a good type-face, and your reader will sit happily in a favorite armchair, reading comfortably for hours on end.

The best typeface to use for long texts is a serif typeface from the Oldstyle Garalde category. Obviously, a major part of the design process is to select a typeface that is complimentary to your content, one that enhances the creative concept that presents your ideas. You'll be able to find such a font within the Oldstyle classification.

> **By the Way**
>
> A way to differentiate between the concept of serif and sans-serif type is to keep in mind that serif type has little extra lines that extend from the letters themselves. Sans-serif type does not have the little lines; the letters are straight up and down.

For instance, if you are producing an emotional self-help book and dealing with depression, you'll want to select a soft typeface such as Adobe Bell or Goudy. If you are writing a nonfiction history book, you might choose a more bookish typeface, such as Adobe Spectrum or Caslon. I don't advise setting a book in a sans-serif type-face, such as Helvetica. Readability is always better with a serif type.

The best rule of thumb in book design is this: if the reader notices the typeface in the body text, then it is a poor design. The best design is invisibility—a typeface that conveys the essence of the message while maintaining its anonymity is the best selection. Titling fonts may be ornate. But for body text, pick something attractive and complimentary, but unassuming and quiet.

Pro Style

Learn more about fonts and what is appropriate for books from Adobe. You can search online for an appropriate font by style, use, classification, and theme. Adobe is the maker of software such as InDesign, Photoshop, and Illustrator. They are also the inventor of Postscript, the printing language that book printers use in prepress. The fonts they have created are all Postscript compatible. Visit http://store.adobe.com/ type/main.html.

Type Size and Leading

Don't make the mistake of choosing a type size that is too small to be read comfortably. Just as the typeface itself makes a difference, so does the type size and overall line length. Unless you are producing a children's book, you can expect to set your text at a size of 10 to 13 points. Now, that is a large size range. The font size for optimal reading is about 10 points. Type styles vary greatly in size. Therefore, you must play with the size of the type you want to use to determine what the best readability will be.

Leading is an old-fashioned term that simply means the vertical space between the lines which allows for maximum readability. Typically you should leave 2 points space between the lines.

Heads and Subheads

We've already discussed the importance of a consistent hierarchical outline. This importance reveals itself when you begin formatting your heads and subheads. Take a look at this very book you hold in your hands. *The Complete Idiot's Guides* series makes great use of heads and subheads, and you can easily see the difference they makes in digesting information. It really moves the reader along, doesn't it?

You will need to select a different weight or size, or italic for each level of subhead. If you have too many levels, you will run out of options. Don't overdo it—use a font that is within the font family you are using for the body text, or a sans-serif font that compliments your body type.

Here are some guidelines and suggestions for formatting heads and subheads:

- Your heads need only one line space before them.
- A type size that is one or two points greater than the body type is effective. (Be conservative—you don't want it to look horsey.)
- The bold family member of your body text font is effective.
- A sans-serif font is effective because it is typically bolder than a serif font.
- A first-level head can be set in bold all caps.
- A second-level head can be set in bold title case.
- A third-level head can be set in bold title case italic.
- A fourth-level head can be set in Roman title case italic.
- A fifth-level head can be set in Roman title case.

General Typesetting Guidelines

This is a lot of obscure information to absorb, I know. I don't expect you to become an expert typesetter overnight (but if you do develop a skill, just think how you might be able to market yourself to other self-publishers). To give you an extra dose of confidence, here are a few typesetting conventions that will help make your book look like it was professionally typeset:

♦ *Never* use TrueType fonts.

♦ Use 9- to 12-point type—the smaller the better, as long as it is perfectly readable.

♦ Never vary the point size of the body text except when setting extracts, which are generally set smaller than general text.

♦ Never use sans-serif for body text.

♦ Try to set no more than 65 characters to a line (on average).

♦ Use consistent leading—always.

♦ For smaller bits of text, such as sidebars, use smaller type set on fractional leading (leading size that is a factor of your main leading). For instance, if your leading is 12 points, your fractional leading could be 9. That means that every fourth line will align back to the leading.

♦ Never use an indent or tab for the first paragraph of a new section or following a head.

♦ Avoid more than three hyphens in a row (stacked).

♦ Avoid leaving any word less than five characters on a line by itself.

♦ Use only one space between sentences.

♦ Always use true em dashes and en dashes.

♦ Always use true quote marks instead of inch marks or hatch marks.

♦ Set extracts indented left and right in a half-point or full-point smaller than the body text size.

♦ Never use the bolding feature available in your software program—always use a true bold.

♦ Never use the italics feature available in your software program—always use a true italics.

- Never underline words.

- Set your acronyms in small caps.

- Never set text in all caps unless it is a head.

- Align your numbered lists so that the numbers line up on the period that follows the number.

- Never strand the last line of a paragraph at the top of a page.

- Use superscripts for footnotes.

Leading

Leading is the line spacing of the text—the space between the sentences. Generally, you can expect to set the leading 1.5 to 3.5 points greater than the type size you select. For instance, if the type size you select is 10 points, your leading should be set to 11.5 minimum or 13.5 maximum. Of course, this depends on the x-height of the typeface and the ascent of its posts. For more information on leading and type sizes, refer to Robin William's book, *The Non-Designer's Type Book.*

Baseline Grid

The baseline grid is a tool in page-layout software that creates a horizontal frame for your text. It is based on the leading you have chosen. For instance, if your leading is 12 points, that is what your baseline grid should be. This will provide a clean structure for all the elements you employ in your book—everything can be aligned to the baseline grid. Furthermore, all body text can be locked to this grid. Why is this important? Well, visually, our brains perceive that the text is better organized if it aligns at the same point line to line, page to page.

Margins

Your margins should be comfortable. Don't economize on your page count by reducing your margins—it will make your book look cheap. These are general rules for margins:

- The bottom margin should be the biggest—close to 1 inch. Remember, you will need extra space to accommodate your footer and folio. That line of text should fall within the bottom margin.

- The top margin should be about .6 of an inch. This should be the smallest margin.

- The outside margin should be about .75 of an inch—enough for a good thumb grip.

- The inside margin (the gutter) should be about .8 of an inch. This is the most volatile margin because it is the margin that is most vulnerable to binding. Printers have different methods for binding books. Some add paper to the inside margin to grind it off to a rough edge for gluing. Some just grind off. Be sure to check with your printer. You don't want a tight inside margin; that will make your book feel squishy.

Producing Your Book

Okay, so you have some design guidelines for typesetting text and preparing your design. Now it is time to get down to business and produce your layout—or consider it time to give up and let the pros do it.

Thankfully, you don't have to do this without benefit of special software. Several page-layout software programs for creating book pages are available today. Printers are familiar with accepting most of them these days; it really is a matter of selecting a program you feel comfortable working with. Do check with your printer to see what they accept, though, before you begin with any software program.

I've mentioned this before, and I do hope you will take it to heart. Please understand that word-processing programs are *not* page-layout programs! The typographical controls and page-flow management are very limited in these programs. It is advised that you not use these programs to create your pages. Furthermore, these programs may create bad problems for printers that will cost you money in the long run. Be warned that the result will appear unprofessional. No major trade publisher uses word-processing programs to create book layouts.

Learning a page layout program takes time and trial and error to become proficient enough to produce a professional-looking book. Don't rush through this process, but take it slow and learn how to use the program. Learn the program thoroughly, and practice using the information you've learned here about layout and typesetting.

Pro Style _____

To determine what layout program might be best for you, visit About.com's Desktop Publishing's website for a full comparison of programs. You'll also find a wealth of information for properly formatting a layout; visit http://desktoppub.about.com/cs/software/f/best_software.htm.

The following are the most common software tools for page layout, in order of preference by designers and printers: QuarkXpress, Adobe InDesign, PageMaker, FrameMaker, and Tex/LaTex.

Preparing the Text for Import

When using a page-layout application, you import your word-processing text into the program. It is important to prepare the text in the proper manner. Your page-layout program's manual will advise you if you need to save the text file in a special format so that it will be recognized by the layout application. The most common format is the .txt format, or the text only format.

Regarding special formatting of the text in the word-processing program in preparation for import, pay attention to the aforementioned typesetting guidelines. We discussed the value of styletagging to preserve your style intentions. Here are the most common preparations:

- Tag italic words and phrases with a <I> tag before and after the instance, to preserve the instance.

- Tag bold words and phrases with a <B> tag before and after the instance, to preserve the formatting.

- Use manual numbering and bulleting.

- Use a space-dash-dash-space for em dashes.

- Use a space-dash-space for en dashes.

- Remove all extra paragraph spaces.

- If you want to preserve paragraph indents, use a tab instead of the word processor's indent feature.

Formatting Trouble-Free Text

When you get a printing estimate, you may see a line that says, "These costs are based on the customer providing trouble-free files for prepress. Additional costs may apply for fixing customer files." Yeah … at $70 per hour! It is critical to create clean layout files for the printer. Keep these guidelines in mind to avoid those charges:

- Always use Postscript fonts.

- Never use TrueType or Multiple Master fonts—they can cause the prepress application to reflow your document or substitute other fonts.

- Never use local bold or italic formatting using the style tool; it may not be applied, or, worse, it can cause doubling or deformation of the font. Always use the actual bold or italic member of the typeface.

Creating Trouble-Free Graphics

Just as the text can be troublesome to prepress if not formatted correctly, imported images must be treated properly so that they do not cause problems. Worse, the images might process correctly, but if the original file type is wrong or the resolution is poor, the image will look terrible. Here are some guidelines:

- Always import graphics according to the proper software instructions instead of simply copying and pasting them into your pages.

- Always crop your photos to the exact usage size in the image-editing program instead of resizing them in the page-layout software.

- If your book is color, always use the CMYK color mode instead of the RGB color mode in your image-editing or drawing programs.

- Always use a resolution of at least 300 DPI for your photo images.

- Always save the photo images as TIF files or JPG files from your image-editing program, such as PhotoShop.

- Always save your clipped-out photo images with a clipping path as an EPS file from your image-editing program.

- Always save your line art as an EPS file from your drawing program, such as Illustrator or CorelDraw.

- Never import a PICT, SYLK, WMF, or PNG file format into your page-layout program. It probably won't print in prepress.

- Always convert your charts, graphs, clip art (don't use clip art anyway), and other third-party program graphics as EPS or TIF files for import.

- Always set your import box to a background of white for photographic images.

- Don't stretch, squeeze, squish, scrunch, crunch, or otherwise distort imported images in your page-layout software. That just looks bad.

This question might have come up in your preliminary discussions with printers: "What is your DPI?" But what the heck does it mean? DPI means dots per inch and refers to something called resolution—how many printing dots or screen dots make up a given line in an inch of a monitor, printer, or scanner. In today's imaging software, it is equated with PPI, or pixels per inch, which is the direct corresponding resolution of the image. The higher the DPI is, the better the resolution is.

It has a close relationship with a printing acronym known as LPI, or lines per inch (or line screen). Rather than geek out over this, all you need to know is that the DPI of the image you are using should be twice the LPI the printer is using. Got that?

For instance, printers usually print book interiors at 150 LPI, so you will want to set the DPI resolution of your image to 300 (150 LPI × 2 = 300 DPI). Be aware that you cannot increase the DPI of a photo image after it has been scanned or digitally photographed at a lower DPI resolution. The correct DPI must be used in originally scanning or photographing the image. Otherwise, you are just shoving more dots into the image without improving its original clarity.

The Round Up—Creating an Even Signature

A signature is a collection of pages. For book printers, they are multiples of 8 or 12. A 32-page or 48-page signature is a common count. If your book is 320 pages, you have ten 32-page signatures.

Why is this important to know? Because printing 320 pages is far less costly than printing 321 pages. It is your job to round out to an even number of pages to fit the signature. Additionally, if your book is under a signature, the printer will add blank pages to the back of the book. That is just ugly and looks poorly planned. Some ideas are sales pages for derivative books, a glossary, a website preview, an expanded author bio, or idea resources for your reader.

Preparing the Layout Files for the Printer

Now that you have properly designed, prepared text for, created the layout for, and typeset the book, your final task is to prepare the files to send to the printer. The key to doing this successfully is to follow the instructions that your printer gives you.

Each printer is different and has its own requirements for submitted files. This is because each workflow is different—they may have different equipment and processes for prepress. The best thing to do is to contact the printer and ask to get a copy of the file-preparation guidelines. You will often be able to download these specifications as PDF files from the printer's website.

Even though each printer will have specific settings for you to use in your page-layout program for creating final files, the majority of printers today require that you create high-resolution PDF files for the interior and provide "live" files (application layout files) for the cover. This is because the printer has great color control over live files than it might in PDF files. The PDF file you will create for the interior will not be alterable.

Creating the Interior PDF

You will be required to print your layout file to a Postscript file within the layout application's print dialog box. Don't panic, it is not as difficult as it sounds. All this means is that you will enter the printer-specific settings into the dialog box and select the print-to-file option instead of sending to your laser printer.

If done according to the printer instructions, this should embed all your fonts and graphics so that everything is encapsulated into one single file and nothing can be moved out of place as it might in live files. When the Postscript file is created, you will be required to "distill" it with Acrobat's Distiller program. Again, there are special printer-specific settings for distilling the Postscript file so that you create a high-res PDF file with all the fonts and images embedded for the printer.

Remember to get the individual specs from the printer you have chosen before you begin this process. Your printer's website will have a plethora of file-submission and preparation information. Don't take it from me—get it from them and produce files they want that are particular to their equipment.

It is always a good idea to send a "test file" to your printer early on in your file preparation process to avoid costly revisions later. The test file will ensure that the printer will be able to use what you provide, or will flag problems that need to be fixed.

The Cover File

Our next chapter discusses book cover design in detail, but let's touch now on how the cover file will need to be prepared. Most printers will want the application files for the cover. This means that instead of creating Postscript files, you will go through your file and collect each image and each font used, and supply them to the printer along with the actual cover layout file. If this is done correctly and according to the printer requirements, the printer should have everything it needs to produce a trouble-free prepress file.

Check with your printer to see how you should send files. You might be able to e-mail them, burn them to a CD, or place them on the printer's FTP site. Printers require that you send them hard copies of your pages so they can reference them during the prepress process.

The Proof Is in the Pudding

When your printer has received your files, it will "preflight" them. That means they will go through them and check each page, graphic, font and line, and image to ensure that there are no output problems and that nothing is missing or in error. If they are missing something, they will contact you and you can supply the missing file or font.

After they have preflighted your files, they will send you a printer's proof and a cover proof. Check these carefully to ensure that there are no missing elements and that the color on your proof is right.

I know, this is a lot of technical stuff to remember, and it's overwhelmingly technical at times. Many self-publishers do opt to work with a book producer. If you elect to do it yourself, just remember the following key points.

The Least You Need to Know

- Examine similar books for design and layout ideas.

- Plan your content carefully and examine the hierarchy for inconsistencies before layout.

- Ensure that you understand the parts of a book.

- Read a few of the recommended books on typography and layout to learn how to do it.

- Play with the layout application to ensure that you know how to use it.

- Obtain specifications from your printer to finalize your files correctly.

Chapter 14

Design an Effective Cover

In This Chapter

- What makes a book cover work?
- Elements of effective cover design
- How covers for fiction and nonfiction differ
- Amateur design bugaboos to avoid
- Working with a professional designer

Oh, we've heard the same trite phrase all our lives: "You can't judge a book by its cover." And when it comes to making snap judgments about people, it is spot on. When you are talking about actual books though, well … there might be some truth to the idea that you *can* judge a book by its cover. In the marketplace, books are always judged by their covers.

When *don't* you need your cover to help sell your book?

- When you are preparing a family history project or a book in which the contents are of sufficient sentimental interest to a small group of people (your family and friends)
- When you are selling your product by mail, or in such a way that you are interesting buyers in the *information* they will gain rather than the way the information is packaged

For everyone else, you'll need to have a *great* cover for your book.

What Makes a Cover Work?

Turn this book back to the front cover for just a moment and take a good, long look at the cover of this book. *The Complete Idiot's Guides* covers have a nice, clean look to them, don't they? An overall white background bordered by a band of orange, strong black type for the title, and the recognizable orange box in the upper-left corner with *The Complete Idiot's Guide* brand. Simple, yet classy and clean. Eye-catching and informative. A simple color scheme—orange, blue, white, and black. A cover with "gestalt" is how cover designer Vanessa Perez describes it. A feeling of completeness: "The design is completed and contained." An effective book cover is one that gets your message across and has a pleasing and polished look to it.

A common mistake that self-publishers make is to find a book they like—*The Da Vinci Code*, for instance, or David Bach's *The Automatic Millionaire*—and then have a book cover done that imitates it. The book world is now awash in novels with dark covers and mysterious eyes, and financial-planning books that show frolicking couples on the beach. You'll need to strike out on your own to develop a design and a look that is uniquely yours.

As with so many other parts of effective publishing, to get a feel for effective book cover design, you will need to spend a lot of time in bookstores. Whereas before you were carefully studying the other books in your category in order to better develop a book that could compete editorially, now you need to study the way these books are "packaged." You will also need to decide whether you want your book to blend in (for greater acceptance) or stand out (for greater visibility).

For a truly great book cover, here are the elements that will need to work together:

- Length of the title and subtitle
- Type size and style
- Color
- Design elements like photographs or icons

Each element is described in the sections that follow.

Your Title and Subtitle

You named your book long ago, but did you ever think about how long it is? Once you put it on the front cover of a book, it might well look a tad too long. Can you shorten it up a bit? First-time authors have a tendency to go overboard with the length of their subtitles, too. With both your title and your subtitle on the front of the book, does the type have to be so small that it is now hard to read?

Pro Style _____

"Most self-publishers don't spend enough time on their book's spine," cover designer Vanessa Perez points out. "Every writer anticipates their book being displayed face out so that the buyer will see the entire cover. Most books end up spine out on the bookshelf, so you need to be very strategic about what your spine looks like." Focus on readability from a distance; make sure that browsers can glance over and easily see what your book is called. And remember, the longer your title, the smaller the print on the spine!

Type Size and Style

Type comes in an incredible array of choices. Make sure that you choose a type style and size that is easy to read and that adds to your image rather than detracts from it. Get the opinions of several folks in your target audience, men and women both. Ask them about "readability" and don't overlook the eyesight of your target audience. Books on retirement issues, for example, should have pretty large size type.

Color

Color can both make your book and harm it. Think of the cool colors like blues and greens—perfect for a health book. Warm colors like reds and oranges are better suited to romance books. Make sure you are using colors appropriate to your topic.

Keep in mind that sometimes a bookshelf is so crowded with fancy covers and elaborate designs that it will make your eyesight swim. When displayed among a large group of fancy covers, sometimes a simple white cover can really pop out and look completely different from the books around it. It is impossible to know just where your book will be displayed and what books will surround it, of course, but when assessing the other books in that category, ask yourself, is simple better than fancy? Is white better than a vibrant color? It just might do the trick.

Cautionary Tales _____

A two-color cover design sounds affordable; a four-color design sounds expensive. So does that mean that a three-color design is somewhere in between? No, it costs more than a four-color design does! Using only three colors will cost more in design hours, prep time, and printing costs.

Design Elements

A well-chosen image can add to a book cover, helping to create emotion and interest on the part of the buyer. An odd or offbeat image that clashes with the colors, theme, or overall look of the cover will seem odd.

Make sure that all four of these elements are in harmony on your book's ultimate cover design. Spend that time in the bookstore wisely, looking not only at the covers of books in your category to see what the standard look and feel seems to be, but also at books in other categories. Why? To better develop your own ability to see what makes an effective book cover. Who knows where you will find the inspiration that will lead to the best cover for your book?

Second Glance

What do you want the casual bookstore browser to notice about your book? The title? Your name? The name of a brand or series? Or maybe the name of a famous celebrity who has endorsed you and your book? Let's get back to the cover of this book. You've seen enough *Complete Idiot's Guides* on the bookstore shelf to be able to recognize the brand look. Your eye zones out the brand identification and zeroes in on the individual book topic, doesn't it? When you look at the front cover of this book, you see the words "self-publishing" loud and clear. Make sure that the way your cover is arranged meets your expectations about what you want the reader to see first.

Image Conscious

Remember the two best-selling book covers I mentioned earlier, *The Da Vinci Code* and *The Automatic Millionaire?* The cover of *The Da Vinci Code* evokes a mood—a brooding, dark, red-brown cover; large gold type; and a strip torn artfully away to reveal the eyes of the Mona Lisa peering out at you. Very effective. Even if you didn't already know this was a popular novel, the images might intrigue you enough to pick up the book and examine it. The colors and image evoke a mood. When deciding on the cover of a novel, you do need to evoke a mood or feeling that leaves the casual browser wanting to find out more about what is inside of your book.

Nonfiction, not so much …. Sure, the happy couple pictured on the front cover of *The Automatic Millionaire* look like they lead the sort of life many of us aspire to (not a care in the world but to follow the sun), but the images aren't as necessary to intrigue the buyer. With a nonfiction book, images are generally less important than words. We would get the point of David Bach's book just by reading the title; the images reinforce the title rather than help draw us in to look more closely at the book.

Not every book cover uses an image. The simplest type of cover, and one much used in the book world, is known as a *type solution*. All that means is that the cover only has words on it, without any major design elements. Just type.

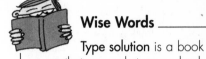

Wise Words

Type solution is a book cover that uses only type and color to get the point across, with no fancy picture or elaborate design.

What Really Belongs on the Cover?

Other than your name and the title and subtitle of your book, what actually belongs on the front cover of your book? A book cover is a marketing piece, really, and what goes on the cover are the things that will most help sell your book. That's information about what it is, who it is from, and what readers can gain from it.

Let's start with a hardcover book first, which will have more space than a paperback cover. The front of the book jacket on a hardcover book should contain …

Front cover:

- Title

- Subtitle

- Author

- Author credential, if important

- Author of foreword, if an important name

- An endorsement quote, if important

"If important?" What I mean is, if the name of the person writing your foreword or endorsing your book is a recognizable name that will help convince the reader to keep looking at your book, then include it, by all means. And if your own description—John Doe, author of the best-selling book *Meet John Doe*—will also be compelling, include it on the front cover.

Back cover:

- Advance praise for the book, if any

- Marketing copy for the book

- Bar code

Inside flap:

- U.S. price/Canadian price

- Marketing copy that describes the book and what it can do for the reader

Wise Words _____

A **colophon** is the logo for a publishing company. Chronicle Books uses a stylized pair of glasses, for instance, and Simon and Schuster a man sowing seeds.

Back flap:

- Author photo (a small one, please)

- Brief author bio

- Design credit for cover

- Publisher's *colophon*, if any

Paperback Cover

A standard paperback doesn't have inside flaps on which to keep writing; it has only the front and back covers. There is a fancy type of paperback with "french flaps" that fold back on themselves, but they are expensive. So let's assume you are producing a paperback with only the front and back covers. What goes where?

Front cover:

- Title

- Subtitle

- Author

- Author credential, if important

- Author of foreword, if an important name

- An endorsement quote, if important

Exactly the same sorts of elements that are on the front cover of the hardcover book. The back cover of a paperback, however, crams in everything that a hardcover could put on the inside and back flaps. So you are left with …

Back cover:

- ◆ Advance praise

- ◆ Marketing copy

- ◆ Author photo

- ◆ Author bio

- ◆ U.S./Canadian price

- ◆ Bar code

- ◆ Design credit for cover

- ◆ Publisher's colophon

Wow, how is all that going to fit? It isn't. You need to be able to look critically at what is needed to sell your book. Is it your bio and credentials? If so, then leave some of that on. Advance praise? Include it, too. Your picture? Maybe not, unless you have a recognizable face. What do you have to have on the back? The price, the bar code, and a description of the book and what it will do for the reader. Sell, sell, sell.

The covers of books are marketing tools. That is why commercial publishers like to control the entire design process and seldom involve the author of a book in the decisions. What pleases an author does not necessarily sell a book.

When designing your book's cover, you need to think 100 percent like a publisher and completely ignore the fact that you are also the author of this book. Concentrate on business, not on ego. A harsh statement, but true.

> **By the Way**
>
> Will your book cover work as a postcard, too? Many authors have their front covers printed up in extra quantities to use as mailers or send the cover design to a company that specializes in making author postcards. You can then use it as an additional marketing and publicity tool.

Inside Front and Back Also?

Now that you are thinking of good cover design for your book, here is another idea to consider: using the inside front and back of your cover to convey additional information.

On a paperback, you can pay an extra printing charge and have your cover printed on the inside as well. Why does it cost more? Simple, it means an extra trip through the printing press. Take a look once more at the cover of this book. Open the inside front cover—what do you see? A note to the reader. What is printed on the inside back cover? The information about the author.

If space is an issue in your book and you want to include as much information as possible, consider printing in these nooks and crannies. Use the space to add pertinent information that will sell your book or hook the casual reader. Run endorsements and quotes from big shots on the inside front and back covers, if you have them! You can also use the inside back cover to run an advertisement for other titles you have available. Consider the extra printing cost, though, when making your decision. Is what you want to add compelling enough to spend the extra money on another trip through the press? Then go ahead and do it!

By the Way

In a commercial publishing house, the cover meetings include folks from all different departments, not just the art department. And they spend a lot of time standing at the back of the room, far away from where the covers themselves are displayed. Why not examine the covers more closely? They do, but seeing a cover from a distance is critical. Notice how in a bookstore most browsers stand back several feet and examine the bookshelf as a whole rather than up close looking at each book at once? Make sure your book can "pop" at a distance. Don't have such a complicated cover that a reader can understand what it is only by getting up close and personal.

Rules to Avoid the Self-Published "Look"

Book-publishing pros will tell you they can spot a self-published book at a healthy distance. While this was certainly true in the past and is now fading, there are still a few obvious self-publishing bugaboos you should avoid.

- **Author's name is *too big*.** Remember, focus on what is going to sell the book, and emphasize that. It is easy to spot an ego at work: big type on a small cover.

- **Type is too skinny.** Don't be afraid to use bold type. Thin and elegant type will disappear on the cover very easily.

- **Title looks too plain.** Some self-published books just look homemade. Make sure you are training your eye by spending a lot of research time on covers in bookstores.

◆ **Inappropriately fancy type is used.** Some type is too hard to read! Again, familiarize yourself with the types that are used over and over on book covers, and stick to one of those. "Avoid Comic Sans and Hobo," advises designer Vanessa Perez.

◆ **Clip art elements on the cover.** This is a sign of a do-it-yourselfer. Stay away from recognizable clip art.

◆ **Amateurish artwork.** Don't use an image you love just because you love it. Make sure that the art you are using is both highly professional and appropriate to your book's topic.

"The cover of my first book really harmed the sales," admits Bob Dreizler, author of *Tending Your Money Garden*. The illustration was unsophisticated, the type wasn't bold enough—it just didn't have a professional look to it. When Bob published a revised second edition, he hired a cover designer.

Book Cover Designers I Recommend

All throughout this book, I have encouraged you to do as much of your own work as possible while self-publishing. If you are considering hiring anyone to help, I suggest that you spend your money on a professional book designer. Spending money here really does make a huge difference in the fate of your book.

How much will it cost to hire a cover designer? Like most things in life, it depends. In addition to the cost of the design itself, there could be added expenses in image licensing, custom illustrators, and prep costs for fancy color work. You might spend anywhere from $1,500 to $4,000 for a design with lots of bells and whistles.

Here are a few designers whom I've worked with over the years. I have great respect for their talents and design sense:

◆ **Vanessa Perez.** The former art director for an imprint of Random house, Vanessa is responsible for the covers of several *New York Times* bestsellers. Reach her at bookdesign@sbcglobal.net.

◆ **Monica Thomas.** Also a former Random House designer, Monica can be reached at Monicathomas@surewest.com.

◆ **Kari Keating.** You can contact Kari at kari@graphicapps.com.

◆ **Mike Tanamachi.** Mike is a brilliant designer, very good with bold, masculine topics and subjects. His e-mail address is Emailforyou@comcast.com.

Remember, the cover really could make or break your book. Please don't squander all of your hard work, time, talent, and money with a poorly designed and ineffective cover for your book. Devote plenty of time and attention to getting this part of your book done right.

Cautionary Tales _____

If you decide to hire some help with your cover, don't just hire a designer—hire a book cover designer. Subtle nuances in effective cover design are learned only after countless covers and are not taught at basic art school. Book designers have a better feel for using type, and they understand what kinds of fonts mix well in a book cover and how issues like kerning come into play when you are trying to fit a long cover title on the front of a book.

Ask for criticism, particularly from publishing professionals like bookstore personnel. Take your sample cover design into the outlets that you hope will stock your book, and ask them what they think. Take their comments seriously. You don't want to wait until your book is finished and printed to learn that the very places you hope to sell your work don't think it is quite good enough.

The Least You Need to Know

- Most people really do judge a book by its cover.
- Great covers balance several elements—type, color, and art.
- Your cover needs to be readable at a distance.
- Make sure you put sales before ego on your cover copy.
- Get feedback on your cover before sending it to the printer.
- Money spent on a professional cover design is money well spent.

Chapter 15

Paperwork and Registrations

In This Chapter

- ◆ All the paperwork you'll need to file
- ◆ Copyright registrations
- ◆ Assigning an ISBN
- ◆ The Library of Congress
- ◆ UPC/EAN scannable marks

While your manuscript is working its way through the various editorial and production phases, and a cover designer is sketching out brilliant ideas for an eye-catching cover, you might be wondering whether this is the point at which you get to sit down and relax. No. Grab a pen because you have a form or two to fill out.

You've met all manner of publishing folk in the last few chapters, and you now understand just how many of those roles you need to assume. Here is one more role for you, and you don't have to hire someone to fill it. You also get to be the lowly assistant who sits and fills out the forms.

If you are publishing a book for sale in the bookstore and library markets, certain forms and paperwork are required. The sooner you start the process, the better. As mundane as it sounds, as with taxes, you just need to sit down and do them. No technical or intellectual prowess is required.

When you're finished, you'll have a book that's officially copyrighted, that can be scanned and sold at bookstores, that is differentiated by all the other books out there by its own code, and much more.

The Debut Party: Publication Date

Have you decided on a *publication date* for your book? The actual day that you expect to receive finished copies of your book is a day you just can't wait for, I know, but don't declare that actual date the pub date, please.

Before you begin to fill out these forms, you need to pick a month and a year. One of the first things to consider—taking into account just how long each part of the publishing process will take—is the release date or publication date of your book.

Interestingly, the publication date (or "pub date," as it's referred to within the publishing industry) is set for a few months after the printing of the work. There are several reasons for this. Certain reviewers—important reviewers such as *Library Journal* and *Kirkus Reviews*—work months ahead and need to review books and write their critiques before a book's release. Later in this chapter, I'll go over the Advance Book Information (ABI) form; you'll need the publication date for this form, too.

> **Wise Words**
>
> The **publication date** is the date your book is "released" to the public—that is, hits bookstore shelves—not the date that your book is hot off the presses and boxed. In fact, often the pub date is up to four months *after* the book is printed, allowing publishers the time to garner advance reviews and press for the book.

Another compelling reason that publishers "sit" on printed books and choose a later launch relates to advertising opportunities. Books themed for specific holidays, for example, may be written, printed, and ready to roll into stores—but why release a book such as *Christmas Miracles* in July? The sales opportunities increase exponentially with a strategic release date sometime in early November. Sports books? A great sell around Father's Day. Sexy romance books? How about Valentine's Day?

Consider your production timeline and advertising opportunities, then choose the most appropriate publication date for your work. You've worked hard, why not plan a big to-do on your pub date? Another good reason to self-publish is that you can throw yourself a party and invite all your friends! Commercial publishers hardly ever throw book parties for their authors anymore, so enjoy the chance to do it up yourself.

When the pub date is clear in your mind, you are ready to move on to filling out the pesky, but necessary, forms. Paperwork is never pleasant, but in this case it can be an exciting process. There you sit, filling out forms that will show the world you did what you said you were going to do—publish a book!

By the Way

More commercial publishers are "embargoing" their hottest, biggest titles, not permitting bookstores to sell them until an announced date. Books such as *My Life,* which is Bill Clinton's autobiography, or the latest John Grisham novel arrive at bookstores and then have to sit in unopened cartons until the date arrives; they can't just be put on the shelves right away as with other shipments. This is really a publicity technique more than anything else. I don't recommend trying to do anything like this for your book.

Up Front and Personal

Open any professionally published book, and within the first few pages, usually right after the title page, you'll find the copyright page, which lists copyright information, publishing history, Library of Congress Cataloging-in-Publication (CIP) data, the International Standard Book Number (ISBN), prior publication, permissions, acknowledgments (if applicable), and the paper durability statement. Remember all the information from Chapter 10? Before you can line up all this info inside your book in the proper order, you first have to get the info from the folks who bestow it.

The proper order of the first few pages of the front matter goes like this:

♦ Book half title

♦ Title page

You will put all your official notices on the copyright page, which is on the backside of the title page. The proper order is this:

♦ Copyright notice

♦ ISBN

♦ CIP/PCN

Cautionary Tales

There is a lot of confusion about the CIP, Cataloging-in-Publication data, which is bestowed by the Library of Congress. According to my e-mail exchange with the Library of Congress folks, self-publishers may not apply for CIP info, but rather a PCN. This stands for preassigned control number and is used by self-publishers instead of the CIP data. Some self-publishers do go ahead and fill out the forms, making sure to use an official-sounding publishing name for their company. I recommend following the Library of Congress rules and applying for a PCN instead. Check out http://cip.loc.gov for more information.

Papers and Forms and Feds, Oh My!

Obviously, you'll already have some of the information you'll need, such as your address. But most of the information requires you to fill out form after form and obtain the information from either a government agency or another party. We live in a world of numbers and paper trails. The following are must-have items for your front matter and instructions on where to go and what you need for the paperwork. Let's begin.

Always Use Protection: Copyright Registration

I touched on this concept in the legal chapter. As the author, you possess copyrights the minute you put ink to page. Your work is your work. To validate your copyrights, always either type the symbol © or write out "copyright" followed by your name and the year of the creation.

You really should make it official, though. Even though manuscripts are protected before they are published, you will want to register the copyright, and thereby protect your rights. You will need to fill out one of two copyright forms provided by the Copyright Office at the Library of Congress, either a Form TX or a Short Form TX.

The fastest way to get started is to visit the website at www.copyright.gov and download the forms. You can also do it the old-fashioned way by calling the Library of Congress at 202-707-3000 and requesting that they send you the forms.

Explicit instructions will accompany the paperwork. You will return the forms with one copy of your original work and the required fee in the form of check or money order to:

Library of Congress
Copyright Office
101 Independence Avenue, SE
Washington, DC 20559-6000

As of this writing, the copyright fee is $30 per work.

By the Way
Make sure you get the correct form from the Copyright Office to protect your literary work. Not only do writers send in their work, but so do boat designers! You'll see a section on the Copyright Office site set up for registering the hull design of ships. Don't absent-mindedly register your novel as a boat. Let your readers decide whether your plot holds water.

Library of Congress Number

After you've obtained your copyright registration, you might think you are finished with the Library of Congress. But, no, there's more!

If you want libraries to buy your book, you'll need to obtain a Library of Congress Number, or LCN. Sometimes you may see it referred to as a LCCN, standing for Library of Congress Card Number.

The Library of Congress requires that you submit your application online. First go to http://pcn.loc.gov/pcn/pcn006.html, where you will set up an account number and password at the Preassigned Control Numbers site. Your account number and password will provide you access to the form you'll need to request your LCN.

This seems simple, but it can be a controversial area for self-publishers. Commercial publishers are assigned something else, you see—a CIP number and data. This stands for Cataloging-in-Publication, and we have all been trained to think that real books have CIP info inside of them. The Library of Congress has established the PCN system because of the growing demand by one-book publishers for official registration. Don't be put off by this; please honor their requests and apply for the PCN. It might interest you to know that many big publishers are also using PCN, too.

ISBN

Just as we all possess Social Security numbers that uniquely identify us, a book is assigned a number to uniquely identify it. This number, the International Standard Book Number (ISBN), is assigned by the R. R. Bowker Company and the International Standards Organization (ISO), and it facilitates all tracking and order fulfillment.

Any bookstore can identify a book by its ISBN. The number isn't arbitrarily assigned or randomly generated. The first digit identifies the country in which the book is published. The second group of digits identifies the publisher. Check out several books from the same publisher, and you'll notice that the second set of digits of the ISBNs is the same. The third grouping of numbers denotes the book, with the last digit as a "check digit."

Book-publishing geeks can rattle off the ISBN prefixes of major publishers. My former employer, Prima, was 7615 (all of the Prima ISBNs, then, started off as 0-7615- and then went on to numbers identifying the actual book).

Bookstores, distributors, wholesalers—anyone who sells or distributes books—will not carry books without an ISBN. It is imperative that you have one if you plan to go this route. If your book is intended to stay within your family or otherwise skip the commercial market, then you really don't need to go through this step unless you want to.

It's easy to procure your ISBN. Log on to www.isbn.org. You may either download the forms and mail them in to the R. R. Bowker Company, 121 Chanlon Road, New Providence, NJ 07974, or register for the number online by using your credit card to pay the fee.

Pro Style

Each version of your title must have its own distinct ISBN. Let's say you produce both an audio book and a hardcover of the same title. Each will possess its own ISBN. Moreover, if you revise a book and produce a new edition with substantial changes, you'll need to use a new ISBN. This is particularly important for textbooks, where students are required to purchase the book. You don't want students to buy the first edition when the third edition is being used in the class.

The last time I checked, the cost of an ISBN was $225. Sounds steep, but that will actually get you 10 numbers altogether. You can use one for your first book, and then you'll have nine numbers left over for your updated editions. But with anything, changes occur. It's best to find out what the fee is directly from the company. You may call R. R. Bowker at 1-877-310-7333. The forms are straightforward, but ask a Bowker representative if you have any questions. In addition to receiving your ISBN, you'll receive directions concerning where the ISBN should appear on your book.

Scannable Marks

No longer do grocers tag products with prices on stickers. We live in an electronic world, where scanning marks hold encoded information such as price, inventory, and more. For your book to find its way to shelves and the bookstore cash register, you'll need to order a Bookland European Article Number (EAN) scanning symbol or barcode.

It took a number of years for the industry to decide which of the scanning systems books really needed. I remember fierce battles in the '90s between a publisher of computer game hint books and the toy retailers who sold the games and also wanted to sell the book alongside it. By the time all of the different bar codes were printed on those books, you could hardly see what it was!

Basically, you are ordering a "graphic" that will be printed on the back cover, right lower side. The barcode will identify the ISBN, the book's price, and the Bookland EAN barcode with a check digit and the title's ISBN again, but without the check digit.

Several design firms and companies will produce a Bookland EAN barcode for you. The cost for the barcode runs between $10 and $40.

Conveniently, you can find Bookland EAN barcode suppliers, categorized by states, online at www.isbn.org/standards/home/isbn/us/barcode.asp. Each listing showcases contact information, e-mail address, website link, and a short blurb about the company. Many also display prices. As always, we recommend networking with other self-publishers and asking for suggestions.

Applying the barcode to your book's cover is a job for your book cover designer. A skilled cover designer will know just how to place it in the proper spot, which colors to use (black and white, please, so the scanner can read it), and how much space it needs around it.

UPC

Do you plan to make your book available in nonbookstore outlets such as grocery stores or drugstores? If so, you'll need yet another type of code on your book: a universal product code, or UPC. The same basic type of information is contained in the UPC as in the EAN (and they look remarkably similar), but they are designed to be read by different equipment.

Beginning around $300, a UPC doesn't come cheap, so don't pursue this unless you really think your book has a shot at being sold in the nonbookstore market. Before you can get a UPC code, you'll need to become a member of the Uniform Code Council. The actual membership fee that you pay will be determined by how many products you need to identify with a UPC, what your gross revenues are, and other specific business questions. Remember, your books are products. And these guys, the UCC, are used to dealing with cereal manufacturers and milk producers, not always one-book publishers. To find out more, visit their website at www.uc-council.org.

By the Way

All of this fuss over the ability to run your book through a computerized checkout. The truly maddening thing is that most of the major booksellers use their own in-house-generated sticker with encrypted information that they apply to each and every book in stock. Look at the back of a book at Border's or Barnes & Noble, and you'll see that another code has been added!

Four Books, Four Styles

Confused yet? It is difficult to know just what your book really needs. I recommend discussing this issue during the early stages of your contact with potential distributors.

Even the big publishers seem to approach it from all angles. I checked four different books on the shelf at a grocery store. Here is what I found:

- *Love Overboard*, by Janet Evanovich: A mass market–size paperback, published by Harper Torch. This book has a UPC code printed on the back and an EAN code on the inside front cover.

- *Embracing Eternity*, by Tim LaHaye and Jerry B. Jenkins: A trade paperback book published by Tyndale. This book has only an EAN printed on the back cover, with nothing on the inside front cover. The book has a UPC sticker added to the back cover, though, by the distribution company, The News Group, which supplies grocery store accounts.

- *Women's Health & Wellness 2005:* An oversize trade book published by Oxmoor House. This book has both an EAN and a UPC printed on the back cover.

◆ *Paul & Phil's Rocket Science Cookbook:* A locally produced book that comes from two radio personalities in Sacramento, sold to raise funds for charity. The two self-publishers work directly with the grocery store itself to set up distribution, so the only code found on the back of the cover (in fact, the only thing printed on the back cover at all!) was a simple UPC bar code.

I'm confused, too! The bottom line is that the different types of encoded and encrypted information found in the UPC and EAN codes are driven solely by the type of check-out and inventory system that the individual retailer owns.

Let the World Know What's Coming

Okay, now. You've been happily filling out forms and joining associations and compiling all of the very specific types of information that you will need to include in your physical book. Is there anything you should be doing now to warn the world that you have a book coming up soon? You bet.

R. R. Bowker, the powerhouse information publisher that controls so much of what goes on in the registration world (the folks you went to for your ISBN, remember?), also has a handy way to let the world know about your forthcoming book. It's called *Forthcoming Books in Print.* Clever name, eh? You will want your book to be listed in *Forthcoming Books in Print,* to generate some advance interest, orders, and publicity.

Remember the day you chose as your official publication date? A sort of, kind of, fake date a few weeks or even months beyond when you actually planned to have finished books? This is the date you will use when filling out the information in the ABI form, which is all that is required to be included in *Forthcoming.*

Just fill out the Advance Book Information (ABI) form and send it in. You should receive the form and instructions when your big books of blank ISBNs arrive in the mail. If you don't, contact R. R. Bowker. You can also go to their website and fill out the form there at www.bowkerlink.com. Plan on filling out an ABI form about six months before your official pub date so that you are in the system well in advance.

Who looks at *Forthcoming Books in Print?* I used to, when I was the buyer for a bookstore chain. It is an important way to know what is coming up in the industry and to stay on top. So you never know just who might notice that your book is waiting in the wings. Thankfully, ABI is much easier than any of the other registrations and forms you've done so far. And it is also free.

The Least You Need to Know

◆ Choose a publication date that gives you time for the production of your work, advance reviews, and advertising opportunities.

◆ Copyright your work through the Library of Congress, Copyright Office.

◆ Apply for your ISBN through R. R. Bowker.

◆ Obtain a Bookland EAN barcode through myriad graphic designers listed online.

◆ If you want to sell to libraries, secure a Library of Congress Card Number.

◆ Give your title free prepublicity by filing an Advance Book Information form.

Part 4

My Book Is Done, Now What? Publicizing and Selling a Self-Published Book

Congratulations, you just had a book! And your next step is—what, exactly? You'll learn all you need to know about how a book gets into bookstores and online so that customers everywhere can buy your new product.

How will they learn about your new self-published book? Publicity, publicity, publicity. From press releases to what to wear on camera, these chapters will turn you into your own best publicity agent and soon have you as polished as a pro.

Chapter 16

Book Distributors and Retailers

In This Chapter

- ◆ Retail bookselling explained
- ◆ Understanding distribution
- ◆ Independents and chains
- ◆ Distributors and wholesalers
- ◆ Exploring the gift market

While researching and writing this book, I had the pleasure of talking to many self-publishers and hearing of their triumphs and challenges. I will tell you straight off that many, if not most, felt that the book-distribution process was the most difficult part of the puzzle—not impossible, mind you, but difficult. Here's what one successful self-publisher said: "Most folks launch their books into a swamp. They have no idea how complex the business is."

I don't mean to frighten you in the first few sentences of this chapter, but I want you to understand how very critical it is to have a firm grasp on this topic. Just as book publishing itself is a business, so is distribution.

Distribution is a very real business with an eye toward profit. The distribution arm of the book world is not there to make you feel good, massage your ego, and congratulate you for having written and published a book. Book distributors want to make money.

Book retailers want to make money, too. You might find the retailers (particularly the independent retailers) a bit more open to you as a first-time publisher, but never forget that they want to make money, too. It costs money to stock a bookstore, and every volume sitting on a shelf represents an investment. The books that they place on their shelves have been chosen with their customers in mind. The kinds of topics that sell well are stocked in healthy numbers; the kinds of topics that don't sell well are stocked sparingly.

The World of Retail Bookselling

If your goal is to see your book on the shelves of a bookstore—any bookstore—you need to understand just how the retail end of the book business works. Unlike other kinds of retail businesses, such as shoe stores or clothing stores, the book business operates on a 100 percent returnable basis. What does that mean? It means that if a bookstore agrees to carry your new book, it will expect that if the book does not sell, it will return it to you for a full refund. Yikes! Long a thorn in the side of book publishers (who rue the day that policy was introduced during the Depression), it is a major perk for booksellers.

Pro Style

Keep in mind that bookselling is one of the only retail businesses in which the product is returnable to the manufacturer (you, in other words). That's another reason to make sure your product is the best and most marketable it can be.

How do books end up on bookstore shelves? A book is first presented to a buyer—not a buyer in the sense of someone who buys a copy of your book from the store, but rather a merchandise buyer in the store who makes decisions on what they carry. Look at it this way: your book has to sell twice. The first time when the bookstore buyer decides to carry it (on a returnable basis, remember), and the second time when a bookstore customer carries it up to the counter and makes a purchase. And only this second purchase really counts as an actual "sale."

The Brave World of Independents

Years ago, I worked as a book buyer and sales clerk at a wonderful *independent bookstore* in Sacramento, Beers Books. When I wasn't meeting with sales reps to pore over their new catalogs or helping a customer find the latest book of Wendell Berry essays, I was happily perched on a stool with my nose in a book. Ah, what clerk at Borders gets to do that for hours on end? Independent bookstores are great for book lovers, and heaven for bookstore employees!

If your plan for your book involves making it available only in your area, in your local independent bookstores, your distribution plan will be simple. You don't need a *distributor*. You don't need a *wholesaler*. You can deal directly with your local accounts. I did this successfully with my first book, *The Sacramento Women's Yellow Pages*. It was carried by two or three independent bookstores (including my beloved Beers Books), by the local outlets of Tower Books (a small national chain, but headquartered in my town so it was easy for me to deal with their buying office), and a small independently owned legal bookstore. At its peak, I had only 10 different accounts to keep track of.

Clearly, my book was only of regional interest. Who else would want a book about businesses in Sacramento? Because it was a regional book, I knew that national book distributors would not be interested. I became my own distributor and handled the process myself. If your book is too small to attract a distributor, you can handle it yourself, too.

Wise Words

An **independent bookstore** is a bookstore that is owned by an individual as opposed to a large corporation. There are small chains with more than one outlet that are owned by individuals. **Consignment** merchandise is left with the retailer with the understanding that the retailer will have to pay for the product only when it has been sold to a customer. A **wholesaler** is a book business that warehouses books and has them available when bookstores call to order them. Wholesalers are passive; they wait for the phone to ring. A **distributor** is a business that calls on bookstore outlets and takes orders for the books it represents. Distributors represent many different publishers at once. Distributors try to create sales.

Your distribution approach will look like this:

- Scout out suitable retail locations for your book.

- Ask to speak to the manager and ask who orders the books.

- Pitch your book to them as one with potential; explain how customers will discover it (publicity, promotion, and so on).

- Ask for an order.

- Ship the books.

- Bill the account.

- Publicize your book to create demand, and let folks know which stores carry it.

- Periodically check the stock and ask for reorders.

Many bookstores will ask that you leave your books with them on *consignment*. Some self-publishers are insulted by this approach, but as a former bookseller, I think it is a reasonable request. If your book sells, you will get paid. If your book doesn't sell, you won't get paid. What could be unfair about that?

Ask the Question!

Please memorize this question and be prepared to ask it often: "Where do you get your books?" Ask anywhere you think your book might sell well. With a fishing guidebook, step right up to the counter of a bait shop and ask, "Where do you get your books?" With a regional restaurant book, ask at the airport kiosk. Always ask "Where do you get your books?" and you will soon learn the name of the local distributors, or the person in charge of buying books for the store, or the wholesaler they call to place orders. Ask, and they will share the information.

The Big World of Chains

What if your town doesn't have an independent bookstore for you to cut your teeth on? What if you have only a chain such as Borders or Barnes & Noble? The manager of the store should be able to explain the buying process to you and put you in touch with the national buying office. Even if you are hoping to have your book carried in only that one store, you will have to deal with the national headquarters.

> **Pro Style**
>
> As you enter the world of distribution, you will need to develop a very thick skin. Try not to take it personally when a bookstore or distributor isn't interested in your book. It's not personal; it's business.

If your plans involve having your book carried in Borders and Barnes & Nobles across the country, gird your loins now for the battle ahead. Your best bet is to interest a national book distributor. I'll explain just who they are, what they do, and how to find them in a minute.

How Does a Book Reach the Shelves?

It seems somewhat miraculous. You read in the paper that the newest John Grisham book has been published and you rush to your local bookstore that afternoon to get your hands on a copy. And there it is! Just unpacked from a box and set neatly on the bookshelf. How did that happen? How did that book get there at the exact right time?

Commercial publishers have their own sales reps who attend the company sales conference, learn about the upcoming titles, and then begin to call on their accounts and meet with buyers in the bookstores to present the titles and take advance orders. When the book is published, the printer ships the books to the publisher's warehouse, where they might sit for a few weeks or sometimes months until the pub date or release date is reached. When the book is officially "pubbed," the publisher ships it from the warehouse straight to bookstores that have ordered the book. The shipping clerk opens the box at the bookstore and puts the books on the shelf. And there it is, ready for an eager buyer.

If the plans for your book are national in nature, you will need a national book distributor to help you reach out to all the possible outlets.

By the Way

Publishing Trends reported in June 2004 that the distribution arm of the publishing business is "doing laps that even the Queen Mary 2 can't keep up with." Why? Because even big publishers with their own sales forces are re-evaluating the most efficient ways to get their product to market. Some publishers are deciding that the costs of handling their own distribution outweigh the benefits and are working with distributors instead.

Who and What Are Distributors?

Whereas a commercial publisher such as Random House or Simon & Schuster has sales reps who present titles to bookstore buyers and large warehouses in which to store and then ship their books, you, as a self-publisher, could interest a book distributor to carry your title. Book distributors are companies that represent a great many small, medium, and sometimes even large publishers; they serve as the sales force and the shipping and billing department. Some distributors also provide help in marketing and publicity, but that will cost you.

Understand that having a distributor for your books in no way guarantees any actual sales. Life is a crap shoot, and so is the book business. Bookstores cannot possibly order all of the books that are published and presented to them. Even a book published by a big house is sometimes skipped by buyers who decide that it won't be a good match for their customers.

When I was a buyer for Beers Books, I looked at each of the books in the rep's catalog and listened to the pitch and then thought to myself, "Who is going to buy this book? Can I see one of my customers buying it?" And if I didn't think it would work for our customers, I would pass. The sales rep for your distributor will try very hard to get bookstores to carry the books that they distribute, of course, but the decision on what to order (and in what quantity) still rests with the buyer.

When considering which books to represent, book distributors ask themselves the very same question: "Who is going to buy this book?" They also carefully consider questions like these: How large is the audience, and how is the author going to get the word out on this title? Be prepared to sell very hard on your own behalf. Most distributors will want to see a fairly complete business plan for your book, one that includes a heavy emphasis on publicity and marketing. No distributor wants to waste time carrying a book that doesn't have potential.

> ### Cautionary Tales
>
> A huge order comes in, and you feel like celebrating! Wait. First ask yourself, can this account really move that many books? Many a self-publisher has shipped hundreds of books to a wholesaler only to see them back on his doorstep (tattered and torn and now worthless) a few months later. Worse yet, some self-publishers have ordered a large, expensive printing to fulfill a large order from a big account, which have also ended up back on the doorstep unsold. Be cautious and realistic.

What They Do

Book distribution is a business, and money is made selling books and taking a percentage. These basic services should be included in that percentage:

- Including your book in their sales catalog or website
- Presenting your title to buyers at their accounts
- Processing orders

- Shipping your books to fulfill orders received

- Billing the customer and tracking down late payments

- Paying you for books sold on a regular basis

- Providing you with sales reports

You might also be given a chance to attend a sales conference (although these days fewer companies hold them) to present your title to the sales force. Some distributors purchase a large booth at the annual publishing trade show, Book Expo America, and let the publishers they represent buy space inside the booth to display their titles.

What They Don't Do

Distributors move books, which is their primary business. It is up to the author to create sales for their own books, and to create demand for the book when it is available in the bookstore. If a book doesn't sell when it is in the bookstore, it is not the distributor's fault. It is the publisher's fault. If you are a self-publisher, the responsibility rests with you.

Distributors can also help you with other functions, but those won't be covered in the percentage of your retail price that they are keeping on each sale. Ask how much they charge for the following additional services:

- Early help, advice, or referrals with design, production, and printing

- Publicity and marketing services such as press releases, author tours, and marketing materials

If you don't want to sign up for extra services from a distributor, don't worry. The next few chapters will give you a good grounding in doing your own publicity and marketing.

How to Interest a Book Distributor

So how exactly do you convince a book distributor to carry your book? Book distributors are interested in carrying books that will work, books that will sell. A self-publisher who has a book with a good topic, a great-looking package, and a coherent plan for getting the word out to the public and create sales will have a good chance of interesting a distributor. National distributors are looking for books with national sales potential. Regional books, personal memoirs, family genealogies, and other topics with a fairly small audience won't be of interest to a national distributor.

Pro Style _____

I asked distributor Eric Kampmann of Midpoint Trade what single piece of advice he'd like to share with self-publishers. "Build a great team," he said. "Book publishing is a team sport; don't be afraid to recruit others who already possess knowledge of the industry and flexibility of mind."

As with real estate agents, distributors don't make money until a sale has occurred, so they save their efforts for products they think will sell. This is not a vanity business, and your ego might well get a bit battered by some of what you might hear when you begin approaching distributors. The best way to avoid heartbreak is to do what you've been doing all along in this book: evaluate your product and your reasons for publishing, focus on creating a professional product, and approach the market with professionalism and pride. Go for it!

Major Players in the Distribution World

When you are ready to approach distributors about carrying your book, start with these well-known distributors. Always start at the top of the field. Put together a business plan for your book that includes information about your audience, your marketing plans, and your promotional budget. With some of these companies, you can approach them online first.

- ◆ Midpoint Trade Books
  www.midpointtradebooks.com
  Midpoint concentrates on selling to the major national accounts.

- ◆ National Book Network
  www.mbnbooks.com/prospectivepublisher
  NBN is the largest independent distributor in North America. They are headquartered in Maryland and ship from Pennsylvania.

- ◆ Biblio Distribution
  www.bibliodistribution.com/distribution
  Biblio was established by the National Book Network specifically to work with self-publishers and small publishers.

What happens when a bookstore decides it wants a copy of your book? At one time, a sales rep or book buyer would fill out a form and then fax or phone it in. Midpoint describes the new high-tech process that has taken the place of other antiquated methods:

> Most of [our orders] come EDI (electronic data interchange) from the major accounts and are automatically entered into our computer systems. Orders are processed through our computer systems and picking tickets, and packing lists

are printed. Books are then picked from the warehouse pick locations and transferred to shipping. There, the barcode of each book is scanned electronically to fool-proof double-check on accuracy as the order is packed.

Picture a large warehouse filled with books from all manner of publishers, and you can imagine how complicated this can get.

This all sounds wonderful, but how much is it actually costing you to have a distributor work on your behalf? Typically, a distributor keeps between 25 and 30 percent of the net from each book—not a percentage of the retail price of the book, mind you, but a percentage of what has actually been paid. When a bookstore orders a copy of your book and pays the distributor, you will get paid by the distributor, minus the distribution fee.

Pro Style

Success breeds success. If initially you strike out with distributors but sell your book well on your own because you've generated media attention and demand, pick up the phone and ask them to help out again.

Book Wholesalers

Somewhat different from book distributors are book wholesalers. They do one thing the same—they warehouse books from lots of different publishers and sell books to bookstores. But the similarity stops there, really.

It is easy to get confused. Why would a publisher deal with both a distributor and a wholesaler? Why would a bookstore get its books in so many different ways? Each one exists for a different reason and has a slightly different function. Let's look closer at the function of a book wholesaler.

What They Do

Book wholesalers sell books to retailers. They carry books from all manner of publishers, not just from select publishers as with a book distributor.

Why would a bookstore order from a wholesaler instead of a distributor, or instead of directly from the publisher? Because a bookstore wants to carry a broad selection of books, not just the titles from a few publishers. If I ran a bookstore and was suddenly out of a best-selling title from McGraw Hill, instead of calling McGraw Hill and ordering 25 copies from them (and even then, I might not have enough to meet their minimum order requirements), I'd call Ingram and order 25 copies of the McGraw

Hill book, plus a few copies of a book published by Ten Speed, and a handful of copies of a book published by Simon & Schuster, and two by Random House, and an extra copy of a self-published book that was doing well. This is one-stop shopping, without the hassle of trying to remember which distributor represents which publisher, and so on. One phone call (or fax, or EDI), one box of mixed titles arrives, all combining for one discount.

What They Don't Do

Book wholesalers are passive. They have warehouses filled with books, but they wait until a bookstore orders from them before they spring into action. Wholesalers do not create sales; they respond to them. Wholesalers do not have sales forces that call on accounts to solicit orders for individual books. Having your books available in the Ingram warehouse is great, but understand that it does nothing to actually create a sale for your book. Until a bookstore contacts Ingram and orders a copy of your book, all you have is a book collecting dust.

> **Cautionary Tales**
>
> Poetry is tough to publish under any circumstances. Small poetry chapbooks (20 or 30 pages bound with staples) are very difficult for bookstores to deal with. Not only is poetry a slow sales area, but the fact that these small chapbooks don't have a spine makes it difficult to properly display on a shelf. Your best bet with a poetry chapbook is to meet face to face with your local independent bookseller and ask them to carry it on consignment. Promise them that you will have a reading night when you'll invite all your friends and family to come and buy copies.

Ingram Book Company

Ingram is the biggest book wholesaler, and Baker & Taylor is No. 2. Ingram used to work directly with self-publishers but has discontinued that practice; they will not work directly with a publisher that has fewer than 10 different titles in print. This doesn't mean that you can't get your book on their warehouse shelves; it just means you need to go a different route.

There are a few routes to Ingram. The Ingram website lists four different ways to go:

- ◆ **Publishers Marketing Association.** PMA has a program for its members that enables Ingram to carry their books. For membership information, visit www.pma-online.org.

- **Lightning Source.** Lighting Source is a POD company that is a subsidiary of Ingram. If you use them to produce your book, you benefit from their established relationship with Ingram. Visit www.lightningsource.com.

- **Biblio Distribution.** As described already, Biblio is an offshoot of the National Book Network that is specifically designed to work with self-publishers. They have an agreement with Ingram. Visit www.bibliodistribution.com.

- **Greenleaf Book Group, LLC.** Greenleaf works exclusively with small and independent publishers. Visit their website at www.greenleafbookgroup.com.

For more information on Ingram and their suggestions on how to best work with them, visit www.ingrambook.com/new/publishers.asp.

Baker & Taylor

Baker & Taylor has long been the powerhouse into the library market, but they also sell to the retail book trade. I had the pleasure of spending an afternoon in one of their warehouses a few years back, and it was an overwhelming sight: books as far and as high as the eye could see.

Baker & Taylor still seems willing to work directly with self-publishers. Their one-page form titled "Establish a Business Relationship" seems straightforward and hopeful. You can find the form at www.btol.com/supplier_info.cfm. Complete the form and fax it to 908-541-7863, and they will contact you for further information to establish a business relationship.

How Much Does This Cost?

If you are being handled by a book distributor, your distributor will, in turn, handle the major wholesalers for you. The percentage that your distributor takes from your sales will already cover what they've had to give up to the wholesaler.

If you are dealing directly with a wholesaler, though, don't be too shocked by the deep discount they will demand from you. How deep? Try from a minimum of 50 percent, upward to 60 percent!

And remember, as in the rest of the book business, these books are also returnable. You might ship books off to a wholesaler and get them back months or years later, in shabby condition and no longer presentable.

Distribution for Print-On-Demand Titles

Most of the major print-on-demand companies, such as iUniverse, Authorhouse, and others, do work with the major wholesalers. Your book will be available through Ingram, but, remember, there is no sale until you create a sale. Having your book carried by Ingram means very little until you personally create a demand through marketing and publicity. That marketing and publicity hopefully induces someone to go into a bookstore and inquire about your book, and then place a special order with a bookstore. The bookstore will then fill the order with Ingram.

I polled several independent bookstores about carrying POD titles. Of course, they would do it for authors they know or customers with whom they have a relationship. But in general, no—no bookstore was willing to order a POD book from Ingram or Baker & Taylor without an existing request for a copy.

Can you get a distributor to carry your POD title? This is a very sticky area for authors who go the POD route. Book distributors are quite upfront about the fact that, to be represented by them, you must "own your ISBN." This issue has come up before in other chapters and bears repeating here. Getting your book issued through a POD company usually means that the ISBN printed on the book and used on all other official forms is an ISBN that belongs to the company, not to you.

If your plan includes getting a national distributor to carry your self-published book, please keep this in mind. Don't discover it later.

The Gift Market

"The gift market!" These words inspire glee in the hearts of book publishers everywhere. Why would a market inspire such delight? Because the gift market operates on a different set of rules than the retail book world. Whereas books sold into a bookstore are ordinarily returnable, books sold to a gift account are not. Publishers like to call this a one-way sale. Those are books that, once shipped to the account, they will never see again. Doesn't that sound like a great deal to you?

In the chapters on design and production, we addressed the needs of the gift book market. More than in any other type of sale, books here are considered "product" and are evaluated strictly on how they look. Books are judged by their covers. And if the cover is gift market worthy, so to speak, then the gift market buyer will consider whether the topic and the writing will work in their store. What works in the gift market is a quirky and unpredictable combination of style and substance.

Regional books can do well in the gift market. If you have published a travel guide to your area, or a history book that brings an event to light, you might have a wonderful shot in getting local gift stores that cater to tourists to stock it. What better way to remember a trip to South Carolina than a regionally published book on Low Country cooking?

How do you find a gift distributor? Remember that question I asked you to memorize— "Where do you get your books?" Any time you find a gift store that looks like the perfect place to sell your book, step up to the front counter and ask away. Some small gift stores will deal with you directly; others may give you the name of the book distributors they work with, and you can approach them about offering your title to all of their accounts.

Don't turn up your nose at any kind of outlet. You just never know where a book might sell, and often a bookstore is the worst place for what you've written. A major gift book distributor in San Francisco confessed to me not long ago that her top account for books was a car wash. That's right, a car wash. What else do folks do while waiting for their car to be washed? They hang out in the waiting room, which is cleverly outfitted as a gift shop.

General Words of Advice and Encouragement

I do hope that you have been reading these words about distribution long before your book is actually finished. A proper distribution plan takes time. Setting up contacts and agreements takes time. Waiting for sales to occur takes time. This can be an enormously frustrating part of the self-publishing business.

You might have noticed that a few of the distributors that represent self-publishers also have consulting services available to help with editorial, design and production, and marketing. If you are open to hiring them for their advice and are open to the suggestions they make, I'd venture to say that you will have a greater chance of sales success.

I'm not suggesting that you need to hire them, or that they won't represent books that they haven't made a little extra money from—not at all. I'm suggesting that if you make them a part of your team from the beginning, if you rely on them for advice from the minute you finish your manuscript, you will have created a team of thoughtful and knowledgeable publishing people who will help you reach your goals.

The Least You Need to Know

◆ Book distribution is critical to your success; don't wait until you have a finished product to learn the process.

◆ Retailers buy from both distributors and wholesalers.

◆ Ask likely outlets where they get their books; they will share the name of the buyer they order from.

◆ Approach a national distributor only if your book has national appeal.

◆ If your book is intended for a local audience, you can handle the distribution yourself.

◆ Understand that most book sales are returnable, but gift market sales are non-returnable.

Chapter 17

Online Book Distribution

In This Chapter

- ◆ What online sales can do for you

- ◆ How to get set up

- ◆ The downside of online

- ◆ Linking your website to an online bookseller

Ah, how did we all exist before online bookstores such as Amazon.com, Borders, or Barnes & Noble? It's hard to remember those foggy days of yore in the 1990s. Online bookselling has been a tremendous boon for the self-publisher. I remember the enormous pride I felt the first time I went to Amazon.com and typed in the words—*The Air Courier's Handbook*. And, boom, there it was on the screen before me! Incredible. The other incredible thing was that it really wasn't that hard to set it up.

Many of the outrageous predictions about how the Internet would change our lives failed to come true. But for self-publishers, the existence of online booksellers truly has made an amazing difference. Before online bookselling, if you had a book you were promoting on a national radio show, for instance, unless you could afford the trouble and expense of an 800-number and the ability to process credit cards, it was very difficult to take advantage of the publicity. Now, get yourself booked anywhere, anytime, and all you need to do during your interview is say proudly, "My book is available on Amazon.com" or a similar site, and watch the sales numbers respond! Headaches over qualifying for a merchant credit card account (a huge deal back in the day), processing orders, and shipping and handling all have disappeared.

Is it all glory and roses? Not at all. There are drawbacks and hassles to sometimes be endured with online bookselling. That's life, and it isn't perfect. But it is an enormous step forward for self-publishers.

Getting Started

Who would have guessed that the one truly strong retailing environment on the web would involve books? Stodgy, old-fashioned, always predicted-to-disappear-soon books. Online booksellers have come and gone in the past decade, but overall, they remain a very strong presence.

How will you choose which online booksellers to deal with? Unlike a distributor—who will want exclusivity—you don't have to choose. Go ahead and have your books available on Amazon.com, on BN.com, and on the wonderful Portland-based independent Powell's Books, at powells.com. You might decide to deal with only one, to streamline your own business processes. If you plan to do a great deal of national publicity, it does make sense to give out only one web address during your interviews.

Amazon.com

The elephant in the living room, Amazon.com, is the highest-profile book business online. Mention buying books, and Amazon.com comes to mind first. Try to buy online from Borders, and you will find that Borders online has gone away and been replaced by a relationship with Amazon.com.

Amazon.com makes it simple for self-publishers to deal with them. Not only can you have them carry your book, but you can also link your own website to theirs so that visitors to your website can click through and buy your book from Amazon. And you'll get a small cut of that sale.

To have your book available through Amazon.com, go to the Amazon.com home page and scroll down the left side until you see "Make Money." Click on Advantage. To be totally informed, you should explore their entire section on Advantage before making up your mind, but the short information is this:

- ◆ Complete the membership agreement.

- ◆ Apply to the Amazon.com Advantage program, which includes sending a sample copy of your book.

- ◆ You should receive an answer on your acceptance in one to two weeks.

Amazon.com requires a $29.95 membership fee, paid on an annual basis (and prorated depending on what month you join). You will need to give them a 55 percent discount off the retail price. Here is their explanation for how the process works:

> You'll first need to apply to the Advantage program and submit one or more titles for consideration. If your application is approved, you simply list your products (along with the appropriate bibliographic information) in our catalog and consign copies of your inventory in our warehouse. When customers purchase your titles, we process the orders within 24 hours and ship the titles anywhere in the world. We monitor your inventory and automatically send you an e-mail request for additional copies based on customer demand.

To become an *affiliate*, an "Amazon Associate" linking your website to theirs, click on the "Make Money" section on the Amazon.com front page, on the left sidebar. Follow the directions and read the agreements to set it up. Again, the process is simple.

- ◆ Complete the online application.

- ◆ Create and post links to Amazon.com using the Build Links tools available in Associate Central.

You'll earn a commission for each book sold through your efforts. If you "direct link" your book from your website, you could earn up to 7.5 percent.

Wise Words

An **affiliate program** is a program whereby you become linked to the sales site of a bookseller and you collect a small percentage from any sales that arrive on their site via your website's efforts.

Barnes & Noble, BN.com

Barnes & Noble is still in the online game and not conceding the entire bookselling space to Amazon.com. What they seem to be conceding, though, is the self-publisher space. Whereas Amazon.com makes it easy for authors and publishers to deal with them, Barnes & Noble is much more fortresslike—not impenetrable, but not flinging open the castle doors in the way the folks in Seattle are.

After much wandering and clicking around the site, I found it. Mind you, I found it only by poking around in the affiliate section and clicking on the affiliate FAQs. And there it was, quite well hidden on the page: barnesandnoble.com/help/pub_selling.asp, the answer to the question "How do I get Barnes & Noble to carry my book?"

> **Cautionary Tales**
>
> The Barnes & Noble website cautions that their review process takes approximately two to four months: "We ask for your patience as we are working with a large number of publishers. All submissions are reviewed in the order in which they are received. Please do not expect an immediate response confirming receipt of your submission."

Their process involves several steps, several downloadable forms (that require you to have Excel) that need to be filled out and mailed in to their distribution center in New Jersey, and then a wait of several months to find out whether you have been approved. Upon approval, they will order two copies on a returnable basis. "Customer demand will be used to determine the proper stocking level and quantities for subsequent reorders."

I like Barnes & Noble as a company, truly I do. But, hey, if you had to choose between paying Amazon.com $29.95 and being up and running in a few weeks, or mailing off a bunch of forms to BN.com and waiting in the dark for several months, I know which one I'm going for. You can also do both if you so desire.

Borders.com

As I just mentioned, Borders now sells books online through Amazon.com. They did have an online store for many years, but they decided that it just wasn't paying off and threw in the towel. Your books will appear here if they are also on Amazon.com.

Other Sites to Keep in Mind

Just as Barnes & Noble is hanging in there, so are a number of smaller sites that you might want to consider working with. If you support independent booksellers in your town, choosing to work with them over the chains, you might want to extend your philosophy into cyberspace.

How do you decide which bookseller to go with? Do you have to decide? You can have your book carried by as many different online bookstores as you want to keep track of. Just remember, it means filling out forms and waiting for approval over and over again, shipping (and paying for shipping) to replenish stock over and over again, and hoping to receive a check over and over again. Although it may be a good feeling to say that your book is carried by multiple online bookstores, personally, I'd skip the hassle.

Booksamillion.com

Booksamillion does not deal directly with self-publishers. They carry only books that are handled by Ingram and Baker & Taylor. If you have a distributor for your book that deals with Ingram and Baker & Taylor, ask your distributor to set you up with Booksamillion.

Powells.com

Powell's Books, in Portland, Oregon, is a well-known bookselling presence. They run a nice online bookstore that sells both new and used books. Like Booksamillion.com, however, they will carry only self-published books that are available through Ingram or Baker & Taylor. An exception might be made for Portland-based authors who can actually deal directly with the bookstore (because their online inventory is drawn from the store itself), so drop by if you are there.

Justbookz.com

Justbookz.com is run by the folks who run BooksJustBooks.com (printing and production services) for their customers as an alternative to Amazon.com. There are no setup fees, and they charge only 25 percent of the retail price on sales, compared to 55 percent charged by Amazon.com and BN.com.

By the Way

You've read glowing reviews on Amazon.com before and thought to yourself, "So, did the author's mom write this one?" Could be. Most authors do ask their friends and family to post good reviews, so go ahead and join the pack. Try not to be too obvious, though. What if really mean and nasty reviews get posted by your enemies? It has happened. It is possible to bring it to Amazon.com's attention and get bad reviews removed if they seem like an orchestrated effort.

Doing Business with Amazon.com

Okay, signing up to have Amazon.com carry your book isn't really that hard, but then what happens? Here is my stern warning yet again: sales won't occur online (or anywhere else, for that matter) unless you make them happen. A reader discovers your book, goes online, orders a copy, and then ….

Ellen Reid Smith, the creator and publisher of *Cowgirl Smarts*, has sold more than 100 copies of her book on Amazon.com in the few months it has been available. She's pleased, of course, but she also sends a note of caution to other self-publishers. "Shipping to Amazon.com isn't always smooth. If you ship media mail to get the best rates that will take a week or so, then it can sit for up to 7 to 14 days at Amazon.com before they get it into their computer database. So if they are out of stock on your book and you ship off a box to remedy that, it could take close to a month before your book is listed in stock again."

She also warns that, despite her success with Amazon.com, she has never been able to get the Barnes & Noble site to carry her book: "I couldn't break the code."

Another word of caution about Amazon.com from Ellen (and I've heard this in the commercial publishing world, too) is that it can also be hard to get Amazon.com to fix problems on your book's page. So be very careful about the information that you input because trying to get it out will not be easy!

Amazon.com requires a certain amount of high-tech savvy on your part, too. "Amazon.com uses FTP upload for book covers; you can't just send a JPEG," Ellen also warns. Make sure you are ready with the right software before you hit Send. If you're wondering what the heck FTP is … it stands for File Transfer Protocol. It is the simplest and most secure way to exchange files over the Internet.

Cautionary Tales _____

Not everything about online book sales is a boon to authors. In fact, a huge percentage of online bookselling activity surrounds used books, which doesn't benefit the author at all. This is quite controversial in the book world, particularly because booksellers make a greater margin on used books than on new books. Some publishers have taken issue with the fact that on Amazon.com and other sites, when a customer types in a book title, they are offered the opportunity to buy either a new or, if available, used copy. If the customer buys a used copy, both the publisher and the author are cut out of the revenue stream.

Online Sales Rankings

When your book is published, you will have a chance to play the game that absorbs authors around the world, although no one will admit to doing it themselves. What's that? Obsessively checking their Amazon.com sales ranking, that's what. I can tell you with great confidence that the lowest number I have achieved (yet) is 42. Not too shabby, the forty-second best-selling title out of the millions Amazon stocks. How did I achieve that glorious number? It was after a Sunday morning appearance on *Book TV.*

How does Amazon.com figure out those sales rankings, anyway? According to their website, it works like this: "The calculation is based on sales and is updated regularly. The top 10,000 bestsellers are updated each hour to reflect sales over the preceding 24 hours. The next 100,000 are updated daily. Any title with a rank higher than 100,001 is updated on a monthly basis."

Does your number really matter? I'd recommend not getting too obsessed over it. Your book is available. When readers want to buy it, they can. Getting all of your friends and contacts to buy it all on one day will make a difference and temporarily get you a small number, but nothing else will come with that. Unlike in a physical store, where books that are selling well might some day get moved up near the counter or otherwise better displayed, there is nothing to be gained in the online world.

> ### By the Way
>
> If you have used a print-on-demand company to produce your book for you, chances are, you won't have to hassle with setting yourself up with an online bookstore. Most companies such as iUniverse and Authorhouse include getting your book listed with Amazon.com and BN.com as part of their basic service.

Whenever I get too puffed up about how well my books are selling on Amazon.com, I bring myself down to Earth by typing in *Mein Kampf* and checking the sales number there. Yep. Most times I'm being outsold by a dead murderous despot. The last time I checked, I was at 7,556 and Hitler was at 3,893. A cold bucket of water, to be lagging behind Hitler in cyberspace.

Selling from Your Own Website

If you have your own website and regularly promote it, why do you have to drive book sales to someone else? You don't. If you want to handle your own book sales and have a way to do it, you will be able to make a far greater profit than if you are sending your customers over to an online bookstore that is keeping 55 percent.

The biggest piece of the puzzle in handling your own sales is a way to process credit cards. Folks are quite wary of giving their credit card information away and might be reluctant to give it to you if you have a less-than-professional sales site.

Check out these companies for credit card processing:

- GoEMerchant.com
- Verisign.com
- Buyerzone.com
- PayPal.com

When you've handled the money thing, the only other real issue is shipping and handling. I used to really enjoy the process of hand-addressing orders I received for *The Air Courier's Handbook*, stuffing them in envelopes, and taking them to the mailbox. It was so satisfying to have an armload of books that had been ordered. Not everyone enjoys that process, however, and if you end up with a lot of ordering activity, you might want to designate someone else in your household to handle it. Hire your kids.

Online bookstores are a wonderful addition to the book-publishing scene. Although they have opened up an easy access to a national sales outlet for self-publishers, they are not the answer to everything. Don't forget that folks won't just stumble upon your book if it's available online. You must make them aware of your book, give them a reason to buy it, and drive them to the online store. Sales happen for a reason. They happen because hardworking publishers and authors create them.

In the next few chapters, you will learn many ways to do just that—create demand and sales for your title through publicity.

The Least You Need to Know

- Amazon.com is the easiest online bookstore for self-publishers to use.
- You can link your own website to an online bookstore and become an affiliate.
- Other than Amazon.com and BN.com, most large online bookstores deal only with books carried by Ingram and Baker & Taylor.
- Few online sales occur without being created by the author; you need to drive demand.
- Set up your own online store by using a merchant account such as PayPal or Verisign.

Chapter 18

Book Publicity 101

In This Chapter

- ◆ What exactly is publicity?
- ◆ Why every book needs a publicity campaign
- ◆ How to plan a publicity campaign
- ◆ The components of a strong publicity kit
- ◆ Effective publicity pitch letters and press releases
- ◆ Going it alone or hiring a professional publicist

For a self-published author, publicity can prove your greatest asset in the sale of your book. Certainly, you may spend some money on your publicity campaign, but there are ways to minimize the expense of publicity and maximize the exposure within the media. In this chapter, you'll learn the difference between marketing and publicity, and how to implement a publicity plan. With a solid publicity plan, you stand a good chance of increasing your sales, which, for many of you, is a primary goal. For those of you who've published a book in the hope of getting your views aired, publicity is where that will happen, too.

What You See Is What You Buy

Plain and simple, you must find ways to let the public know your book is out there, or they won't buy it. A person can't buy what they don't know exists. Take a new teacher, for example. That teacher may be frustrated with the many pitfalls of his first job in education. He needs help, or he's certain to end up looking for another profession, joining the ever-increasing attrition rate of educators. Suddenly, he comes across an article in the newspaper about a local educator who has written a book for neophyte teachers, a book to help navigate the bumpy inaugural teaching road. The next day, he tunes in to a morning show on television and sees the author talking about techniques listed in her book to help new teachers with classroom management. The teacher runs out to buy the book. The author just received a direct hit—the sale of the book through *publicity* channels.

When you find ways to garner editorial coverage of your book—whether on television, radio, or in print—without paying for that coverage, you've made a publicity hit and put your work center stage in the public's eye.

> **Wise Words** _____
>
> **Publicity** is the process of drawing attention to a person or thing. The key element of publicity in publishing, however, is that it's *free* exposure. It's the difference between paying for an ad in a magazine like *The New Yorker* for your book and having a reporter write about your book launch within the "Talk of the Town" section of a prestigious magazine without charging you a cent.

Hook, Line, and Sinker

Books sell because the public is interested in the topic or the story. When it comes to nonfiction titles, the best-selling books usually have somehow managed to propel the title into the public eye with a socioeconomic, sociopolitical, cultural, news, or celebrity "hook." Take a book like Hilary Rodham Clinton's *It Takes a Village*. The former First Lady had both celebrity and a sociocultural hook to sell the book. Her book's "hook" transcended her celebrity with a cause that touched many people—our children and their success. When headlines rage about the deterioration of our youth, a book like Clinton's could "use" those headlines as a "hook" to show readers why they must read her work.

But let's look at another best-selling title, *The Rules: Time Tested Secrets for Capturing the Heart of Mr. Right,* by two unknown authors, Sherrie Schneider and Ellen Fein, two women who thought they had something to say about dating success. The book turned into a pop-cultural phenomenon. The authors found themselves on every major talk show and saw their little title's sales explode, spawning a series of books. Their hook on the first book? Again, blaring headlines helped their sales. They were able to hook into the research study that showed that, as women age, their chances of marrying decline and that fewer men are available after a certain age. They also recommended some tactics that seem arcane in our day of women's liberation. They used the "hook" of the latest statistics on male/female relationships, the fear of loneliness, and the sensationalism of their "traditional" techniques. Voilà! The hook propelled their book into the public eye. Hence, publicity ensued, and the ultimate goal, sales, was generated.

Career counselor Helen Scully, proprietor of Scully Career Associates, has self-published a CD-ROM and online course, *Elevations,* geared at self-counseling your-self to your dream job—a lot less expensive than going to a career counselor. What's Scully's hook? Every time the unemployment rates plunge or major layoffs occur, she has a "hook" that gives her the chance to pitch herself as an expert to the press and gain more exposure for her products.

Do you need a "hook" to sell prose to the media? Fiction and poetry are different beasts—kind of. Certainly, social commentary and relevant themes with prose and poetry are their own "hooks." But propelling a self-published work of fiction or verse into the public eye and selling those books require some imaginative publicity. Fear not, soon you'll be able to put together a fabulous press kit and know how to target your reviewers, editors, and others. Perhaps the next time a story breaks about how high the American public's stress level is, you'll be able to jump right in there with the media and suggest that reading poetry will bring down blood pressure!

By the Way

Begin thinking about all possible hooks for your work. As you come across any head-lines or stories within newspapers and magazines that tie to your work, clip them and keep them in a separate "hook" file. As I write this, the TV show *Desperate Housewives* is all the rage. Publicists across the country are all hard at work trying to peg their product, expert, or book into that hot angle. Maybe there is a novel with similar themes or a self-help book for frustrated women?

The point of this hook stuff again? Books sell because there is relevance for the information within the public. But you've got to let the public know *why* your book is relevant—what trends your book falls into. How do you let the public know your book has a hook and is a topic "du jour" or a literary accomplishment of its day? Publicity.

Vanity Sells

The first step in your book publicity begins with you. Even before your book hits the shelves, you need to start preparing your publicity materials. I already told you to keep any headlines or stories that somehow relate to your topic. But before I get into the other elements of clippings and files you're going to need to keep in the formation of your publicity campaign, let's talk about you. A big key to publicity is who you are. Here is a four-step plan to gather the information you will need for your publicity campaign.

- ◆ **Step 1.** Put together your biography. Include honors bestowed upon you, previous works, personal interests, and even family, if applicable. This is your chance to laud yourself. Be careful. Don't sound haughty—just secure in your accomplishments. In fact, have a good friend or editor review your biography for "tone" to make sure you come off as a professional, not an egomaniac.

- ◆ **Step 2.** Have a professional portrait taken for publicity purposes—especially because potential television programs will want to see how "mediagenic" you are. If there's an imaginative way to take your headshot (color or black-and-white picture from the shoulders up, used in publicity packets) without seeming cheesy, go for it. To promote my lifestyle books *Wear More Cashmere: 151 Ways to Nurture Your Inner Princess* and *The Martini Diet,* my author photo shows me coyly holding up a martini glass with pearls spilling from it. A cocktail glass of expensive jewels! I would suggest that you really indulge yourself on this step and hire a very good photographer. Don't cheat yourself by going to some outfit in the mall; spend money on a very professional photo and enjoy the experience.

- ◆ **Step 3.** Get your resumé or curriculum vitae together. If you have a list of published works or appearances and speaking engagements, list them in chronological order. Include your education, if applicable to your work. Let's say you've written a book on relationships and you're a counselor. List your professional credentials. If you're a novelist who has attended an acclaimed university writing program, list it.

- ◆ **Step 4.** Start collecting any media on you that's already aired, that's been written, or that's in the works. Let's say you're writing a cookbook. Your church's ethnic bazaar has booked you on the local morning show to give a cooking demonstration on baklava. Ask for a copy of the aired tape, or have someone tape it for you. You'll want it for your publicity tape (and to have it on hand when and if a national show calls). What if you make the most original furniture in your hometown and the paper prints an article about you—and your book just happens to be *Small Town Decorating?* Clip the article and put it in your "Me" file.

Keep steps 1–4 organized and together in an accessible folder or within a file cabinet. Soon I'll be showing you when you'll need to pull it out (that'll be in the press kit section) and what you'll need to do with it.

Cautionary Tales

Jen Pfeiffer, a former publicist for Prima Publishing turned freelance publicist, recalls a publicity campaign on a book for recovering alcoholics. The author, unfortunately, sent in less than flattering publicity photos. "The publicity department couldn't use the shots because the author looked so scary," recalls Pfeiffer. As harsh as it may seem, television, due to its nature, typically requires what they term "mediagenic" looks and personality. In fact, many producers insist on preliminary interviews or videotapes of authors, to determine whether they look good on camera and can handle themselves on the air, especially if they are to be cast as the expert on the program. The author needs to be seen as credible to the public. "It's important for an author to get a stylist, if necessary, and really make themselves look as attractive as possible and work on their public speaking skills, too," contends Pfeiffer. With better photos, the author earned the television time he needed to promote the book. Superficial, but true.

Operation Publicity Storm

Now that you know publicity sells books and you need to be thinking about a hook, we'll get into the nitty gritty of planning a publicity campaign—the first step to your book launch and tour. You'll notice that many of the words of publicist seem military—as in *campaign, media blitz,* and *publicity storm.* Like a coordinated air and land attack, for purposes of your book, you'll be implementing a blitz—but a media blitz. You'll coordinate a print, television, and radio attack, where the only thing left in the minds of the producers and editors is your title. So hunker down in your Hummer because the publicity vehicle moves like a well-trained troop, with you as the general in charge of all operations.

Strategy and Risk

Just as all good plans of attack require a thoughtful approach, you'll need to sit down and plan your publicity. Begin with your hook. Ask yourself and actually *answer* these questions:

- Who is my audience? Women, men, children?

- What age is my audience?

- Has anything happened in the news recently to which I can "attach" the concept of my book?

- According to my audience, do I know or have an idea of what cities or areas my book will sell well in (if the audience knows it exists)? Is there a connection with my book and any particular city?

- What's the most important and compelling reason for anyone to buy my book?

These questions are strikingly similar to the questions I wanted you to ask yourself in Chapter 3. These questions are important once again because you're going to need to form a clear idea in your mind about where your press kit will go and who will be interested.

Just as a general needs to know his troops, so does a publicist. The publicist also needs to know where to concentrate the *blitzkrieg* of media materials. It doesn't do any good to send a press kit to a magazine editor who handles only finance for a publication when your book deals with fashion—unless, of course, your book is about the finance of fashion. It doesn't do any good to send a review copy of your cookbook to *Family Circle*, a leader in listing recipes, if your cookbook has a focus on bawdy designed desserts for passionate lovers. *Family Circle* is clearly a family-oriented magazine. You'd probably do better blitzing *Cosmopolitan* and *Glamour*, right? So your first step in the publicity campaign is strategizing. In the following chapters, we'll look more closely at strategizing for different media venues, like magazines, radio, and television. For purposes of this section, answer the questions and start thinking like a publicist ready to "Charge!"

Battle Plans

Once you've answered the questions and have a good idea of your market, you can begin to plan your campaign.

Essentially, you'll need to decide where you're going to send your press kit—complete with media hook—within these media arenas:

♦ **Print.** Newspapers, magazines, journals, newsletters, online publications, and so on

♦ **Electronic.** Media outlets that disseminate press releases, online sources

♦ **Radio.** National and local programs, shows, and stations

♦ **Television.** News stations, talk shows, lifestyle shows, and more

Your campaign will determine each outlet that will receive a press kit. Just how do you know to whom you should send your kit? Well, there are several ways to identify prospective editors and producers with an interest in your topic.

Remember that file with clippings of articles related to your book? Dig those out now and look at the publication and the writer. Put those people on your list. Next, the Internet is a great source for finding "media" services, like Barron's and Burrell's, which offer writers customized lists of publications and producers around the globe. They do charge for the service, but the fees (which can range into hundreds of dollars for annual subscriptions) are well worth the information. In the next two chapters, I'll explain the services and the process comprehensively. I'll even show you how to find free media lists. But right now, just know that you need to list the publications and media you'd like to reach with your book in your publicity campaign. You'll also need to know the department (travel, food, business, hard news, and so on) in which your book best fits.

By the Way

You consider yourself a writer, an author. But in order to sell your book, you need to put on the publicist hat also. The key to any publicist's success is reading a multiplicity of newspapers and magazines daily. Publicists need to keep their pulse on news, health, pop culture, and the trends of our world. Why? To keep a hook in mind for every book they publicize. A publicist at a large publishing house who preferred to remain anonymous admitted to poring over at least 12 publications a day as part of her work routine. Top 10 on her list of must-read publications: *The New York Times, The San Francisco Chronicle, The Christian Science Monitor, People, Newsweek, The New Yorker, Vanity Fair, Rolling Stone, USA Today,* and *Forbes.* Don't limit your reading to your specialty area; open up and read general news so that you can find the hooks.

Effective Eventing

To tour or not to tour? That is the question. Most authors consider a book signing as the event that seals their arrival as a legitimate author. Be warned: book signings are brutal. Unless you are a celebrity name, a book signing is a two-hour-long opportunity to feel humbled as you sit alone at a table, hopeful pen in hand and a stack of books at the ready, praying that someone (anyone) walking by will stop and take a look.

If part of your campaign is a book tour, think strategically about it. Don't necessarily plan signings at bookstores across the United States or even locally. Instead, plan book events—talks or demonstrations that relate to your book. If your book is fiction, plan a reading and a talk. A collection of essays by contributors? Plan on gathering a group of the contributors to read from their stories.

Events really are the name of the game. Not long ago, I helped two self-published authors write a press release for a bookstore appearance in Oregon. "A book signing?" I asked quietly. "But your books have been out for years, and all of the friends and family who were going to attend a book signing and buy a book already have." So with their permission, I wrote the following press release for the calendar section of their local newspaper:

> Is There a Book in You?
>
> According to a recent survey, 81 percent of Americans would like to write a book someday. Two local authors saw their book dreams come true and are happy to share their knowledge with others. Carolyn Amneus's romance novel *Dream Mender* was released in 2002 and has gone into a second printing. Ray Sims has written and self-published several local history books, including *Loon Lake* and a book about the Methodist Church. Come hear them talk about their publishing experiences and ask questions about your own projects.

Why did I write it this way? To give complete strangers a reason to come down to their local bookstore on a Saturday afternoon to meet these writers. Because it tells the newspaper readers that here are two people who can help you achieve your dreams, too. That's a much more powerful reason to go to a bookstore than to meet someone you've never heard about before, with a book you don't yet know you want! Why will strangers want to come and meet you? Think of a way to position yourself and your topic that will draw a crowd.

Here are a few more examples:

♦ Learn how to cook for allergic children: meet the author of *Allergy-Free Cooking for Kids.*

- Relax and enjoy a mini-retreat: listen to the meditative nature poetry of John Doe.

- Master the art of guilt-free indulgence: let the author of *Wear More Cashmere* convince you to treat yourself better.

Where Else?

The obvious location for your book event seems like a bookstore—particularly a Border's or Barnes & Noble. But depending upon the material in your book, numerous other publicity opportunities exist. Some of my best events for my lifestyle books have been at spas! I was even invited to teach a "How to Indulge" class at a Ritz-Carlton. Think about organizations or groups that have an interest in your topic, and put them on your publicity campaign as prospective venues to host the event. Typically, these organizations will possess mailing lists of people interested in your material—and you'll have a built-in audience, instead of sitting aimlessly at a table as people drift by, not knowing whether the content of your title is something that might pique their interest.

For example, let's look at a sports book. Where might the author book appearances besides a bookstore in the cities he or she plans to visit on the tour? How about these:

- Stadium stores during games

- Little league games

- Ice rinks and pro skater stores

- Sporting conventions

- Amateur league meetings

- Fitness centers and gyms

- High school and university athletic departments

These are just a few ideas outside the box that show a more "targeted" approach to the writer's publicity tour. By seeking out those venues where people who are interested in sports hang out, the writer has a better chance of a positive reception and publicity for the book than a "hit or miss" approach by booking on a bookstore calendar, where a sports enthusiast may or may not notice the appearance.

Let's try it again with a fiction title, let's say a poetry book. A few ideas outside of a super bookstore might include these:

- The poetry department or club at a university
- A professional poet's society
- Writer's organizations
- Book fairs

Finally, let's look at a cookbook. Now narrow the cookbook to a tome that teaches parents how to cook allergy-free foods for children suffering from food allergies. The author might …

- Give a talk on the ingredients in allergy-free cooking at a natural food store.
- Demonstrate several recipes from the book at a cooking store.
- Provide a lecture to teachers about food allergies in children.
- Offer to give a presentation to allergy support groups.

By all means, plan a tour—but don't limit yourself to "signings." Instead, thoughtfully consider other venues to tout your title, venues with built-in audiences interested in your topic—who are ready to buy!

Pro Style

Want to save money on your book tour? Think about cities in which you may have upcoming business, perhaps conventions you may be attending or other trips on your calendar, like a family reunion, for the year of the release of your book. Book tour dates in those respective cities when you'll be there anyway. Plan a signing/ presentation at the bookstore in the town in which you'll be (if time permits, of course, and it doesn't conflict with the duties of your career), and sell a few books. This is a technique that any successful small business owner can use. Handbag designer Jackie Christie is married to basketball player Doug Christie of the Orlando Magic. When she goes on his road trips, she plans ahead and books an appearance on a local program or a showing at a boutique; she may even conduct an interview with a print reporter. Use Jackie Christie's business savvy and apply it to your book.

The Press Secretary Is at the Podium

Now that you've determined *who* you'll be notifying about your book, *where* you plan to tour, and *what* your campaign plan will be, you'll need a press kit. The press kit will go to reviewers, editors, journalists, and producers at least three months prior to the release of your book and prior to the date you want to book events on your tour. Event planners' calendars fill up months ahead, and editorial calendars and schedules are the same. You'll especially want to get your campaign in its first phase at least four months prior to publication.

At the least, a press kit contains a new book release (press release). But a comprehensive kit may contain these elements:

- **A pitch letter.** This is a letter addressed personally to each individual and specific area magazine or newspaper editor, or television and radio producer. The letter is meant to pique the reader's interest into reading further within the kit and provides all contact information. Many times, the pitch letter reads much like a release, providing the same hard-hitting information to entice the recipient into digging further into the topic.

- **A new book release.** This is the press release announcing your book and what it is all about.

- **An appearance press release.** This release announces signings, tour locations and dates, and events at which you may appear; it's the "who, what, when, where can we meet the author" release.

- **An author biography.** This is a look at you. It tells the recipient of the press kit why you're the expert he or she needs to book on the show or write about. This is where your resumé or curriculum vitae comes into play. Dig it out of that file.

- **Suggested interview questions.** This is approximately 20 to 25 questions that a radio host or interviewer may ask you about you, the evolution of the book, and the contents of the book. The questions provide any interviewer a springboard from which to begin the conversation. They also provide you with an idea of what you may be asked and the ability to practice your responses.

- **Suggested show/story ideas.** Primarily used by television talk show producers, these provide recipients with the different "ways" or themes that may tie into your book. This component is where that big "hook" folder comes in. You'll want to give four or five ideas in comprehensive paragraphs that a producer may be able to use on camera, as a story, or with you as an expert.

- **Mini-feature.** This is an article written about you and the book, always with a news hook, which reads like a newspaper article. Papers are given permission to print the piece within their publication without having to pay a writer or reporter. For publications that are actively seeking good information but that don't possess a big budget, a mini-feature is the perfect fit for the editor. Local and neighborhood papers love mini-features. The key to a good mini-feature is writing a story that is compelling and that "incidentally" mentions the book or uses you as an expert in the story. Many authors may run their whole campaign but actually hire this one component out to a freelance journalist to write. The mini-feature must be free of bias, must follow *AP style*, and must depend on several sources.

◆ **Photo of the book cover.** These are 3×4 or 5×7 color prints of the book cover; these will be used if a publication "picks up" the mini-feature, or they may be affixed to the front of the press kit folder cover.

◆ **Author head shot.** This is a 3×4 or 5×7 black-and-white photograph of you. Television producers use this to assess your potential on-air appeal, and the photo may be printed in publications.

◆ **DVD of other media clips.** If you have a history of television appearances already and have saved the tapes, edit the clips of your appearances (or snippets of the appearances) together on one DVD.

◆ **Copies of recent press clips or stories that display your "hook."** Make sure you photocopy any positive reviews or stories about your book or you as a writer. Include the clips in the kit. You may also want to include a clipping of a news story that reinforces the headline of your press release or the "hook" of your book. But be careful—don't overload your kit with too many of these clippings. Too many clippings that feature the topic but don't feature you can be distracting.

◆ **A review copy of the book or a *galley*.** Not everyone will need a copy of your book, but certainly national publications, writers, and producers will. Shortly, you'll learn what to put in a release where a review copy is not included.

Wise Words

All press follow the same grammar and construction rules in news writing, considered **AP style.** You'll find the press rules in the book *The Associated Press Stylebook and Briefing on Media Law*—the bible for all journalists. Familiarize yourself with this style and use it in your contacts with the press.

A **galley** is the uncorrected proof of your book, bound but not yet in its final form. It's also called an ARC, or advanced reading copy. If you don't have a galley or ARC, it's just fine to send a finished book.

All these components may not be necessary for every media outlet on your publicity campaign—but many outlets, especially editors and producers, who find an interest in your book will appreciate the information you provide. It makes their lives easier.

> **CAUTION**
>
> ### Cautionary Tales _____
>
> Don't inundate an editor or producer with more than two clippings of stories that relate to your book. Because of the copious amounts of mail they receive, producers and editors barely have time to read through your kit—and will do so only if your pitch snags their interest. Be kind and don't send superfluous information. One strong, reputable story that reinforces your book's relevance will be enough. Two is good. Your kit will quickly end up in the circular file instead of the prospective story file if you throw too much their way. If the editor bites for a story, then offer more "research."

Effective New Book Releases 101

When we get deeper into the different media venues in the following chapters, I'll show you how to customize releases and pitch letters for different editors and producers. In this chapter, you will learn the basics of a press release—a release that you can fax to your local stations if that's all you have time for, or a release that you can send to the media world if it's part of your plan.

A press release is a one-page announcement that is meant to grab the interest of the person to whom you sent it and thus generate a story on you and your book. Take a look at a press release I used during the holiday season to successfully generate television, radio, and newspaper exposure for some of my books:

10 Little Christmas Indulgences to Give Yourself

The gift-giving season is upon us. You have a terribly long list of folks to do wonderful things for, but why ever should you leave *yourself* off of that list? "Don't think of leaving yourself off of your to-do list," says Jennifer "Gin" Sander, America's Affordable Indulgence Expert. The author of *Wear More Cashmere: 151 Luxurious Ways to Pamper Your Inner Princess* and *The Martini Diet: The Self-Indulgent Way to a Thinner, More Fabulous You* (both from Fair Winds Press), Jennifer believes that the more you do for yourself, the more you can do for your friends and family. Here are her suggestions for ten small ways to indulge yourself this Christmas to make that holiday mood last on and on.

1. Tea Time—Pause amidst your frantic shopping and treat yourself to afternoon tea at a luxury hotel like the Waldorf-Astoria in New York, The Windsor Court in New Orleans, or the Ritz-Carlton in Chicago. Less formal tea shops have sprung up around the country, some even have a closet filled with big hats, lady like gloves and feather boas guests can borrow to enhance the mood.

2. High Style/Low Price—Indulge in your haute couture fantasies this Christmas without emptying your bank account by shopping for used designer clothing online or at your local designer consignment store.

Jennifer might be swanning around town to holiday parties this year in her sparkly Badgley Mishka gown, bought from a designer consignment shop for a fraction of the original cost. Or she might slip into the vintage Carolyn Roehm cocktail dress she found on eBay. Either way, no one will guess that someone else owned it first.

3. Be Ready for Your Christmas Close-Up—Take advantage of the trained makeup artists at department store beauty counters. Haughty as they sometimes can look, the truth is they are standing there all day waiting for you to come up and ask them to give you a new look. There is seldom an obligation to buy, of course, but the polite thing is to at least purchase a tube of the twenty dollar lipstick that looks so very good on your professionally made-up face.

4. Party by Mail—Why not indulge in a catered party, catered by upscale catalogs and delivered to your door before your guests are due to arrive? Start with crab cakes ($54.00) or handmade tamales ($49.50) from the Williams-Sonoma catalog, move on to the stuffed chateaubriand from the Neiman-Marcus Christmas catalog ($86.00) and finish up with King Leo Peppermint Bark ($19.95) from the Restoration Hardware catalog.

5. A Private Concoction—You could always invent a new variation on a holiday drink and then name it after yourself. While writing *The Martini Diet*, Jennifer concocted the GinSander (a dry gin martini with a twist of lemon and a sprig of lavender). A delicious way to celebrate you!

6. Black Velvet—Who doesn't feel like a movie star when your hips are wrapped in a sexy sarong? Fashion your own sensuous holiday sarong by buying velvet or heavy silk (62 by 42 inches should do it), then wrap the long side around your waist, grab the two edges up, and tie it across your

hips. You are dressed and ready for an indulgent December evening at home.

7. Exercise in High Heels—Explore your inner Katerina Witt by spending an afternoon alone skating to the music in an ice rink. Not only is it exercise, but you are instantly taller and slimmer and moving with grace. Much more indulgent than race walking in your neighborhood.

8. Share the Pleasure—Dreaming of drinking a rare bottle of wine but dreading the bill that will accompany it? Why not round up another few wine-loving friends to splurge together on an expensive bottle. A bottle of Opus One can cost $225 and is well worth it, split four ways you can each indulge for only $57.

9. Feet First—How often do we get to enjoy the regal feeling of having someone at our feet. Do your fingernails yourself and spend the money instead on a long and luxurious pedicure. It is far more indulgent than a manicure and the results last for weeks. If you feel too guilty spending money on yourself this time of year, try a beauty college ($18).

10. By the Light of the Silvery Tree—Splurge on a good bottle of champagne and an incredible dessert, but wait until the children have gone to bed to indulge. Turn out all of the lights in the house except for the Christmas tree lights and spread a blanket on the floor to enjoy your treats beneath the tree.

###

Books by Jennifer "Gin" Sander:

The Martini Diet: The Self-Indulgent Way to a Thinner, More Fabulous You (June 2004, Fair Winds Press,) ISBN 1-59233-046-0, $19

Wear More Cashmere: 151 Luxurious Ways to Pamper Your Inner Princess (October 2003, Fair Winds Press) ISBN 1-931412-34-0, $18.95

To interview Jennifer "Gin" Sander about indulgence, call 916-791-2101

About Jennifer "Gin" Sander: A longtime fan of self-indulgence, martini-sipping Jennifer (known to her friends as Gin) is the best selling author of more than 30 books, including *Christmas Miracles*. The busy mother of two young boys, she posted a note on her computer years ago reminding herself to "wear more cashmere," and the rest is history. Jennifer and her books have been featured on *The View, Soap Talk, Fox & Friends,* and C-Span's *Book TV.*

This wasn't a press release to announce the initial release of a book, which would have been written in a style that not only piqued the interest of the press person that received it, but that would have filled in more about the books themselves. Notice how I gave these media folks an easy lead that they could use—"10 Little Christmas Indulgences to Give Yourself.."It was picked right up and run that same way in a number of newspapers. Make their job easier, and it will pay off!

You'll find a few more sample press releases in Appendix B. Just follow the style of the samples for your release and full kits in order to learn where you place the things like the dateline (the release date of the information), contact names and phone numbers, and formatting rules (like placing three centered #'s at the end of the release to denote the end of the release.

All press releases should start out with a "catchy," even sensational headline. Just like my "10 Little Christmas Indulgences" appeared in print as is, don't be surprised if you see your headline lifted and used in a subsequent article. That's the point! You want editors to believe in the validity of the information you're providing and believe that their readers desire that information.

Check out these headlines (and what the book might be about) to give you a quick idea of what I mean:

- ◆ "In Wake of Recent Plane Crashes, Pilot Offers Flyers Life-Saving Tips"

    This book details everything from what to pack and what to wear, to optimize safety on an aircraft.

- ◆ "Mommy Cooks So Even Kids with Wheat Allergies Get a Cookie"

    This cookbook offers yummy recipes for children suffering from food allergies.

- ◆ "Eat Your Way Through Italy on Only Ten Euros a Day"

    This travel guidebook shows the reader where to eat across the country of Italy without spending a ton of money.

After the headline, meant to grab the attention of even the most jaded and information-glutted journalist, you need to succinctly provide details of who, what, when, where, and why. Most important is "Why?" Why is it important for the editor to propel the information you're offering into the public eye? What's the purpose of your book, and how does it fit into our current world? Aha! The hook. What's your news or cultural hook? Remember Helen Scully, the career counselor? Her hook was the rising unemployment rate—a topic always on the front page of the newspapers. Her CD-ROM/book offered readers/buyers a way to stay off the unemployment rolls and find their dream job. Her press release substantiated *why* editors should let readers know about her and her product.

As we break down the different media outlets (print, electronic, radio, and so forth) and how you approach publicity with each in the next chapters, we'll look closely at nuances of content within releases for each—like the difference between announcing an event to a paper and attempting to gain a feature article.

Help! I Need Somebody, Not Just Anybody

What if after reading all of this you decide that the whole publicity gig isn't your cup of tea? Not everyone is cut out to be their own publicist. It takes a certain nerve to promote yourself to the media. The idea of appearing on *Oprah* is one you can handle, but not the legwork to get you there. Perhaps you'd rather hire someone with experience, a freelance book publicist or book publicity firm, to handle either all of your campaign or individual components of it.

By the Way

A freelance book publicist contracts with individual authors or book-publishing companies to plan and implement the publicity of their book. Same goes for publicity firms. Most freelance publicists will provide packages of services—everything from complete campaigns covering full service for a certain number of months to components of the plan, like mailing out your kits and following up with magazine editors. A firm typically requires a retainer before beginning any publicity services. Monthly retainers average a thousand dollars.

If you do decide to hire help with publicity, your choices are almost limitless. Start first by asking anyone you know who has successfully used the services of a publicist. Without a personal recommendation, try Googling "book publicity" online. You'll find hundreds of hits—everything from professional publicist organizations with listings of members to publicity firms that list clients and services. I've listed several freelance publicists in Appendix E. These are folks I know and have worked with in the past.

The choice to hire a publicist is an individual decision. You'll want to interview prospective publicists and find one that you really think believes in your book. You'll need to weigh the expense versus the services offered, and also consider the time you're willing to expend on the publicity of your book. If you have a full-time job, for example, it may prove cost-advantageous to hire the publicist over taking a month off work to devote yourself to the publicity. And most publicists maintain personal contacts with editors, writers, and producers that can open doors more quickly than if you go it alone.

You may ultimately decide that you can do this without a professional publicist, and I would encourage you to try. The process of successful book publicity will help you develop copywriting skills you might not have known you had and discover conversational skills you haven't had to use since you were trying to talk your parents into something years ago. You may have the time for it and relish the thought of forging your own media contacts. After all, you decided to write and produce your own book. Why not take the knowledge about publicity within these pages and blitz away to coverage and sales?

The Least You Need to Know

- ◆ Publicity generates exposure for the author and helps sell books.

- ◆ Unlike advertising, you do not actually pay for publicity, although it can take money to create it.

- ◆ Invest in professional elements for your publicity kit—an author photo, CDs or videos of media appearances and interviews, and a well-written press release.

- ◆ A press release announces your book to the media and gives them a compelling reason to cover it.

- ◆ Book signings are passive and often don't work; create events instead.

- ◆ If you don't feel comfortable promoting yourself to the media, hire a freelance publicist to do it for you.

Chapter 19

Reaching the Print Media

In This Chapter

- Why it's important to know about the various print media
- Learning about the different genres of articles
- The pitching process
- Etiquette when writing and calling editors
- The power of editorial mentions and the longevity of the written review
- Using the expertise of freelance writers

As a self-published author, you can never get enough publicity. Each successful piece of coverage will whet your appetite for more. Print media is every bit as satisfying and effective as television or radio.

Reaching print media editors may well be your best tool in selling your book—because so many people, millions, read everything from newspapers to magazines, to trade journals every day. The key is getting editorial copy—even a few lines or a mention—within these publications. As you already know from the last chapter, these mentions equate to free advertising and free publicity.

The Art of the "Know-It-All"

Mom may have told you that everyone hates a "know-it-all," but in the world of print media, you need to know everything about the publications in which you may be thinking of pursuing a story or review. You also need to know as much as you can about the stories and events prominently in the news—remember the whole hook thing?

Ah, and you thought you only needed to be the expert in the topics covered in your book or the characters and themes in your novel. Guess again. In order to know where to pitch an editor without wasting his or her time, and to keep your book and publicity kit out of the "circular file," you must know the demographics of the readers, editorial calendar topics slated for the publication, and who the publication's major advertisers are.

> **Pro Style**
>
> A freelance writer usually sends a "query" letter that offers an idea for a story he or she would like to write for the magazine. In publicity, however, you are "pitching" an idea for a story based upon your book or offering yourself up as an expert—not as the writer of the story. In fact, offering to write the story about your own book may seem a conflict of interest because then you'd be asking to get paid. In publicity, you offer *free* information and thereby get *free* editorial coverage.

The Three R's

The three R's of publicity research: reading and reading and reading. The best way to get your pulse on the publications that might suit your publicity needs is to read. But don't just revel in works that seem to fit your topic—read everything you can get your hands on. Let's not be silly here. You're probably not going to get a "publicity hit" in *Thrasher* magazine, a skateboarding publication, if your book is a memoir of your time as a chef in Paris. But there are certain newspapers and magazines you should read regardless of whether you think they fit the genre of the work.

It's Black and White

First reads first: newspapers. Years ago, independent newspapers reigned. Fewer companies own increasingly more newspapers collectively. The big players within the newspaper industry include The Hearst Corporation, Knight-Ridder, Gannett, McClatchy News, and The E. W. Scripps Company. These big boys, like Gannett, which owns *USA Today*, all produce papers of influence in which any section—not just the book review section—may prove the perfect place for a story about you and your book. Let's take *The Sacramento Bee*, a McClatchy paper based out of the state capital of California. Each Saturday, the paper produces a pull-out magazine devoted to home and garden—the perfect place to pitch a story if your book focuses on beautiful bird feeders or decorating the smaller home.

Within each of these newspaper chains, you'll find papers with national appeal, within the "Top Media Markets" and local papers.

> **Pro Style**
>
> Want to know a little more about professional newspaper writing—especially in the wake of the Jayson Blair scandal and the ethics of papers? *The Columbia Journalism Review* (and The Columbia School of Journalism) have long been revered as the authority on great journalism. Take a day and check out the journal's website at www.crj.org. Just exploring the site will make you a more knowledgeable writer.

Locally Grown

Local papers are a great way to start your publicity blitz. As "one of their own," residents are interested in people from their communities doing great things—like writing a book! You'll want to read your local city paper cover to cover, along with papers from the surrounding suburban areas.

As you come across columns, stories, or sections that may fit the intent of your book, clip them. Keep these clips and include the editors of the section on your media blitz list. How do you find the name of the editor (information you'll need for top media market publications like the *Los Angeles Times* and glossy magazines, like *GQ*)? On the *masthead* and by calling the paper or magazine— don't skip either step. You'll also find writer's names with the story: their byline.

Start with the masthead, a listing of all editors (and now often their respective phone numbers and e-mail addresses) within the first few pages of a paper or magazine or each section of the paper.

> **Wise Words**
>
> A **masthead** is a printed list of all the editors, artists, designers, editorial staffers, and advertising executives for a publication, typically found within the first few pages of the publication.

Clip the masthead, too, and keep it with your clippings from each story. But before you send anything out, call and double-check that the editor or writer to whom you plan on sending your kit is still employed with the publication. Editors move around, especially with smaller, local suburban papers. But they also move around within large, glossy magazines. Years ago I established contact with Kara Corridan, then the Health editor at *Child*. In four years, Corridan has jumped to three other national magazines—from *Seventeen* to *Modern Bride*, and I've pitched her at every stop!

But let's talk about those neighborhood papers again. Neighborhood papers are *always* looking for stories. Your very first coverage for your book will probably be the local newspaper. As a homegrown author, you can expect a longer feature and a good addition to your press kit.

By the Way

Steve Sax, an All-Star Major League baseball player in the 1980s and '90s for the Dodgers and Yankees, knows the power of homegrown appeal and publicity. The athlete-turned-stockbroker is now writing a book on sports and money. The former player, born and bred in West Sacramento, now living in a suburb near the foothills called Roseville, pitched both the *Sacramento Bee* Business Editor and the *Roseville Press-Tribune* about his writing a book—the book isn't even sold or out! The business section of *The Bee* devoted a short column to his upcoming book, and the *Press-Tribune* wrote a feature-length article. Take Sax's lead and head first to your local newspapers for publicity. The prepublicity stand he took garnered him some cool stories for his press kit once the book hits the shelves, and helped his negotiating ability!

Shopping the Markets

Just what is a media market? Well, every community has its media, right? The populations and circulations upon the populations of the cities determine the media market. Tyler, Texas, for example, a tiny town in East Texas, is low on the media market list. Meanwhile, New York City is, you guessed it, number one.

In your publicity campaign, you decide what markets will prove most effective in achieving readers. Let's say you've published a book about crossbow hunting, or cooking wild game, or foraging for mushrooms. Why not plan on pitching papers in those areas less populated—smaller media markets first? Chances are, their editors will recognize a topic that will appeal instantly to their readers. But you may have a universal book that requires a strategic kit that goes to top markets, like Chicago, Detroit, Miami, Los Angeles, Philadelphia, Dallas, and more.

It's easy for you to research your local papers :just buy one off the newsstand. Researching out-of-town papers isn't as easy and will cost more than a quarter or two. You may not have access to all the papers or magazines that are well suited for your story ideas based upon your book within the markets you plan to approach—or know anything about the sections and the editors. I've mentioned this before, that several media services exist online—both for which you pay a service and for which you may receive free lists.

Here are just a couple of places to begin your search for print (and television) media directories:

◆ **www.mediapost.com.** Offers free lists but no editors' names—just publication names, addresses, and phone numbers by cities, topic areas, and markets.

◆ **www.gebbeinc.com.** A fee-based service offering comprehensive books and DVD directories of publications, but without editors' names. Publications are updated with information frequently, and lists are maintained.

◆ **www.bacons.com.** A fee-based service that offers online, daily-updated lists of publications and editors. Expensive but comprehensive, detailed and accurate. This company provides myriad services that others don't, making creating your media lists an easy task.

◆ **www.bookmarket.com/directories.** Helpful pages of information as you put together lists of print media, including a book marketing home page.

Don't forget to check your newspaper online, many (if not most) newspapers now have an online version. Sometimes it is free to access, sometimes not.

So Many Articles to Pitch!

Now that you've got an idea of how to find locations to place your book within newspapers and magazines, you'll want to think about the story ideas you'll include in your kit. Here's a mini-course on the type of articles found within newspapers so that you'll be armed with a little more information when approaching editors.

◆ **Opinion editorial (op-ed).** Opinionated essays on topical subjects. Does your book possess a topical slant that the op-ed editor might find intriguing?

◆ **Personal essay.** For publicity, not a good choice. But if you'd like to write a personal essay that a newspaper or magazine may publish that somehow intrigues the reader about why you wrote your book or that is an excerpt of sorts from your book, this may be a way to gain publicity.

◆ **Review**—Critique of your book. Be careful and think about the appropriate editor to do the critiquing. Many authors think they should send their book to the "book review editor." Not a wise choice for a nonfiction writer. The book review editors deal with serious fiction, typically, and sociopolitical nonfiction. It's more difficult to find your book in the book review section than another section of the newspaper. Look carefully at what each editor of magazines discusses, too, because the choices are often eclectic. Understand that the real estate in the review section is scarce, as many newspapers have cut back considerably.

◆ **Service piece.** An informative or educational piece, including phone numbers and contacts that relate to the piece. If your book has a service hook, it's a great way to garner publicity and help the public. You win. The readers win.

◆ **Q&A.** An interview, most likely with you the author. To gain this sort of article, you need to establish yourself as an expert on a topical subject.

◆ **Profile.** Again, you'd be interviewed and "profiled" for a feature-length article. The question to ask yourself is "What do I have to say that an editor will want to hear and then pass on to the readers?"

◆ **News story.** Here's where you take out the hooks and engineer a story that uses you as an expert or your book as an informative publication on the topic. Did you write a book on serial killers, and your town is suddenly the venue for a sensational murder trial with national coverage? You could offer your expertise to writers in the newsroom covering the trial.

Pro Style

Most every author thinks that the place to send his or her book and kit is to the book review editor—not true! Book review editors typically review fiction. Look more strategically at the sections within the paper that "fit" your topic. Don't arbitrarily send your book to the book review editor; do so only if it's an appropriate title for the editor.

◆ **Round-Up.** An entertaining, informative piece that usually offers readers several ways to do something or places to go. Could your book be listed as a tool in a round-up? For example, let's say you know that *Glamour* magazine is devoting an issue to serenity and your book is all about relieving stress. Your book might be the perfect fit as a book to read to gain serenity.

◆ **Cultural commentary.** These stories deal with a cultural phenomenon, often with an opinionated slant. Does your book deal with a cultural phenomenon? Then pitching the culture/lifestyle editors of newspapers might prove advantageous.

◆ **Humor piece.** All that's funny finds its place here. Is your book comical? Does it find humor in an aspect of our world? You'll be pitching editors funny letters!

Although newspapers are continually on the hunt for material, remember that magazines work very far ahead on their issues, several months ahead of publication.

Also, never pitch a book review or story idea unless you've read at least three issues of the magazine or newspaper and have a feel for these publications. Let's say you have written and published a traditional parenting book. You see a magazine for parents and blindly pitch your book as a possible topic to be covered, not knowing that the magazine is devoted entirely to the niche of blended and nontraditional families and their lives. Oops. A waste of energy and a waste of money. Chances are, you don't have enough of either to make these kinds of mistakes.

Etiquette at the News Desk

Before you send out your kit, you need to know that there is an etiquette to publicity. Newspaper editors are always, always on *deadlines*. They work in a fast-paced world where readers want their news up-to-the-minute—but in ink. It's one thing to report on the scene in television; live satellites make it possible. But newspapers need to be printed and delivered to newsstands and homes. If there is a breaking story that relates to your book, go ahead and call the editor. But be warned: it had better be that you are the expert they need to talk to right then. Make sure your input is immediately what they need.

Otherwise, here's the protocol:

Newspaper editors are a little more flexible than magazine editors. Because they work on quick deadlines, they are more inclined to accept pitches by phone. Have notes ready and, when the editor answers, say, "Hi, I'd like to pitch a story idea to you. Are you on a deadline and should I call back later?"

The editor will let you know if he or she can't talk. They may say, "Shoot. Go for it." Tell them clearly that you are the author of a book on Topic X and that you have an idea for a story that is timely and will interest their readers. Be specific about the hook. Ask the editor if they would like a kit.

The editor will either say, "No, not something we are interested in right now" or "Sure, send me the kit."

Send the kit.

Wait a week.

> **Wise Words**
>
> A **deadline** is the final day (or even hour within a newspaper) that a writer/editor needs to turn in an assignment.

Call back and ask if the editor received the kit—but not before asking if he or she is on a deadline!

Hopefully, you'll begin a rapport with the editor and start to formulate a story in the paper.

Sometimes your first pitch will yield a story.

No Calls, Please

Magazines don't like cold pitch calls at all. Always send your pitch within a kit. Mail it to the appropriate editor and wait about two weeks. Then make a follow-up call, also following the "Are you on a deadline?" etiquette.

Leave a Message

If you get a message machine, leave a brief message giving your name and the title of the book, and say that you are sending a kit and will call in a week or two to follow up. Don't besiege the editor with calls, three is your maximum.

Pro Style _____

Follow-up calls are a must. When writers and editors are inundated daily with information, sometimes they need a little jog of the memory to move forward on a good idea. But there's a difference between a stalker and a follow-up call. Don't stalk. Make one or two follow-up calls, no more. Make sure your voice is pleasant, always "smile and dial" so that you are in the right frame of mind.

Editorial Copy Is Power

You may think that television is the way to go for publicity exposure. Look at Oprah's Book Club, after all. But there are several great reasons to concentrate your publicity on the written word.

Editorial copy establishes you as the expert. Television can, too, but within print you have a better chance of being quoted than a newscast, in which an anchor may mention your book only a few times over days.

Next, print circulates on tables, in coffee houses, in doctor's offices, and in other places well past the date of the publication. There's a chance that people will be reading the stories about you or your book well after a television hit. Some papers are weekly, and some are monthly, too, adding to your publicity longevity. The same goes for magazines. How many times have you picked up a magazine from a year ago in the dentist's office? Well, your publicity hit may be in that magazine, and a year later you may sell even more books.

Going in the Back Door

Just a short note on freelance writers, writers who are not on the newspaper or magazine payroll—they work for themselves and are always looking for good story ideas. The publication pays them; that's how they make their livelihood.

If you can, find out some of the names of freelancers within the publications you want publicity. Pitch the freelancer into pitching an article to his or her editor. You never know, the freelancer may like your book and your ideas, and then should have an added interest, in that he may gain some income.

You might try navigating online and looking for writing groups or organizations to make your contacts. It's a long shot, but the benefits can prove great.

Does some of what I'm saying about pitching editors sound a lot like sales? It does indeed. One reality that all authors—self-published and commercially published alike—need to get used to is that we need to be able to sell ourselves and our books. At times, it may be distasteful, but just put your head down and keep on going! Success may be as close as that very next phone call ....

The Least You Need to Know

♦ Read a plethora of publications; know what's going on in papers and magazines.

♦ Keep a file of clippings and editors' and writers' names—but double-check once you begin the pitch process.

♦ Consider using a media list service to find the publications you want to target.

♦ Become a student of the different kinds of articles in publications you aspire to.

♦ Understand the etiquette when contacting the media.

Chapter 20

Television and Radio Publicity

In This Chapter

- ◆ How television and radio are powerful tools in the sale of your book
- ◆ What works on television, what doesn't
- ◆ How to interest a producer
- ◆ Looking and sounding good on television
- ◆ Sounding great on radio
- ◆ Advice from national television and radio producers

Could it happen? Your pearly smile on television, laughing with Ellen DeGeneres, or providing information to Dr. Phil's audience? Your voice broadcast across the airwaves on National Public Radio? What author doesn't see himself publicizing his work in an interview with Katie Couric or even Howard Stern? Oprah proved with her talk show that television does sell books—big time. And radio has always been a venue that attracts readers and book buyers. In this chapter, I show you all you need to know to navigate the slippery world of television and radio news and entertainment. From what to wear when in Technicolor to what to say on those radio waves, this chapter gives you the know-how to go from unknown to "it" author.

The Power of TV and Radio

Television and radio are integral to our culture. People start their day with the morning news and may even tune into national morning shows. On their drive to work, they surf radio stations for interesting talk, news, traffic, and music. Meanwhile, on the tube, the talk shows run all day—everything from Maury Povich to Ellen DeGeneres, to Dr. Phil. And each year, more names are added to the mix, providing you, the book author, countless opportunities to draw attention to your work. Moving images and sound are all over. It's been estimated that we are hit with more images in 20 minutes than someone in Middle America received in the 1920s in his whole life. We are information junkies, and we get our fix through constant television and radio. If you are promoting your book on a radio or television talk show, thousands of people are out there listening and watching. If the show is national or syndicated (in radio), millions may be tuning in.

I hope you get the chance to hawk your book on *The Today Show* someday (I know I hope I do, too!), but understand that the appearance does not necessarily translate to sales. Even on a huge show like *The Today Show*, it's up to you to put your best foot forward and try to hedge your bets with each guest spot. Radio and television can prove powerful publicity tools—and in cases like the *Oprah* phenomenon, you just may find yourself on the bestseller list.

All of Cable Is Your Oyster

And then there's always cable. With the rise of cable television and the hundreds of channels devoted to the interest of everyone from bow hunters to fashionistas, railroad fans to farmers, there's a good chance that there is a channel and a show just waiting to talk about your book. Cable blew open the world of 24/7 news and unlimited channels. Although viewers of a CNN show still don't reach the numbers of a network broadcast, cable still reaches hundreds of thousands and even millions of viewers, depending upon the show. With cable, you really can find your niche.

With my girlie gift books, *Wear More Cashmere* and *The Martini Diet*, I've done a few national shows. But the show that asks me back on a regular basis every few months or so is *Soap Talk*. That's right, a talk show on ABC's Soap Opera channel. I've been teased about this by my snootier friends (and my even snootier mother); I just smile and cite the viewership. The Soap Opera cable channel has even bigger viewership among women than Lifetime and Oxygen, two cable networks created to cater to women. Never turn up your nose at cable.

By the Way

Whether it's her book club or just a book mentioned within the topic of a show, Oprah's seal of approval tends to sell books. According to *Who Owns the Media?*, by Benjamin M. Compaine and Douglas Gomery, "Consider that in May 1997 TV talk show hostess Oprah Winfrey had promoted six novels on her television show that went on to the bestseller lists. To the book publishing industry, having a novel picked by Oprah was akin to winning the lottery." By 1999, a book appearing on her show, could expect sales to exceed 1 million. Here is one glitch for writers: Her book club is strictly fiction and has now moved on to fiction from dead people! That doesn't mean you shouldn't pitch nonfiction books as topics for her show—just be realistic. A hit on *The Oprah Winfrey Show* does sell nonfiction books—but not necessarily to the extent that a fiction hit on her show might fuel sales.

What the Heck Are They Looking for?

It seems like a daunting question: "What are producers looking for?" But really it's quite simple. Producers are all looking for information—topics and guests that grab their viewers and listeners. What varies and where it becomes more complicated is the show. Let's look first at television and take a crash course in a few of the "types" of programming out there and what producers within each genre are looking for. Here are the types of television programs that air regularly:

- Hard news
- News magazine
- Morning show
- Talk show
- Entertainment talk
- Documentary/educational

Hard News

Producers in hard news are working fast and furiously for the latest story, the scoop. Unless *you* are the serial killer on the loose, chances are, the hard news producer doesn't want to talk to you. But hold on a second. What if you are a former police investigator who has just written a book on the mind of criminals? A reporter may want to talk to you for a sound bite for a *package* that will air on the news broadcast. This kind of spot won't really promote your book, though. The best you can hope for on a hard news program is to be identified onscreen as "author of ...."

So you get booked on to a hard news show. Don't celebrate yet. Wait until after you've actually appeared. Hard news shows will cut you the second a better story needs to be aired. It has happened to me twice on *Fox News*. Once I was actually in a cab coming in to New York from the airport when my publicist called to tell me they'd canceled my spot on the Sunday news due to a big story in the Middle East. I had the driver turn around and take me back to the airport for a fast trip back to California.

> ### Wise Words
>
> The term **package,** in broadcast news, refers to a story that has been written, shot, and edited into a few minutes or less and then airs on the broadcast. A package isn't live. Often you'll see the reporter live, who does a bit of live chatter to set up the story—and then the filmed "package" rolls.

News Magazine

These programs, like *20/20*, *Dateline*, and *60 Minutes*, are typically investigative in nature and showcase longer packages that deal with stories or trends currently in the news. They also air celebrity interviews and entertainment news. News magazine shows often rely on experts to fill out and provide credibility to their stories.

Remember when Kobe Bryant was accused of assault and rape? Virtually every news-magazine covered fidelity in the NBA. Each story included "experts," and several authors were interviewed. Pitch a news magazine producer a story that has a "news hook" but needs more elaboration. Or even better—are you an expert? Send in a resumé of your expertise to producers asking them to call on you whenever they're looking for a "talking head."

Morning Show

Morning shows are like a perfectly balanced cup of coffee. You'll find mellow notes with items like cooking segments and the best educational toys for the kids coupled with political interview and stories. Entertainment is always a focus, too—everything from movies to fashion, to reading. Producers for morning shows usually each have their focus—but some go all over. The health producer, for example, will be looking for health stories. The technology producer will be looking for anything interesting in gadgets or computers. The cooking producer? Anything to do with cookbooks, cooking, and food. You get the idea. Don't think in terms of only the book producer—think about how your book fits into other categories and what stories can be extrapolated from your book.

There are several towns with morning shows on their local stations. My own hometown, Sacramento, has a great one, *Good Day Sacramento*, which has a whopping three hours to fill every day. Do they book authors? You bet they do!

Talk Show

We all know these! A live audience reacts and asks questions of a panel covering a topic. Talk shows are not all created equal. Something like *Maury Povich* might be looking for mothers with more than six babies by different fathers, while Dr. Phil's show covers homemakers who are addicted to prescription medications. Each show will need an expert. As we've learned in the past decade, no topic seems taboo for many of these programs. At the same time, many of these programs offer viewers great information and help. Ask yourself, "How can my book help others?" and see if there's a talk show producer looking for your expertise and information. There are very few regional talk shows left; most are national shows.

Entertainment Talk

Live with Regis and Kelly comes to mind when I think of entertainment talk. Entertainment talk focuses more on celebrity interviews and doesn't cover hard news like a morning program of the *CBS This Morning* variety. It's all fun on these shows with light information, but it is very hard to get booked unless you are a celebrity.

Documentary/Educational

You'll find these programs on PBS and on many of the cable channels, like The History channel or The Discovery channel. These outlets often have series that producers are constantly looking for topics to consider and experts to call on. Are you a Ph.D. in ancient Rome with a specialty in gladiators? Perhaps there's a producer out there looking for your book and your sound bite.

As you can see, the opportunities are as endless as the number of programs out there. The difficulty is determining what shows really "fit" your book.

How Will They Find You?

How does a television producer find you? Because you told them about yourself through your cover letter and press kit. Remember that press kit list from Chapter 20? The one that included a pitch letter, a book release, an author bio, suggested questions ... sounding familiar? Get the producer's name (double-check the spelling, please!), write a catchy pitch letter, and send it!

Make sure you make your follow up calls and let the producer know that you have an interest in appearing as an expert if they should ever need you. You may not find yourself immediately in front of the camera, but a month up the road, you may receive a call that whisks you away to New York City to be interviewed.

> **By the Way**
>
> For effective TV, there needs to be more than just your talking head on the screen. Always think about what a television producer can have the photographer shoot—what pictures can be used to tell the story. Without moving pictures, you have no story on television.

The key is interesting the producer in your story ideas—you learned how to do that in Chapter 19 on working with the media. You need to find a hook that appeals to the sensibilities of the producer and his or her audience. You can't pitch a story on your book about the ancient ruins of Petra on *Maury Povich*. Look for producers and shows that cover the Middle East, tie in today's conflicts, and run to a news magazine producer who looks at historical and political pieces.

Is There a Show in Your Area?

I mentioned that my hometown has a great live morning news show. What's on the air in your town? Before you pitch yourself to the big guys, start small. Just like you should pitch yourself to your hometown newspaper first, pitch your local TV first. It gives you a chance to gain skill and comfort in front of a camera and to practice what works best to promote your book. Best of all, it gives you a tape that you can copy and send out with your press kit to shows in bigger markets!

You never know where it might lead ... I ended up as a regular, doing spots twice a month as the Lux Lady on the local UPN station in town. It wasn't a paying gig, but I got great experience in front of the camera and have a much better sense of how to write a TV segment. I also made good contacts. The producer I worked with in Sacramento now runs the morning show in Seattle, and I have a standing invite to appear there.

Video Didn't Kill the Radio Star

Radio is still rocking and talking strongly all over the world. But unlike television, radio depends more on expert interviews than on full-blown stories. Radio producers are looking for interesting topics that can be discussed by engaging people in a way their listeners will enjoy. You don't need to worry about your looks as much as how you convey yourself by the microphone. All news stations will book guests any time of the day, depending upon their program, whereas predominantly music stations want guests during the all-important drive time in the morning and evening as people go to and come home from work.

Because of the sheer number of local programs all over the globe, booking a telephone interview on an appropriate radio program isn't difficult. Usually a crisp and well-written fax will open the floodgates of producers. As with television, however, choose the programs you send your kit (or fax) to wisely. Otherwise, you're just spinning your wheels.

You Look (and Sound) Marvelous!

To some extent, television and radio are unforgiving. You'll want to look and sound your best when you stand behind the camera. Many shows even require "test interviews" before booking you as a guest on their show. The producer wants to know how you handle yourself and what you look like on camera. Let's say you are a renowned geneticist and the producer wants you as an expert on genetics and fertility—but you show up in something looking more suitable for an outdoor travel program than a suit-and-tie science show. Chances are, another geneticist with a book will get the gig.

There are a few simple things to remember for on-air work that every newscaster knows:

- Don't try a new, drastically different hair color or style before a television appearance. You may hate the way it looks on camera.

- Do get a healthy trim, if necessary. Make sure you don't sport flyaway or split ends. You'll look unkempt if your hair isn't in place.

- Do touch up roots, if needed, before a television appearance; you don't want your roots to be so distracting that no one hears what you're saying.

- Stick with a simple style for the day of the show—blow-dried sleek or pulled back neatly for women, and combed neatly for men.

Pro Style

Every man on the set who sits in front of the camera uses makeup. Guys, you may feel a little funny powdering your face or using a base makeup, but you'll need to move past it. You think Tom Brokaw goes on air before a makeup check? Never.

Cautionary Tales

George Clooney and Brad Pitt may be able to pull off the tie-less, casually buttoned shirt with a sports coat for their appearances, but you shouldn't even try. They are entertainers, whereas you are a writer and an author who wants to be perceived as an expert. Look the part. After all, Clooney and Pitt dress their parts in the movies, right?

◆ Wear more makeup. A little color is good on camera. Use a darker shade of makeup than you normally would. You'll notice that all the talent seems "painted" when you arrive. That's because they cake their face with a darker makeup to mitigate the "white-out" effect of the lights and camera. You may feel stupid, like you have too dark or too much concealer and foundation on, but it will help you look healthier behind the camera.

◆ No frosts allowed! Women, do not use frosty eye shadows, blushers, or lipsticks. Frosts increase the visibility of lines on the face and appear gaudy on camera.

◆ Choose flat colors that complement your skin tones, and definitely wear lipstick. Men should apply a little Chapstick to their lips before going on camera

◆ No dangly earrings (shoulder dusters) for women; again, they're distracting. Sure, a few anchors on the cable networks may sport the shoulder dusters, but it takes an inordinate amount of style and bravado to pull it off. Err on the side of safety and professionalism, and wear only smaller earrings. You don't necessarily need to wear a stud.

◆ Wear a suit with a blouse (women) or a button-down shirt (men). Make sure you have a collar; it just looks cleaner, crisper, and more professional on camera.

◆ Skip wearing white; it makes the cameras go haywire. Even off-white should be avoided. And pass on the sequins or any kind of shiny material; it will reflect all of the studio lights, and you won't show up at all.

◆ Check your shirts and jacket for stains, and have an extra in case you do accidentally spill something before show time.

◆ Choose something fitted but not tight.

Fun with Makeup

The makeup thing is a big deal on TV. You will need to wear so much more than you usually do, and if you get the chance to be made-up by an in-studio makeup artist (all the big national shows have them), you will learn how very different the TV techniques are. I've taken lessons from a top media makeup specialist, Jeanne Marie, founder of International Media Cosmetics. She has done everyone from Peter Jennings to Bill Clinton, to Arnold Schwarzenegger, powdering their noses for on-camera work. I have a little black bag that I carry everywhere to media appearances with all of the special makeup she has selected for me. Check out her website at www.jeannemarie.com.

You May Have a Wardrobe Gimmick

Of course, you want to look your best—even attractive—on air, and you can! Look at the myriad anchors, both male and female, who are gorgeous but still look professional. Keep them in mind when putting together your look.

The only elements that may cause a deviation from the suit and collar rule might be the topic of your book. Let's say you're a zoologist who has written a book about primates and will be appearing on *The Tonight Show with Jay Leno*. Let's add a few baby primates to the mix. You, of course, will want to wear something indicative of your work—perhaps a safari shirt and slacks might work your topic nicely. Plus, you'd want something durable in case the monkeys get to your clothes.

The key, ultimately, comes to dressing appropriately for your title and the situation. Just because you wrote a cookbook on pies doesn't mean you should dress in a giant slice of pie Halloween costume with each food demonstration—but do wear a chef's apron.

If you are being interviewed or are a guest on a show and will strictly be answering questions about your book or topics related to your book, look like an anchor. Study anchors. Study their makeup, their jewelry, and their clothes. Find an anchor that you'd like to emulate, and attempt to follow in that person's fashion and makeup footsteps.

Finally, check your nails. Typically, there won't be a close up of your fingertips, but you never know. Nails that have been bitten down to the quick or with chipped polish won't show you're polished to the producer.

You Sound Marvelous!

On radio, you can't depend on your perfect suit and tie to make the audience stand up and listen. You need to sound professional. There are several ways to improve your public speaking skills:

1. Strike "like" and "um" from your vocabulary.

2. Practice your spiel to anyone who will listen (pets included).

3. Tape-record yourself and listen to the way you speak. Make notations of things that bother you, and work on improving them.

4. Join a public-speaking organization like Toastmasters.

I can't say enough about Toastmasters as a way to improve your speaking skills. It has helped me in front of crowds, in front of the microphone, and in front of the camera. You can find a group in your area by checking out the Toastmasters International website, www.toastmasters.org.

The Least You Need to Know

◆ Television and radio draw in millions of viewers and listeners—that could all hear about your book!

◆ Producers are looking for information; what's important is to know what type of information each genre of show desires.

◆ Look closely at where your book fits in the television and radio markets, and send materials only to those producers at shows you know will find an interest in your book or your talent as an expert guest.

◆ Practice your speaking and presentation skills. Make sure you look and sound professional on camera.

Chapter 21

Marketing Online

In This Chapter

- ◆ Websites and online publications
- ◆ Why writing for e-zines is a powerful tool in the marketing of your title
- ◆ Pumping up sales with niche catalogs
- ◆ Creating blog buzz
- ◆ The power of an e-mail database
- ◆ Networking your friends and family

Now that you are in hot pursuit of exposure for your book and yourself as an author through the "old-style media" of television, radio, and print, it is time to move into cyberspace.

Although books are cherished and revered, in many ways, we are now a world of paperless information—especially when it comes to sales and marketing materials. Just look at the success of the Internet and sites such as Amazon.com. The world is wired together with endless marketing opportunities at our fingertips—literally at our fingertips! Consequently, you can't self-publish a book and expect to *not* market it online. A huge chunk of your audience moves within the online community. You just need to get the buzz out about your book on the Internet. And there are varied ways to accomplish this.

In this chapter, you'll learn, among many marketing strategies, how to get a website going, how to develop an e-mail sales list, how to create buzz with *weblogs* (or *blogs*), and how to find *e-zines* perfect for the online marketing of your book. Strap yourself in because we are taking a fast ride on the information superhighway.

Wise Words

A **weblog, or blog,** is an online journal, diary, or dated postings on a certain topic created by the weblog's originator. Essentially, blogging is like an archived chatroom. The postings don't go away when the room is closed. An **e-zine** is an electronic magazine or an online publication that is sent directly to the e-mail addresses of readers who have requested it.

So Many Ways, So Big an Internet—Pumping Up Sales Online

The Internet is really unlimited. Every day new blogs, e-zines, and catalogs pop up—many just waiting for information contained in your book. You can do everything from freelance articles that will garner you marketing venues to begin your own blog on a topic related to your work. There are so many ways to market online these days that the enormity of the opportunities may seem daunting. That's why I've put together a brief overview of the best ways to market your book online. When you have a good idea of the sales and buzz opportunities out there, you can plan your marketing strategy by picking and choosing from the ideas and implementing them.

Build It and They Will Come—Websites and E-zines

Nowadays, who doesn't have his or her own website? Just as with the ubiquitous nature of a cell phone, websites are becoming de rigueur, with many Internet service providers offering their members free web pages and step-by-step instructions on how to create them.

Your website need not be elaborate. It's enough to have one page showcasing your book and providing either a link to another site to buy it or a way on your page to buy it, coupled with your biography and perhaps a review of the work. But you may want to consider building something a little more inventive—perhaps an entire online publication, an e-zine.

If you provide information on the area of your expertise and create a "niche community," where people with an interest and need for the information you provide go, your traffic will most likely increase. Increased traffic to your site means more people seeing your book and more people *buying* your book.

> **By the Way**
>
> You can find information on building your own website online, of course. One great place to visit for help is Cnet.com, a site devoted to computer technology.

Though you may want to begin by designing your own web page, put some thought into hiring a webmaster/consultant if you really view your website as an integral aspect of your book business. I really recommend using a pro to get the best-looking website you can afford. My own website, www.goalsandjewels.com, was designed by a talented designer who made certain that the site reflected my own philosophy and the personality of my books. It comes as no surprise to visitors that it is pink and girly in feeling!

According to Alan Ludington, owner of *Nine1-6 Creative* and the webmaster and designer for clients such as the NBA's Sacramento Kings, the reasons an author might want to hire a professional website creator are many. "Someone like me can ensure no glitches, the proper layout, and branding, and make the text and images visually appealing," says the web professional. "I can also insert metatags, words commonly searched on engines, so your site will receive a greater number of hits. Basically, the more sophisticated and detailed a site you desire, the more you need someone who can translate your vision to the Internet."

Web consultants abound, and you need not limit yourself to consultants in your area. By the nature of their work, they can provide you with service from miles away. Navigate online and search for "web consultants" and "web designers" for innumerable listings.

Giveaways

A great way to attract visitors to your website (who, in turn, will be exposed to your book) is to give something away. On my goalsandjewels.com website, I have a blank goals form that visitors can print out and fill in with their own personal goals. They can hang it on the wall next to the mirror to be reminded of their goals, and at the same time remember the goalsandjewels website that gave it to them. Having a page like that gives me the chance to periodically market to the world. I can send out a press release about a free blank goals page (needless to say, it is a beautifully designed and bejeweled page that fits the rest of the feeling of the website) in January when

New Year's resolutions are a big news item, or after April 15 and tax day. I've gotten several great mentions of my website that way over the years.

What can you give away in connection with your book? How about a well-designed blank page that someone can put to good use? Or a handy info item such as "Four Great Ways to Get Your Kids to Study" or perhaps "101 Ways to Put Romance Back into Your Marriage." You get the idea. The info on your web page should not be solely centered on your book, but broken up into parts and pieces that can be used as smaller bits of free info.

> **Cautionary Tales** _____
>
> Rhonda Sharp, an entrepreneur in pharmaceuticals, decided to self-publish an e-book and build a website to promote the book and her business. Because she wasn't proficient in HTML and web design, and her company was just in its infancy, she initially chose the least expensive web consultant she could find. Unfortunately, "you really do get what you pay for," says Sharp, who required a complete overhaul of the site with a different and more expensive webmaster soon thereafter—but is pleased with the results. "I highly recommend that anyone looking to create a website as a marketing tool not only look at the expense, but also require recommendations from other clients. Ask around about potential web consultants. Not all are created equal—or have the experience and knowledge to make your site pop!" cautions Sharp. "If you don't do it yourself, you'll want to find someone with a proven track record of satisfied clients and save yourself the headache of an overhaul later."

Is there money in websites? My husband always asks me this question. Years ago, I was convinced that my website would create an active revenue stream. Now I'm not so sure. Does it drive book sales through the link at Amazon.com? Yep. Does it position me as a public speaker and expert on my topic, thereby attracting speaking jobs and consulting work? Yes. But do website visitors send me money? Nope.

Be certain that you understand clearly the role that having a website will play in your overall book-marketing strategy. Otherwise, you might set yourself up for costly disappointment.

Man for Hire—Writing Articles for E-zines and Excerpting Opportunities

Another way to market your book online is by placing it on other people's web pages. In addition to or instead of building your own e-zine, why not provide content for another e-zine? The effect is the same: your book gets out there for all to see. You can go about getting marketing hits basically three ways:

- Send a pitch to write an article for the e-zine.

- Send a review copy, for a possible "book review" on the site.

- Offer an excerpt from your book.

A good place to look for online publications that fit your topic is *Writer's Market* at www.writersmarket.com. Whether you choose to use the book or the website, *Writer's Market* now lists the online versions of many magazines and offers a comprehensive and categorized look at your freelancing opportunities. The really great thing about getting an article published that relates to and markets your book is that you generally also get a paycheck! Not only are you marketing your book and fueling sales of the work, but the e-zine is paying you for your piece.

Writing for other online venues gives you the chance to create an "about the author" at the end that promotes you and your title. For many years, I wrote a column for the *USA Today* website, and down at the bottom of every one of those pages my books were always listed. The name of the game is online exposure, folks!

By the Way

A simple way to get your work mentioned in an e-zine is by faxing or electronically sending your "New Book Release" to the online publications editor. Send a cover letter, too, with the offer to mail a copy of your book, if requested. With the hit of the Send button, hundreds and even thousands of e-zines appropriate to your topic will now know about the title. Sit back and wait for the calls.

Love to Link You, Baby—How Links Fuel Sales Hits

Reciprocal links are a great way to market your book. If you decide to build your own website, link sites that have reviews of your book or articles by you or about you to your site. In many cases, the sites you link will link back to you if you ask.

By the Way

Start your banner advertising search at HyperBanner.net, or go to Google.com and search for "banner advertising" to come up with numerous sites to peruse.

As with links, banner advertisements can help move traffic toward your book. Many websites will host your banner advertisement in return for your hosting of their advertisement on your site. Numerous "banner-building" sites are abound—all with free services—and worth checking into.

Shopper's Paradise—Online Catalogs and Stores

The web these days is truly a virtual mall. Online catalogs compete with each other for content and the best pricing. Book distribution for Amazon.com is one thing, but getting your book sold to an online catalog and store may prove less tricky. Let's say you've written a book with a military theme. Search the Internet for companies and catalogs online that offer like-themed products. Contact the company with a letter and an overview of your book. The catalog can either buy the book through you to sell to its customers or get it through your distributor. Either way, yet another prospective buyer is alerted to your work. I highly recommend spending a day researching all the online outlets in your book's category. Have you written a business book? There are plenty of electronic catalogs catering to the businessperson. Is your tome on tornados? Natural science sites might find a place to sell your work.

What's That You Write? The Power of Blogging

What better way to get the word out about your book than to start a weblog conversation related to the work. Blogging, as it's called, has become the latest online craze. Blogs are so up-to-the minute that news hits blog sites before networks. Because blogging has become such an international success at getting the word out, educators are even using weblogs in the classroom—either as a way for students to keep journals or as the creation of a blog as an assignment to further delve into a topic of research.

Needless to say, creating a blog is relatively easy. All you need is the hosting service and the topic. You've already got the topic; you've written a whole book on it! Now it's time to talk about it with other bloggers who have an interest in your work.

Many of the hosting services provide a free account—much like free e-mail through Yahoo! or Hotmail. But as with free e-mail, the premium services aren't free. You pay a premium. And don't worry about your computer-programming expertise; most services come with easy-to-use software or step-by-step instructions through the online process.

To get you more familiar with blogging services, surf around to these sites and check them out:

- www.weblogger.com

- www.angelfire.lycos.com

- www.livejournal.com

By the Way

Think we've come a long way with the Internet and marketing? Think again. Consider this, from a December 7, 2004, story in *The New York Times*, "One day, before long, when your mobile telephone sounds, it could be a novel calling to recount how the headstrong heroine dumped the handsome heartbreaker. Or it might be a guidebook surfacing at a critical moment in a crowded bar to provide you with a pickup line in Spanish, French, or German." Soon cell phones might be the newest wave in electronic marketing and a way to reach millions in an instant.

Build Your E-mail List

What an amazing sales tool e-mail can be. Think about it: there are lists of addresses at your fingertips to whom you may send notification of your book. How do you get the list, though? You probably already have quite an address book of contacts that are looking forward to receiving an e-mail announcement. So send everyone in your address book an announcement! But you'll need to dig a little deeper to find the electronic addresses of those who share an interest in the topic of your book. If your website is up and running, you may have chosen to have a register feature—or simply asked visitors to provide you with their information. Ah! You have the beginnings of a potential customer database. Find ways, therefore, on either your website or your weblog, to capture information—most important, the e-mail addresses—of your target audience. Generally, a weblog will require anyone who posts on it to have registered, thereby providing you with an automatic list of all members.

You might want to provide a registration area on your website much like the weblog to gather more e-mail addresses in order to send marketing materials. If this is a feature you want to include (and it can be a powerful one), be sure your web designer knows exactly what you have in mind.

E-zines have been around for a decade, and they are not as effective as they once were. I encourage you to write one, but I also want you to be realistic about their effectiveness. Azriela Jaffe, the author of 12 books and currently self-publishing a cookbook, had this to say: "Spam has really watered down the effectiveness of online newsletters. I've been sending one out for many years to a steady group of around 3,000 readers, and I have noticed how much trouble there is now in getting it into people's mailboxes."

Friends and Family—Ask for Help

Guess what? Your family and friends provide an excellent way for you to market your book online. How? It's easy. Send them your electronic book announcement and ask them to forward it on to all their contacts in their address books. Chances are good that your family will be more than happy to show off your accomplishment.

A gentle word of warning: Nobody likes to be spammed, and you shouldn't ask your family and friends to pass on a message to folks who won't be interested. But if your book is about dogs, say, ask them to send it to fellow dog lovers. Just like the Faberge shampoo advertisement with Farah Fawcett in the 1970s—"And I told two people ..." —an exponential effect will occur. You may have 50 family members and friends in your address book—and they have 50 also. If almost everyone forwards on your announcement, you've just reached thousands of people. Pretty powerful. And don't forget to thank those closest and dearest to you for their help and vote of confidence.

The Power of Emotion

In an earlier chapter, I mentioned the e-book that I was a part of several years ago, *A Glimpse of Heavenly Miracles.* The primary way that the book was marketed was through online newsletters that excerpted a story and built in a sales link at the bottom. Our biggest hit was a wonderful online e-zine called *Heartwarmers* that is always looking for good material. By allowing them to use our story for free, we were able to reach thousands of people in moments. It was a far more effective marketing technique than other kinds of press coverage simply because readers who were moved by the stories cut and pasted them and sent them on to their friends as well. That was *viral marketing* at its finest.

Understand that viral marketing can sometimes leave you behind, though, in a very literal sense. Candy Chand is the author of several collections of inspirational stories. Every Christmas an inspirational story that Candy wrote makes the rounds on the Internet, passed from friend to friend. One charming tale you might have received in your in box was about how a young child holds up his sign the wrong way in the Christmas pageant to spell the words "Christ Was Love." An online link back to Candy's Amazon listing would sell tons of books, except that Candy found over and over again that the folks who circulated her story online actually cut and paste it without the author information attached! So the story has become anonymous over the years rather than credited to Candy. The Internet giveth, and the Internet taketh away. Once something goes out to thousands of people, you will lose control over your material and might end up not benefiting from it at all.

> **Wise Words**
>
> What does a virus have to do with marketing? **Viral marketing** describes any strategy that encourages individuals to pass on a marketing message to others, creating the potential for exponential growth in the message's exposure and influence. Like viruses, such strategies take advantage of rapid multiplication to explode the message to thousands, to millions.

The One-Day Special

A very common online book-marketing technique nowadays is to send out a request to friends, family, and colleagues asking that they all buy your book on one particular day. Why? Because the greater your sales volume is, the greater your chances are of achieving a low sales number on Amazon.com (a low sales number does not mean low sales on Amazon!). In fact, the desire of everyone who sends out one of these letters is, "Help my book go to no. 1 on Amazon.com."

Should you try this? Go ahead! I'd stick with close friends and family, though, and not ask them to send your message to strangers. What was a very effective technique a year ago has become hackneyed and overdone very, very quickly.

The Plan, Man

Not all of these online marketing ideas will appeal to every author. Then again, you may want to try them all. Do what seems reasonable and fits your plan. Pick and choose the tasks that work with the time available. I strongly suggest pursuing one of the marketing ideas thoroughly rather than trying to do them all haphazardly. Concentrate on implementing one marketing opportunity at a time until you have each running on autopilot—something quite feasible with the nature of the Internet.

The Least You Need to Know

◆ The Internet provides a marketing-rich environment and the means to reach thousands of people interested in your topic.

◆ A few of the best ways to market your book online include websites, e-zines, weblogs, and an e-mail database.

◆ You don't need to be a computer wizard to get a website or weblog up and running. Hosts provide step-by-step instructions for creating whatever you desire.

◆ If you want something more sophisticated, however, you might want to hire a professional web consultant to run your site.

◆ Spread the word fastest by including your family and friends and asking them to spread the word in turn.

Chapter 22

Meeting With Success

In This Chapter

- Best practices—marketing techniques from the pros
- Adopting an independent marketing mind-set
- Grabbing marketing ideas from other industries
- Deciding your next move—sell out or second edition?
- Should you start a publishing company?

Hey, look! You've made it through 21 chapters on how to self-publish. I know it has been overwhelming at times (particularly all of the book production and design aspects, sheesh!), but I'm confident that you now have what it takes to go forward with your idea and create a successful self-published work.

As I approach the end of this book, I stopped and asked myself this: if I had to boil it all down to one single lesson, what would it be? My best piece of advice is this: if you are going to self-publish, you need to learn to sell.

To make a book happen, you need to take action. To make a book sale happen, you need to take action. Without action, you won't have a book, and you sure won't have a book sale. Book publicist Kim Dower sums it up this way: doing nothing does not sell books.

Let's spend our last bit of time together examining what has worked well for other successful self-published authors. And let's discuss a few options that you might consider for your next move. Because now that you've published one book, I know you are already thinking about where to go from here.

Best Practices

My husband, Peter, came to book publishing from the world of corporate jargon. I learned the term "best practices" from him. Best practices are the things that have worked for other people, and I'll show you how you can make them work for you. I've found that the best way to get ahead in this world is to ask for help, pay attention to what other people do, and learn how to do it. Instead of reinventing the wheel, learn from a guy who is already zipping down the hill on a go-cart. Ask other authors who are flying downhill with their books what has worked for them. And when you get them talking, don't forget to ask about what techniques flopped so you can avoid them.

One of the wonderful aspects of self-publishing is that the sky is the limit. You won't have to deal with a stodgy publisher in the front office who balks at every enthusiastic suggestion you have for new and creative ways to sell your book.

Here are a few best practices I'd like to share with you.

Ellen Reid Smith

Ellen has been in the marketing business a long time and has created many a high-profile program for corporate America. So when it came time for her to move her own product, she was ready.

"I knew that my book, *Cowgirl Smarts: How to Rope a Kick-Ass Life*, was really too small a package to be spotted in a bookstore. So I spend more time and effort taking it to horse shows, where I can sell it directly to the very folks I wrote it for."

Ellen had been through the commercial publishing routine before with a business book and was surprised by how scatter-shot the marketing was. Her whole focus this time was to market directly to the folks she knew were interested, horse women.

She was also savvy about building up a speaking business based on the content of her book. Ellen now gives Cowgirl Smarts talks to business groups, and you know she is selling her book in the back of the room!

Jennifer Basye Sander

Hey, look, it's me! Okay, I'm vain enough to add my own ideas here in this section. The last few years, I've been writing gift books for women. *Wear More Cashmere* and *The Martini Diet* are both small, cute little packages that make readers squeal with delight. Early on, I realized that a perfect way to sell these books would be in a "home party" setting, as with a Tupperware party or a Pampered Chef night. You've been invited to those, right? Well, would you women rather spend a night out with friends buying things for your kitchen, or indulging yourself and feeling special?

I team up with other entrepreneurs who have products that will appeal to the same kind of woman—scented lotions and feather boas, And then we encourage women to host a party and invite their friends to an evening of indulgence. I give a funny talk to warm up the crowd and put them in the mood to spend on themselves, and the fun begins. Needless to say, the woman who hosts the party gets a cut of the sales and a lovely gift.

Does your book topic lend itself to a home party setting? Ask your friends if they'd be willing to host one. And if it turns out to be a fun evening, chances are, other guests at the party will want to host their own. It can snowball from there.

I also make it a point to announce that I'm happy to attend book groups. Women's book groups or book clubs are everywhere nowadays, informally organized women who get together and read a book a month. If a book group wants to read *The Martini Diet* as their selection, I'll come and lead the discussion. Women, weight, and martinis—what could be more fun? Each meeting sells 10 or more books and ramps up the word of mouth. I also do it long distance; I "attend" the book group meeting via speakerphone.

By the Way
Seeking to stay in continuous contact with the kinds of women who might buy my books, I started a blog in 2005. "The Black Dress Manifesto" is a way for me to write a short weekly piece on one of the sassy topics that tie into *Wear More Cashmere* and *The Martini Diet,* and remind hundreds of women about who I am and what I do. From start to finish, it took only five minutes to set up for free on blogspot.com. Check me out at http://blackdressmanifesto.blogspot.com.

The Indie Mind-Set

Early in this book, I pointed to the similarity between "indie" films and music and the self-publishing world. You can be so much more creative in this indie world than in the uptight we-don't-do-it-that-way world of corporate publishing.

When I first attended the big self-publishing seminars that Mark Victor Hansen puts on, his MegaBook Marketing University, I was an uptight editor from the world of corporate publishing. I was just there looking for hard-working self-published authors that I could poach over to my list. I was shocked, shocked by what I heard from the stage. Mark made me blush with his tales of aggressive publicity and outrageous marketing ideas. "That simply isn't done!" I thought, shaking my head in annoyance at much of what he was suggesting. "So naïve!"

But as the days wore on, the scales fell from my eyes. Turns out that I was really the naïve one—naïve about how much farther creative thinking could take the whole book world.

I was swept up in the creative ideas that energized the room. Sure, maybe only two or three would really work for other authors and other books, but, hey, all you need is one good idea to sell a bunch of books. I saw that I'd been too stodgy in the way I was thinking about book promotion and marketing, that there was no reason not to try something wild and fun. That day I moved away from the idea that "if it hasn't been done before in this business, it won't work." I adopted the slogan "Just Try It!" Being wild and outrageous and thinking far, far out of the box has worked for *Chicken Soup* folks: they long passed the 80-million copies sold mark and are closing in on 90 million.

So let yourself think up crazy schemes for selling books. Go ahead and set up a stand by the side of the road and wave a sign at passersby. Maybe you won't sell any books, but you might end up on the news! Go ahead and make calls to corporate giants and suggest yourself as a spokesperson and your book as a promotional giveaway. You'll never know unless you try!

Let's not overlook the marketing wisdom that so many professionals are willing to share. Brian Jud of Book Marketing Works e-mails a free biweekly newsletter with regular columns from self-publishing gurus such as Dan Poynter, John Kremer, Eric Kampmann, and Rick Frishman. You'll pick up all kinds of new info and tips on selling to special markets. To subscribe, send an e-mail to brianjud@bookmarketingworks.com with the note "subscribe" in the subject line.

Keep Your Eyes and Ears Open

Just as I had my imagination blown open by Mark Victor Hansen, your mind might expand over an idea that comes to you in the newspaper. Don't limit your observations to what other authors and book folks are doing. Keep an eye on what is happening in music marketing, grocery sales, and computer marketing. You just never know where a good idea will come from. A few days ago, I glanced up at the cartoon channel my children were watching and caught a short infomercial selling a "Sleepover Parties DVD and Booklet." Wow! Now there is a product that will sell. And what a smart idea to sell it directly to the teenage girls who are watching. What about your book? Is there a short and catchy infomercial to be planned around it?

Every morning I read the business section of *The New York Times* and all of *The Wall Street Journal.* I'm not trying to show off here—I'm just showing you that writers shouldn't exclude themselves from the business world. We are not above commerce. Perhaps while reading an article you will stumble across the name of the very marketing person you've been trying so hard to find, or realize that a new business entering a competitive field might be interested in using a book like yours as a giveaway. My *Wear More Cashmere* book once ended up in the goody bag of a party at Neiman Marcus that a high-end cashmere company was giving. I'd run across a mention of the marketing woman in a *Vanity Fair* article and tracked her down with the information I gleaned.

Cautionary Tales

What if your book doesn't sell up to your expectations? Have you failed? I don't think so. You have managed to do what so many people only dream of doing—you wrote a book and brought it to life. The very fact that you saw it through to completion is a victory and a success in itself. And now that you know the ropes, just think how much easier it will be to do it again.

Your Book Is Successful—What's Your Next Move?

Throughout the preceding chapters, I've asked you to examine your goals for your book. Money? Fame? A higher professional profile? A lasting legacy for your family? Whatever your goals have been, I hope the information here has helped you achieve them. If your goal was to create a book of family history, your task is now done. But you might now be looking at helping your spouse's family create a similar book, or perhaps setting up a consulting agency that helps folks research and write their family story. Who knows where this new knowledge and talent will take you?

If a higher professional profile was your goal, I hope you have put the publicity chapters to good and valuable use! From now on, your colleagues won't be able to pick up a trade magazine without spotting a quote from you, or attend a conference without seeing you sitting up there on the dais next to the master of ceremonies. One book has done you good, but won't more books keep your name out there even longer?

When your book has been out for a while, you will find yourself thinking, "Hmmmm, maybe I'll try that self-publishing thing again." There are a few different routes that successful self-published authors take, and one of them might be the path for you.

Sell to a Publisher?

The history of self-publishing is rife with examples of writers who were able to attract the interest of a commercial publisher after publishing themselves first. The more successful the self-published book, the bigger the offer they were able to attract. Among the more recent examples are these:

◆ "Zane," the pseudonym of a 37-year-old writer who began by e-mailing erotic stories to her friends, first self-published them in story collections and attracted the attention of Simon & Schuster. She has now done 14 books with them since 2001.

◆ *Melting Pot Memories* began as a family project for Judith Bart Kancigor. The collection of her family recipes, old photos, and maps of Russia had a first printing of 500 copies and took off from there. Judith sold 10,000 copies of her self-published edition before signing with Workman Publishing.

◆ Suzanne Hansen self-published *You'll Never Nanny in this Town Again* about her experiences as a nanny to high-profile folks in Hollywood, and sold it to the Crown division of Random House.

♦ Pacific Northwest native Patrick Carman self-published his trilogy *The Land of Elyon* and sold more than 5,000 copies in just three months by visiting schools and giving talks. Based on stories he told his own children, Carman sold his trilogy to Scholastic.

How do you make the decision? For some, it is easy: take the check and run! For others, the potential downside needs to be examined. As a self-publisher, you have been 100 percent in control of your own decisions. From the front cover design to the layout of each individual paragraph, this has been your baby. You might want to refresh your memory about how little control authors have over their work when it is published by commercial houses. Will you be happy with this situation when you've been in charge? Possibly not. The more successful your self-published edition has been, however, the more bargaining power you will have over the contract you sign.

Another area in which one-time self-publishers can hit bumps is when they sell out on the money side. If selling your book has developed into a substantial and regular income stream, you should understand that the stream can experience major interruptions. Yes, you will get a royalty advance check, but if you see any money after that is up in the air and not in your control. The book might not do as well in its second life and not earn out the advance. You might experience times when you won't be able to get copies of your book (if it is out of stock and the publisher is waiting for orders to build before they reprint). You might experience shipping delays or malfunctions when trying to keep yourself stocked up during speaking appearances. It is awfully hard to sell your book from the back of the room if it never arrived from your publisher's warehouse.

Consider all of these things very carefully before making the decision to sell out to a commercial publisher.

Start Your Own Company?

Some self-publishers enjoy the process so much that not only do they continue to self-publish their own work, but they take the next step and publish the works of others as well. My old boss, Ben Dominitz, started his company to self-publish a travel book that he and his wife had written. Within a short time, the company, Prima Publishing, was a full-fledged publisher of many types of nonfiction books and grew into one of the largest independently owned publishing companies in the nation.

If you decide to take the step, go for it! What should you publish? You might start by publishing other books in the same category as your own. Now that you understand the distribution and publicity for your area, you could easily duplicate the process with another book. If your own book was about fly-fishing, you can easily publish another book on the same topic and sell it into the same accounts you've already established. If you have kept records on your individual customers, you can go back and market to them directly.

The major difference between publishing your own work and publishing the work of others is that instead of keeping all of the profits yourself, you need to pass on some of the money to the other author. Dang. Take a look at standard contracts to see what the going royalty rate is, and fashion your contract and policies after what is already out there.

Another Life

Other than starting your own actual publishing company, what else can you do? You can publish your own book all over again! That's right, many self-publishers bring out new editions of their work every few years. This can result in a new burst of publicity, a new crop of sales, and a new group of readers.

My little travel booklet, *The Air Courier's Handbook*, was updated and expanded every year for six years. I kept current with the companies who used couriers, where the routes were, how much the current tickets cost, and what the requirements were. I also asked my own readers to submit their stories of traveling as a courier so that I could continue to make the book bigger and more useful. It also gave me a reason to write yet another press release and send it out to the travel editors of magazines and newspapers. Every year I would get picked up in new media outlets, and some places wrote about me every single year. Even *Cosmopolitan* magazine wrote about it twice!

In earlier chapters, I mentioned Jack Everett and his book, *The Truth About Trusts*, and Bob Dreizler and his book, *Tending Your Money Garden*.

Jack is just now evaluating his book for a second, revised edition. The information in the trust world changes constantly, and Jack doesn't want to have a book on the market that is not 100 percent current. In fact, that would be a business liability for him, from a professional credibility standpoint. Keep this in mind if your book is a major part of your professional image.

Bob made considerable strides between the first and second editions of his book. Some of the biggest were cosmetic. He feels that by using professional designers the second time around, he was able to gain a greater level of acceptance from reviewers and distributors that the homemade look of his first edition discouraged. If your finished book is disappointing and doesn't look quite the way you'd hoped, start planning now on how you can revise it into a fresher book that might gain acceptance as Bob's did.

Developing Spin-Off Products and Services

Who says you need to stick to selling books? It might be that your book will lend itself to a natural side product or spin-off. Ellen Reid Smith and her *Cowgirl Smarts* book spawned a side business of chocolate cowboy boots. The erotic self-publisher Zane is now working to create a line of lingerie. Laura DuPriest, who I mentored some years back, recently morphed her book *p* into a line of cosmetics that she sells on the Home Shopping Network. And I'm hard at work on a line of pearl jewelry to sell along with my indulgence gift books. Is there a natural product that will develop out of what you've written and published?

How do you develop a spin-off product? You might find inspiration in the setting of your novel for a perfume, perhaps, or a travel company that books tours of the romantic region in which your book is based. Or is there a theme or image that can be used, the way that Ellen used the cowgirl theme to create chocolate boots? Perhaps an image from your cover or a character in your book will inspire something. Ellen used her book to develop another spin-off product, a matted and framed copy of the Cowgirl Creed with rules such as "Rein in Your Fears." Check out Ellen's products at www.cowgirlsmarts.com.

When you have a product, it could open up new markets for you. My silver pearl bracelets will soon be available in Hawaiian gift shops, and I'm hoping my books will be, too!

By the Way

For many years, I worked for an amazing publishing entrepreneur, Ben Dominitz. He and his wife, Nancy, wrote and self-published a book called *Travel Free!* and enjoyed the experience so much they decided to publish more books. And more books. And even more books. Their company, Prima Publishing, grew over the course of some 20 years to almost $100 million, at which point they sold it to Random House. Ben now enjoys his post-publishing life playing his violin in his house on a lake, freed from ever worrying about the business again. Who knows where self-publishing might lead you in your life's journey?

The book business is fun, and I hope you get that sense from some of the ideas I've shared with you. Fun, but demanding. What makes it work in the end is continual effort. Every day you need to do something, somewhere, to make your book work. Make marketing and promoting your work a part of your everyday life, and the results will be evident.

Well, you've done it. Congratulations are in order. You have undertaken and completed an enormous task. To write a book is an amazing feat. To then go on and publish it yourself is an even more amazing feat. Take the time to bask in the feeling of accomplishment. Enjoy what you have done. But don't bask too long because, remember—you've got to get out there and sell some books!

The Least You Need to Know

- ◆ The most important part of self-publishing is learning to market and sell your books.

- ◆ Keep your eyes open about where good ideas come from; it might not be the publishing industry.

- ◆ Consider carefully all offers from publishers; you will give up almost all control of your self-published work.

- ◆ You have the knowledge and skills to now publish others; remember that you will have to give them a cut of the money.

- ◆ Keep your book current and viable by bringing out new revised and updated editions every few years.

Appendix A

Glossary

affiliate program A program whereby you become linked to the sales site of a bookseller and you collect a small percentage from any sales that arrive on their site via your website's efforts.

back matter Anything and everything that comes after the final chapter of a book—the appendixes, glossary, bibliography, index, and so on.

bastard title page Also known as the half-title page. The half-title page is a front matter page that contains only the title of the book, nothing else.

board book A book that has pages made of thick, stiff paperboard. The printed papers are glued to the boards.

book doctor A professional writer who works to improve another's book.

case binding The process of combining paperboard, glued or sewn gathered pages, and covering papers or cloth to form a hardcover book.

CIP Cataloging-in-Publication, information that you file with the Library of Congress, which then supplies you with a formatted description and catalog number to help librarians catalog your work. The CIP is always printed on the copyright page.

colophon The logo for a publishing company. Chronicle Books uses a stylized pair of glasses, for instance.

commercial publisher A book-publishing company that assumes the full costs of producing, distributing, marketing, and selling the books it publishes. Commercial publishers pay authors for the right to publish their work.

consignment Merchandise left with the retailer, with the understanding that the retailer will have to pay for the product only when it is sold to a customer.

copyright "The right of authors to control the reproduction and use of their creative expressions that have been fixed in a tangible form," according to *The Associated Press Style Book and Briefing on Media Law*.

curriculum Courses of study offered by an educational institution. In publishing, it refers to a set of books developed for a particular study and geared to a specific age group. The books might be a themed series or a self-contained set including a textbook, a workbook, a teacher guide, reproducibles, and manipulatives.

deadline The final day (or hour, with a newspaper) that a writer/editor has to turn in an assignment.

distributor A business that calls on bookstores and takes orders for the books it represents. Distributors represent many different publishers at once. Distributors try to create sales.

e-book An electronic book. Information that can be downloaded and read later on a computer screen or handheld device such as a cell phone, personal digital assistant, or electronic reader.

editor A catchall description for anyone who works with words that he has not written. There are a dozen different types of editors, from acquisitions editors to developmental editors, but their focus is always to work with written material that they have not authored.

epigraph A motto or quotation, as at the beginning of a literary composition, setting forth a theme.

e-zine An electronic magazine, newsletter, or online publication that is sent directly to the e-mail addresses of readers who requested it.

fair use Circumstances in which you may use a limited amount of copyrighted material without the owner's permission.

finishing The process of applying foil stamps, die cuts, embossing, varnishes, and similar embellishments to a dustjacket, book casing, or softcover. Finishing may also include insertions, stickering, wrapping, and anything else that occurs after printing.

first printing Refers to the books that are produced in the first run of the presses.

folio Another word for a page number in a book. A "blind" folio is a page that has no visible page number. The word *folio* can also be used for a group of pages in a signature and can be used in reference to a group of 100 pages.

front matter Everything that comes before the actual text of the book, including the title and half-title pages, copyright information, acknowledgments, dedication, table of contents, preface, introduction, foreword, and any other tables, charts, or introductory text. The front matter is typically numbered with Roman numerals.

galley The uncorrected proof of your book, not yet in its final form. Also called an ARC, for advance reading copy.

genre A particular type or style of literature.

groundwood   A low-quality paper used for printing mass-market paperbacks, marked by its course texture. Generally not an acid-free paper. It has a life expectancy of less than 25 years.

high-bulk paper   A slightly thicker paper that increases the thickness or bulk of the overall book. A high-bulk paper decreases the pages per inch, or PPI.

independent bookstore   A bookstore that is owned by an individual instead of a large corporation. There are small chains with more than one outlet that are owned by an individual.

infopreneur   A publishing entrepreneur who sells information in a variety of ways—in printed books, electronic books, web courses, seminars, and so on.

libel   A published false statement that harms or injures the subject's reputation. "Words, pictures, cartoons, photo captions, and headlines can all give rise to a claim for libel," cautions *The Associated Press Style Book and Briefing on Media Law.*

masthead   A printed list of all the editors, artists, designers, editorial staffers, and advertising executives for a publication, typically found within the first few pages of a magazine.

merchandising   The promotion of merchandise, which is accomplished by coordinating production and marketing and developing advertising, display, and sales strategies.

nonfiction   Works that are fact based, containing true information or observations.

perfect binding   The process of gluing gathered pages to form the interior A hardcover case or paper cover (softcover) may cover the pages to form the finished book.

P&L (profit and loss)   A worksheet that considers the financial aspects of a project and the costs attached, balanced against all the potential revenue sources, to determine whether a project is likely to produce a profit or a loss.

plagiarism   According to the Modern Language Association, "[T]o use another's ideas or expressions in your writing is plagiarism. Plagiarism, then, constitutes intellectual theft."

PMS spot color   A spot color is one specified ink that is used instead of or in addition to black or standard four-color printing. PMS is an acronym for Pantone Matching System, a set of numbered inks that are used for spot color.

press release   A one-page announcement distributed to the press. It contains the five W's—who, what, where, when, and why.

print-on-demand (POD)   A new process by which books are printed as needed on a copy-by-copy basis rather than in large quantities.

printed case   Covering the paper boards of a book casing with printed papers rather than cloth, like a textbook cover.

publication date   The date your book is "released" to the public—that is, hits the bookstore shelves—not the date your book is hot off the presses and boxed. Often the pub date is up to four months after the book is printed, allowing publishers the time to garner advance reviews and press for the book.

publicity   The process of drawing attention to a person or thing. Publicity is free exposure rather than paid advertising.

recto   The right-side page of a book; page numbers are always odd numbered.

retail price   The price that a retail store charges its customers. Many bookstores discount the retail price, but they use the retail price as a starting point.

royalty   The percentage of the proceeds a publisher pays the author for each copy sold.

run-in head   A bolded word or phrase that forms the beginning of a paragraph. It is used in lieu of subheads and is used primarily for paragraphs that are intended as lists. If this is used in your book, make sure you use it more than once or at least once in every chapter, to achieve a balanced look. Run-in heads are sometimes set in italics, depending on the design.

self-promoter   A person who is able to promote himself and his work unapologetically and without hesitation.

self-published   A book that the author has paid to have produced, printed, promoted, marketed, distributed, and sold through the efforts of the author.

signatures   Books are divided into sets of folded pages, termed signatures. Industry standard for books is 16-, 32-, or 48-page signatures, depending on the press.

storyboard   A rough draft of one page or a two-page spread in a children's book. Drafted for spatial planning and artistic concept in the early stages, before illustrating the story. This provides an opportunity to budget pages, copyfit the story, and ensure that the page-by-page visual concept is logical and contiguous.

three-piece case   The three pieces of cloth or paper that cover a book's casing. These papers are not printed. The first is the back, or spine strip; the second is the outside front and back panel covers; and the third is the interior front and back paper that is glued to the board and the book pages (called an endsheet).

type solution   A book cover that uses only type and color as its design. There are no graphics, photos, or other illustration.

verso   The left pages of a book, which are always even numbered.

viral marketing   This describes any strategy that encourages individuals to pass on a marketing message to others, creating the potential for exponential growth in the message's exposure and influence. Like viruses, such strategies take advantage of rapid multiplication to explode the message to thousands or to millions.

weblog   Also known as a blog. An online journal, diary, or dated postings on a certain topic created by the weblog originator. Essentially, blogging is like an archived chatroom. The postings don't go away when the room is closed.

wholesale price   The discounted price needed by any reseller to make a profit when selling your book to its customers.

wholesaler   A book business that warehouses books and has them available when bookstores call to order them. Wholesalers are passive; they wait for the phone to ring.

Sample Press Kit Materials

Here are solid examples of three types of press kit materials you can use to style your own materials. Pay attention to the format, the tone, and the hooks employed throughout.

Sample Pitch Letter to Magazine Editor

Editor
CHILD
375 Lexington Ave.
New York, NY 10017

Dear Editor:

In May 2003, the Economic Policy Institute (EPI) sent out a "brief" on long-term unemployment—people unemployed for more than six months. According to the EPI, most unemployed Americans don't find work for 19.8 weeks, a number not seen in the United States in 20 years. Those long-term unemployed from executive, professional, and managerial occupations reached 20 percent. The older, more educated and skilled workers used to enjoy much shorter periods of unemployment—but not any longer. Dismally, the nation's unemployment rate hit an all-time high of 6.4 percent in June 2003. Women who are the main breadwinners in a family were hit even harder; with rampant downsizing and layoffs, their unemployment ranks swelled to 8.7 percent.

Recent research from University of Maryland demographer Suzanne Bianchi suggests that 11 percent of marriages feature an Alpha Earner female, where the woman in the home is the major wage earner. Moreover, according to the U.S. Census Bureau, 55 percent of mothers of infants were either working or actively looking for work.

The unseen numbers in this crisis are the children of all the parents losing their jobs. So many of the unemployed also have little mouths to feed. The collapse of the dotcom industry and the events of September 11 have left previously secure and prosperous families—your readership—without livelihoods and in a panic. Finding a job—especially a career you love— is difficult and time consuming. Many parents, who may have worked for years in one career, now find themselves laid off and searching for not only a job, but a career transition—a job that will bring them satisfaction and success. According to Helen Scully, a Nationally Certified Career Counselor (NCCC) and Master of Science (M.S.) in Psychology, "After the events of the world in the past two years—September 11, the war on terrorism, and the war in Iraq—people aren't willing anymore to sell their soul for a job. They want to do something fulfilling, that they love, that will also bring in an income to support their families."

So even with the exorbitant unemployment rates, where you'd figure that anyone with a job would be happy to have a job, it's not the case. Interestingly a recent Gallup study found that only 29 percent of workers are "fully engaged in their jobs," professing job satisfaction.

It seems we're spiraling into a crisis concerning career fulfillment and unemployment. People are not willing anymore to stifle their career passion just to ensure a paycheck. I propose an article, therefore, that explores why unemployment may be a good thing, how a layoff just may catapult one into finding his or her dream job, and that uses Helen Scully, the author of *Elevations*, as an expert. The feature will examine four career-development resources:

1. Organizations and support groups—like the 5 O'clock Club, one of the nation's most respected, career-development organizations. I plan to answer the questions "What do career organizations have to offer?" and "How can an unemployment support group offer networking opportunities?"

2. Nationally Certified Career Counselors. This section will explain the services that a NCCC offers and who can best utilize those services. I will also show the going rates for a counselor's services across the nation.

3. In-home career-assessment tools and books. This section will explore a few of the strongest, most recommended books and other tools to help one find his or her dream job, inexpensively and from the comfort of his or her own home.

4. University or community college career centers and career-development classes. This section will answer what classes establishments of higher learning offer to help the unemployed get back into the job game.

Sources already in place for this piece include:

1. Kate Wendleton, founder and president of the 5 O'clock Club (based in New York).

2. Helen Scully, M.S., NCCC (Nationally Certified Career Counselor) and the author of a home-based assessment tool (based in California).

3. Matthew*, husband and father of two daughters, Gabby, 5, and Ashley, 7, who, as the main breadwinner for the family, lost his law enforcement job; his wife, Alisa, is currently in her last year of nursing school. Although Matthew has been out of a job for four months and has been applying for police work, he admits wanting out of law enforcement and perhaps pursuing something in kinesiology. "Truthfully, I hated my

job. I hated police work," he said, as he sat and watched his girls swim in a neighbor's pool two days ago.

I'm sure your readers would appreciate this timely and informative article. I look forward to hearing from you.

Best,

Author/Publicist
[Address]
[Address]
[Phone]

Sample New Book Release

New Product Release   Contact: Helen Scully
August 8, 2003   916-XXX-XXXX

Dare to Wake Up Your Career Dream with Elevations

– – –

Fun and uncomplicated assessment tool identifies the best career for your personality and then offers a roadmap to actually achieving your dream job

The headlines are everywhere. The nation's unemployment rate hit an all-time high of 6.4 percent in June 2003; nearly 1.6 million Americans are out of work. The irony is this: most of the unemployed may not even know what job it is for which they should be looking. What job would provide fulfillment and make working a dream instead of daily drudgery? And what about all those people stuck in a job they hate? How can they, too, _wake up their career dreams?_

Enter _Elevations_, a career-discovery tool authored by a Nationally Certified Career Counselor Helen Scully, that allows you to privately, inexpensively, and at your own pace determine the best career for you, based upon your values, personality traits, skills, and interests.

Here's how it works: first you sort through a series of reusable card decks that systematically define career aspirations and capabilities. Career alternatives are identified and described in skill-based terminology. Over 160 careers are explored through the cards, while Internet sources lead you to over 60,000 choices! Next you complete an uncomplicated self-scoring and worksheet and prepare a career profile summarizing the results. Finally, the comprehensive _Elevations_ workbook guides you through career research, obstacles analysis, and action planning.

Once you finish your _Elevations_ process, you'll know whether civil engineering, zoology, personal training, freelance writing, telecommunications, or anything else fits you perfectly. Moreover, you'll know how to move toward your new career and seize the job that really will provide you with satisfaction and success. With _Elevations_, you won't waste valuable time or money going down the wrong educational or career-development path. You'll quickly know where to focus your energies.

Facing the day won't seem so daunting anymore once you're doing what you were meant to do. And the job search won't seem so haphazard and confusing once you've clarified what job you're meant to look for.

Elevations is available by calling 1-877-TOELEVATE or by navigating online to www. elevatemycareer.com. The media may procure product samples by faxing a request on letterhead to 916-443-4539. The author of *Elevations*, Helen Scully, M.S., NCCC, is available for interviews or to comment on career development and employment issues by calling 916-443-8225.

Sample News Hook Approach

August 4, 2003

[Name]
[Title]
[Publication/Company]
[Address]
[Address]

Dear [Name]:

In May 2003, the Economic Policy Institute (EPI) sent out a "brief" on long-term un-employment—people unemployed for more than six months. According to the EPI, the current average number of weeks most people are out of work is 19.8, a level not seen in the United States in 20 years!

Dismally, the nation's unemployment rate hit an all-time high of 6.4 percent in June. Couple these stats with the fact that a recent Gallup study showed that only 29 percent of those employed feel "fully engaged in their jobs," and it seems we're spiraling into a crisis concerning job satisfaction, career fulfillment, and employment (or lack thereof).

Plainly, people can't find the jobs they want—and don't even know, in most cases, what they're looking for.

Enter *Elevations*. *Elevations* is a solution, a powerful career-discovery tool that helps users *wake up their career dreams* with an inexpensive, home assessment card sort and workbook.

Thus, with our nation's economic woes and the rising unemployment rates, career devel-opment is a timely and helpful topic for your readers. I urge you to peruse the kit that includes the following:

A new product release

A fact sheet on the state of unemployment and career dissatisfaction in the United States

Suggested interview questions

My biography

A "mini-feature" that you may print in the career sections of your publication

For over a decade, with an M.S. in counseling and as a Nationally Certified Career Counselor, I've assisted clients seeking career direction using various available assessments and, quite frankly, have been frustrated; each card sort, online test, or career inventory operates from its own theory and produces its own reports. In the end, the confused career explorer is left with a pile of good information that is not integrated. The lack of coordination between what a person values and his or her interests, personality traits, and skills works against the goal of helping people achieve clarity in career choices. *Elevations* integrates everything and propels people toward finding out what their dream job is—and then puts an action plan in place for seizing the position!

I am, by my own accord, deeply passionate about helping people find career satisfaction. I want to do for a person's career what Suze Orman did for a person's money. Where she helped people understand how they perceive money, I plan to help people understand themselves and their desires in order to gain a fulfilling career.

I am available for interviews. I look forward to discussing *Elevations* with you. Please do not hesitate to contact me with any questions at 916-xxx-xxxx.

Sincerely,

Helen Scully, M.S., NCCC
Scully Career Associates, Inc.
2618 J Street, #2
Sacramento, CA 95816
www.elevateyourcareer.com

Appendix C

Self-Publishing Groups and Websites

www.authorlink.com. Author Link is a networking site for serious writers. It showcases great publishing news stories and links to help you on your self-publishing quest.

www.bookmarket.com/selfpublish.html. This site provides an "inspirational" factor that few other sites do by listing a "Self-Publishing Hall of Fame." You'll notice some big names that started out small.

www.horror.org. Whether looking to self-publish or find a publisher, the aspiring horror writer will find a host of information about this genre.

www.nwu.org. This is the site for the National Writer's Union, the only labor union to represent freelance writers in all genres, formats, and media. Check out your rights as a self-publisher on this site.

www.onlinepublishingnews.com. You'll find a plethora of information on the publishing industry—especially hard news that can help you navigate your way from self-publisher to small press owner!

www.pneumabooks.com. This site pledges to help "publishers succeed through education, inspiration, and the creation of excellent books." It focuses on the self-publisher and the small press publisher. This site also lists free reports, free seminars, and free manuscript critiques.

www.pma-online.org. This is the website for the Publishers Marketing Association, a group that helps small publishers and self-publishers market their books.

www.publishingcentral.com. Publishing Central offers the self-publisher everything from helpful editorials to book binding, to e-book publishing and beyond. It even features a section on self-publishing comic books!

www.shawguides.com. The consummate guide to writers' conferences and workshops can be found here—more than 1,500 are listed! A great source for conference networking.

www.smallpress.org. Although this group originates in New York City and all conferences and workshops for the self-publisher are held there, you can buy CD versions of the workshops through the site. Moreover, you'll find handy information and editorials here.

www.spannet.org. This is the site of the Small Publishers Association of North America. The group states that its "purpose is to bring success to small publishers, self-publishers, and authors." Full of educational materials, this nonprofit professional trade association's site is well worth your time.

www.spawn.org. The Small Publishers, Artists and Writers Network "encourages the exchange of ideas and information among writers" and is a fantastic online community resource. You'll find newsletters, self-publishing help, and other items to both set you and keep you on track.

www.writenews.com. Brought to the Net by The Write News, this site provides the self-publisher with news, features, and resources for the media and publishing pros—including industry insider info like hires, fires, launches, and closings within and of publishers and the industry. Keep yourself up-to-date on the goings-on within your new endeavor.

www.writershelper.org. Free writer's tools abound on this site, along with "fee-based" help. The courses all possess a Christian focus and range from mentorship to the basics of beginning your self-publishing goals.

www.writing-world.com. Formerly Ink Spot, this site lists classes, contest, and even a "Writers Wanted" section. The self-publishing section is comprehensive and also offers success stories.

Sample Agreements

These sample legal forms may be used to suit your own needs and projects when working with others. These are provided for example only, please check with a publishing attorney before you enter into legal agreements.

Sample Release for Story Contribution

Use the following release if you are publishing a collection of stories by many contributors. Each one needs to sign a separate release form:

For good and valuable consideration of **[fee, if any]**, to be delivered after the book's publication, I hereby grant and assign to **[your name here]**, during the full term of copyright and any extensions and renewals of copyright term, the sole and exclusive rights to print, publish, distribute, and sell (and license others to do so) the enclosed materials **[attach story or contribution]** in the book **[named here]** and in any magazine, newspaper, or other media in which the book is excerpted or promoted, which right shall extend worldwide in all languages and in all media, including electronic and audio rights.

I warrant that this material is original (I have not obtained the materials from anyone else) and I have obtained any necessary permission (in writing and after providing sufficient information regarding the use of the materials for an informed decision) from other persons to grant the rights herein, including, without limitation, permission for use of all material belonging to others and all facts which, if published, could invade the privacy of others. The materials which I am providing contain nothing that is libelous, injurious, or otherwise actionable or contrary to law, or that will infringe any copyright, proprietary right, or right of privacy, unless informed written permission has been granted by appropriate persons. I understand that **[the publisher, you]** has the right to edit my story as they see fit.

Signed and dated _____

Sample Work-for-Hire Agreement

The agreement that follows is used to hire a ghostwriter for a business book:

This WORK-FOR-HIRE AGREEMENT ("Agreement") is entered into as of the date first written above and between **[name of person hiring ghostwriter]** ("Commissioning Party")and **[name of ghostwriter]** ("Contributor") regarding the services to rendered and work to be created by Contributor for the Commissioning Party ("the Contributor's Work") in connection with a work described as **[describe project here]**.

1. The Contributor's Work shall consist of the following: to help develop the structure and detail of the book, research such information as **[fill in as needed]** where needed, conduct interviews, and write the work with the Commissioning Party. Contributor agrees to meet deadlines as discussed and set forth by the Commissioning Party.

2. The Commissioning Party shall pay Contributor as follows for the Contributor's Work upon delivery of Contributor's Work in a form reasonably satisfactory to the Commissioning Party: **[insert sums and terms here]**.

3. To the extent that Contributor's Work includes any work of authorship entitled to protection under the laws of copyright, the parties acknowledge and agree that (i) Contributor's Work has been specially ordered and commissioned by the Commissioning Party as a contribution to a collective work, a supplementary work, or such other category of work as may be eligible for treatment as a "work made for hire" under the United States Copyright Act; (ii) Contributor is an independent contractor and not an employed partner, joint author, or joint venturer of the Commissioning Party; (iii) Contributor's Work shall be deemed a "commissioned work" and "work made for hire" to the greatest extent permitted by law; and (iv) the Commissioning Party shall be the sole author of Contributor's Work and any work embodying the Contributor's Work pursuant to the United States Copyright Act, including but not limited to the Commissioning Party's Work, and the sole owner of the original materials embodying Contributor's Work, and/or any works derived therein.

4. To the extent that Contributor's Work is not properly characterized as "work made for hire," then contributor hereby irrevocably grants to Commissioning Party all right, title, and interest in and to Contributor's Work (including but not limited to copyright herein), and any and all ideas and information embodied therein, in perpetuity and throughout the world.

5. Any ideas, information, formats, methods, procedures, programs, data, or other matter which might be disclosed by the Commissioning Party to Contributor, or which Contributor may learn or observe in the course and scope of the Contributor's Work ("the Confidential Matter") are private and confidential, and/or proprietary trade secrets of the Commissioning Party. The Confidential Matter is made available to Contributor in strict and complete trust and confidence. Contributor shall hold the Confidential Matter in trust and confidence, shall not make any copies of Confidential Matter, shall not disclose the Confidential Matter to third persons, and shall not use the Confidential Matter at any time except with the prior written permission of the Commissioning Party.

6. Contributor has not prepared or published, and shall not hereafter prepare or publish, or participate in the preparation or publication of, any work that embodies or is derived from the Contributor's Work or the Confidential Matter.

7. Arbitration. Any dispute arising from this Agreement shall be submitted to binding and confidential arbitration under the rules of the American Arbitration Association in the county of **[your county]**, and any award issued in such arbitration may be entered and enforced as a judgment in any court of competent jurisdiction. The prevailing party in any such arbitration shall be entitled to recover attorneys' fees and costs.

8. Termination. Contributor and the Commissioning Party acknowledge and agree that Contributor's independent contractor relationship may be terminated at will by either party. Upon such termination, Contributor shall be entitled to a proportionate share of the compensation described above based on the portion of Contributor's Work that has been completed in a form satisfactory to the Commissioning Party at the date of termination. The terms and conditions set forth above shall survive the termination of such relationship.

Signed and dated _____

Sample Collaborators' Agreement

The following agreement is used by two or more writers to collaborate on one book project:

The Undersigned **[names here]** agree in good faith to collaborate on a book titled **[book name]**. The following terms detail their collaboration on the Work.

1. Authorship. The Work is a joint project and collaboration of both authors. The names of both authors will appear on the cover and interior pages of the book and on any and all reference materials, publicity, and other identifying materials. The authors will share copyright.

2. Division of labor. **[detail your plan here]**

3. Approvals. In all cases, the content of the Work will be subject to mutual approval by both authors. The final copy shall be subject to approval by both authors. Both authors shall review, jointly or separately, any corrections or changes that may be suggested or made by copyeditors or the publisher.

4. Conflicts. Harmony shall be the goal at all times. However, in the case of a misunderstanding or disagreement over editorial content, **[name]** shall have the final decision. In the case of misunderstanding or disagreement on financial or other issues, both authors shall agree on an arbitrator to resolve the issue.

5. Defaults. It is not anticipated that there should be a default. However, should either party be unable to complete his/her portion of the project, the other party shall have the right to proceed using the work completed to date and compensating the defaulting partner or his/her representatives in proportion to the percentage of content used in the final book.

6. Prior commitments. It is agreed there are no prior commitments with other collaborators on this specific project.

7. Contracts. Any contract with a publisher shall be reviewed, approved, and signed by both authors.

8. Royalties, advances, and other payments. Payment shall be made to each author individually and be divided in the following manner **[insert % here]**.

The above is understood and agreed upon by these parties. A witness shall sign for each party.

Signed and dated _____

Witnessed by _____

Recommended Resources and Experts

Book Development

Author's Team
Mahesh Grossman
1-866-7author
www.authorsteam.com

Pneuma Books
410-996-8900
www.pneumabooks.com

Book Doctors

Big City Books Group
Jennifer and Peter Sander
916-791-2101
basyesander@yahoo.com

Andrea Hurst
916-736-3745
ahawrite@aol.com

Book Production

Professional Publishing Services
Robin C. Hood
916-771-9668

Book Publicists

Annie Jennings
908-281-6201
www.anniejenningspr.com

Planned Television Arts
Rick Frishman
212-593-5820
www.plannedtvarts.com

Katherine Sansone
510-553-0188
sansonepr@sbcglobal.net

Kim Dower
www.kimfromla.com

Anthony Mora
323-874-2933
www.anthonymora.com

Smith Publicity
215-547-4778
www.smithpublicity.com

Cookbook Producer

www.heritagecookbook.com

Cover Designers and Interior Designers

Kari Keating
kari@graphicapps.com

Vanessa Perez
bookdesign@sbcglobal.net

Opus 1 Design
1-800-590-7778
www.opus1design.com

Mike Tanamachi
emailforyou@comcast.com

Monica Thomas
monicathomas@surewest.com

Developmental Editors

Author's Team
Mahesh Grossman
1-866-7author
www.authorsteam.com

Anne Basye
773-334-0028
aebwriter@cs.com

Big City Books Group
Jennifer and Peter Sander
916-791-2101
basyesander@yahoo.com

Editorial Services

Editorial Freelancers Association
www.the-efa.org

Ghost Writers

Author's Team
Mahesh Grossman
1-866-7author
www.authorsteam.com

Lynne Rominger
lynne_rominger@yahoo.com
916-792-1036

Big City Books Group
Jennifer and Peter Sander
916-791-2101
basyesander@yahoo.com

Melanie Votaw
718-230-1927
www.ruletheword.com

Marketing Resources

PR Leads
Dan Janal
952-380-1554
www.prleads.com

Mega Book Marketing University
www.megabookmarketing.com
949-759-9304

Radio-Television
Interview Report
1-800-989-1400

National Publicity Summit
www.nationalpublicitysummit.com
1-800-989-1400

Media Trainers and Coaches

Michelle Anton
323-353-3922

Success in Media
Jess Todtfeld, "The Pitch Doctor"
631-431-8251
www.successinmedia.com

Susan Harrow
www.prsecrets.com

Print Brokers for Off-Shore Printers

Fei Chen
360-944-7648

Palace Press
415-526-1370

Printers

Banta Book Group
1-800-933-9612
www.banta.com

BooksJustBooks
www.booksjustbooks.com

Morris Publishing
1-800-650-7888
www.morrispublishing.com

Central Plains
1-877-278-2726
www.centraiplainsbook.com

BookMasters
www.bookmasters.com

Publishing Attorney

Ivan Hoffman
www.ivanhoffman.com

Lloyd Rich
www.publaw.com

Publishing Consultants

Author's Team
Mahesh Grossman
1-866-7author
www.authorsteam.com

Andrea Hurst
916-736-3745
ahawrite@aol.com

Big City Books Group
Jennifer and Peter Sander
916-791-2101
basyesander@yahoo.com

Lynne Rominger
lynne_rominger@yahoo.com
916-792-1036

Television Make-Up

Jeanne Marie
International Media Cosmetics
Custom photo/media make-up kits available
1-800-854-1106www.jeannemarie.com

Index